2nd Edition

Gentle Hikes *of*
Minnesota's North Shore

THE AREA'S MOST SCENIC HIKES LESS THAN 3 MILES

Ladona Tornabene, Ph.D., MCHES
Lisa Vogelsang, Ph.D.
Melanie Morgan

Adventure Publications
Cambridge, Minnesota

Acknowledgments

This book's second edition builds upon its first, as do our acknowledgments. We are grateful to the following for their role in shaping *Gentle Hikes*: the Department of Applied Human Sciences and College of Education and Human Service Professions at the University of Minnesota Duluth (UMD); all Minnesota North Shore state parks; the Superior Hiking Trail Association (SHTA); the Gitchi-Gami State Trail Association (GGST); the Minnesota Department of Natural Resources; and the City of Duluth Parks and Recreation. We also wish to thank Mark Morgan (Melanie's husband), and Brenna Jordan of Brenna Jordan Calligraphy, for their assistance in reviewing selected trails in this edition.

A very special thank you to AdventureKEEN for their continued and unwavering support of the *Gentle Hikes* series.

And last, but certainly not least—The Creator of it all—to whom we give our utmost gratitude. Truly, "The heavens declare the glory of God and the firmament shows and proclaims His handiwork." Psalms 19:1

Please use caution and good sense when participating in outdoor recreational activities. The authors and AdventureKEEN assume no responsibility for accidents or injuries occurring on the trails, Almost Hikes, waysides, overlooks, scenic locales, and picnic areas described in this book.

Learning as much information as you can about the activities and destinations can help prevent accidents and make your recreational experience more enjoyable.

Dedication

This book is dedicated to the glory of God.
As beautiful as His creation is, it pales in comparison to Him.
It is our hope that you experience both.
Megwich Kchi-Manitou.
Pasa Gweeg!

10 9 8 7 6 5 4 3

Gentle Hikes of Minnesota's North Shore: The Area's Most Scenic Hikes Less Than 3 Miles
First Edition 2002
Second Edition 2018
Copyright © 2002 and 2018 by Ladona Tornabene, Ph.D., MCHES, Lisa Vogelsang, Ph.D. and Melanie Morgan Published by Adventure Publications
An imprint of AdventureKEEN
310 Garfield Street South
Cambridge, Minnesota 55008
(800) 678-7006
www.adventurepublications.net
All rights reserved
Printed in China
ISBN 978-1-59193-728-9 (pbk.); ISBN 978-1-59193-729-6 (ebook)

TABLE OF CONTENTS

INTRODUCTION

This section gives an overview of our book's main co[...] [...] the back-story of its development. We hope you enjoy reading [...] [...] [...] writing it! May your heart be moved by your "sole" . . .

GENTLE HIKES BACKSTORY

Gentle Hikes was created out of a desire to share the outdoors with people of all ability levels. And some of those people are two of the authors, who needed the amount of detail herein because of their athletic-related injuries, one temporary and the other permanent. Furthermore, their visiting family/friends wanted to explore the trails, but many had a very limited stay here. They needed short hikes where they could see the most scenery in the least amount of time. Some had small children. They too needed short hikes in addition to safety information and restroom locations. Others had certain physical challenges. They needed greater detail about what to expect on a trail in order to assess if it was within their capacity.

Finding that there was no hiking book that detailed all of this information for each trail, *Gentle Hikes* was born. The vision grew to encompass the Lake Superior regions of Wisconsin and Michigan (Recommended Reading and Resources, pg. 206) as well.

INCLINES, SURFACES, STEPS, BENCHES, AND RAILS— ALL DISCLOSED FOR EACH OF THE TRAILS

Gentle Hikes aspires to help people "Know Before They Go." All trails are less than 3 miles roundtrip, and for each trail, we provided details such as trail width and surface type, rock/root rating, the number of inclines, including their steepness and length, the number of steps/bridges, the presence of handrails or benches, plus applicable safety concerns, all while adhering to an objective rating system (see "How to Use This Section," pg. 22). This information gives readers the opportunity to decide if a trail may be compatible with their ability level/circumstance and enables them to preplan accordingly.

We also specify which trails are multiuse, non-motorized paths (i.e., permitting bicyclists and in-line skaters but prohibiting any motorized vehicles with the exception of motorized wheelchairs). Additionally, we provide a chapter (pg. 194) that contains information designed to be helpful for readers with physical challenges (e.g., trails that meet Universal Design Standards, as well as trailhead/scenic locale, restroom, and picnic table accessibility). Plus, we also wrote a chapter (pg. 200) that contains helpful parking information for our readers who travel in RVs.

THE NORTH SHORE'S DIVERSE TOPOGRAPHY MANDATES DIFFERENT SHADES OF GENTLE

Due to the diverse topography of this area, trail conditions vary considerably. In this book, we include three trail ratings: the Lighter, Moderate, and Rugged sides of gentle. For example, trails that meet Universal Design Standards (i.e., accessibility standards for persons of all abilities) as well as sections of the paved Gitchi-Gami State Trail are rated on the Lighter side of gentle. However, most sections of the Superior Hiking Trail, by virtue of the terrain, are rated on the Rugged side of gentle. More often than not, the North Shore region naturally involves inclines/declines, rocks, roots, and uneven terrain.

While trail ra████████████ective criteria, our readers may or may not agree with ou████████████ s why we provide significant trail details. If in doubt about a trail's diffic██ ████ad through its entire description prior to heading out.

SAFETY FIRST

When scouting new trails, we use hiking poles, as they help immensely in navigating rocks/roots, uneven terrain, and declines. We also bring other items to ensure our safety, comfort and enjoyment (see Safety and What to Bring on pg. 7).

FOR BETTER HEALTH ON THE INSIDE, GET OUTSIDE!

Hiking has tremendous health benefits, and nature enhances those. To highlight these benefits, we've included a chapter (pg. 190) where we share some of the physical, mental, emotional, spiritual, and social benefits of physical activity, including how a connection to nature positively impacts well-being. Furthermore, throughout the entire book we have inserted "Says Who?" snippets that communicate health-related information. We especially had fun when such info relates to sites on the trails. For instance, a section of Duluth's Lakewalk parallels multiple taphouses (pg. 32), so our "Says Who?" piece relates to . . . wait for it . . . the health benefit of hops (not kidding!). Additionally, the whimsical "Bear Trail" Almost Hike (pg. 154) is on the property of Great! Lakes Candy Kitchen, where we were quick to point out the health benefits of dark chocolate. The most important health snippet we can give? "All things in moderation."

WHERE THE TRAILS ARE AND HOW TO FIND THEM

Whereas most of the trails in this book are well marked and easy to follow, please be aware that in order to meet our *Gentle Hikes* criteria, we sometimes use parts of existing trails to create our own. When this is the case, the trail's title will be marked with an asterisk, indicating that it is a *Gentle Hikes* name. Please pay attention to those descriptions to ensure you stay on course.

Our book includes trails/scenic locales in Duluth, Two Harbors, Silver Bay, Finland, Schroeder, Tofte, Lutsen, Grand Marais, Hovland, and Grand Portage. It also showcases hikes in all eight North Shore state parks, plus selected scenic sections from the Superior Hiking Trail (SHT) and paved Gitchi-Gami State Trail (GGST). For each trail, we provide a small map of the hike and directions to each trailhead, plus phone numbers/websites for entities who maintain the trail.

RESOURCES TO ENHANCE YOUR DULUTH/NORTH SHORE EXPERIENCE

We are excited to share more with you about these wonderful places and the amazing entities that maintain these beautiful trails. In addition, we provide information to help you maximize your Duluth and North Shore experience (pg. 208).

WHEN SNOWFLAKES FLY

If you want to hike in winter, consider Duluth's Lakewalk. The paved path is plowed during snow season; however, ice may accumulate on access ramps and in various places along the path. The section Canal Wall to Bayfront Festival Park may not be plowed.

If using the Lakewalk in winter, we recommend calling ahead for conditions (Duluth Parks and Recreation, Maintenance: 218-730-4303). Also, many of the waysides are closed during snow season, as they are not plowed and many portable toilets are seasonal.

BE LURED TO THE SHORE BY VIRTUAL TOUR!

In order to get you excited for a Duluth/North Shore visit, we've included links to virtual tours of the area. Created by the state parks and other entities, look for these websites in the Foot Notes section. We've also been inspired to create our own virtual tours! Two of this book's authors (Ladona and Lisa) photograph on a professional level, and the other (Melanie) is really, really good behind the lens. Our website (www.d.umn.edu/~ltornabe/gh/) will be constantly updated with our photos from the trails, almost hikes, and scenic locales, so check back often. It will also have tips for healthier living.

A FEW OF OUR FAVORITE THINGS . . .

Be sure to check out Authors' Corner (pg. 10) for themed lists of selected trails and hikes. There we call out the best trails for waterfalls; excellent Lake Superior/river views; spectacular vistas; prettiest woods; the best hikes with kids; the gentlest hikes; and even the best walks/scenic locales for art lovers or history buffs! To discover a few more of your favorite things, peruse our Recommended Reading list (pg. 206).

Whatever your passion, this book has it and so much more!

Healthy trails to you however you may travel them,

—*Ladona Tornabene, Ph.D., MCHES, Lisa Vogelsang, Ph.D., Melanie Morgan*

Safety and What to Bring

Since all of our hikes are less than 3 miles and are on well-marked trails, we list fewer essentials than you'd find in your average hiking guide. Still, it's always wise to be prepared, even on a short hike. Remember to choose trails that are appropriate for your ability and fitness level. Start out slowly and gradually increase your walking speed to a comfortable level, pacing yourself throughout the hike.

STRETCH

Stretching before a hike prepares the muscles for activity, and stretching after can prevent muscle soreness. Not only does it feel good to stretch, but if your muscle is flexible you're less likely to strain it should you move suddenly or accidentally trip.

RAIN GEAR

We thought we could make it back to the car in time, since it was such a short trail. Then it started to pour. Lesson learned: always pack a rain jacket! Even though you may start out on a beautiful day, weather conditions can change very quickly on the North Shore. All three of us have been caught in rainstorms on trails less than a mile long. Waterproof fabrics that are breathable work best for rain gear.

CLOTHING FABRIC TYPE

There are many choices in clothing fabric in today's market. Wear something breathable that also dries quickly. Cotton feels great on a hot day, but when it gets wet, it stays wet. Newer nylon and blended synthetics are breathable, help wick perspiration away from the skin, and dry much faster than cotton.

HATS AND CAPS

Since your head is obviously closest to the sun, it is important to protect your scalp from the sun's burning rays. Many styles of wide-brimmed hats and billed caps offer head protection and shade your eyes. Whatever your style, choose a hat that offers adequate protection from weather conditions and allows for personal comfort.

SUNSCREEN

Sunscreen is a necessity to prevent sunburns and reduce the risk of skin cancer. Use a waterproof sunscreen with a minimum of SPF 15. Apply before hiking and reapply about every hour depending upon perspiration levels. Don't forget to apply sunblock to your nose and ears and use sunblock lip balm, as well as good quality sunglasses to protect your eyes.

FOOTWEAR

The shoes and socks you wear can make the difference between an enjoyable outdoor experience or a hike filled with possible blisters and discomfort. Athletic shoes are great for paved or flat trails without many roots or rocks and are appropriate for trails with a Lighter Side of Gentle rating. Sturdier shoes or hiking boots are a good idea for trails with a Moderate or Rugged Side of Gentle rating. When it comes to shoe or boot fit, don't compromise. Purchase your footwear from a merchant who is knowledgeable about hiking, and try on the boots with the type of socks you plan to wear on the trail. After purchasing boots or athletic shoes, it is important to break them in prior to hitting the trails.

Cotton socks are not recommended because they absorb moisture and hold it next to your skin, which may cause blisters or cold feet. Synthetics or other natural fiber socks that are thick or made specifically for hiking are ideal. Some people prefer using a liner sock as well, to ensure comfort and reduce the risk of blisters.

THE BIG STICK

There are several styles of hiking sticks and poles available. Many types have been shown to improve balance and reduce the risk of knee or ankle injury. They are especially useful on declines, inclines, and when hiking through uneven terrain. There are advantages and disadvantages within styles, as well as between poles and sticks. If you are considering using a stick or pole, do some homework and talk to local merchants who carry such items. Keep in mind that although most poles are adjustable and some have shock absorption capabilities, their tips can damage tree roots. Hiking sticks are not adjustable and may be heavier to carry, but cause less damage to roots. Whichever you choose, being knowledgeable about proper usage is a must for your safety and the well-being of the environment.

BUG BEATERS

Mosquitoes, black flies, gnats, biting flies, ticks, chiggers, and sand fleas are all realities to consider when going outdoors. Prevent yourself from being the main course for the bugs' supper by testing which repellent works best for you. Whether you go natural or traditional, we recommend a product that is healthy for you and the environment (please see Foot Note). Remember to use repellent on clothing as well as exposed skin. During times of high foliage, it is recommended that you wear pants tucked into your socks, to prevent tick and other beastie bites. Also check yourself for ticks after any trek into the woods, and know how to remove embedded ticks. Know the signs and symptoms of Lyme disease.

WATER

When hiking, drink water whether you're thirsty or not because if you wait until you're thirsty, you are already dehydrated. A good rule of thumb is to bring 8 ounces (1 cup) of water for each 15 minutes of hiking expected. The Superior Hiking Trail Association and other sources recommend allowing 1 hour for every 1.5 to 3 miles of trail covered. Since all of our trails are less than 3 miles, this means taking a minimum of 32 ounces of water with you (more on a hot day).

Sports drinks are OK, but soft drinks are not recommended, nor are any beverages containing caffeine or alcohol because you will lose more fluid than contained in the drinks. Do not drink water from streams, rivers, or lakes unless you have a water purification device to clean the water of bacteria and other impurities.

SNACKS

Bring food on hikes lasting longer than an hour. Suggested snack items include dried fruits, crackers, granola, cereal, energy bars, and trail mixes. To help keep trails beautiful, pack out anything you take in.

SAFETY ITEMS

A readily accessible, genuine survival whistle is a necessity, even on short hikes. The volume and pitch can scare away unwanted animals or alert others of your position in an emergency. Other items not previously mentioned that we recommend bringing along are personal identification, a small first aid kit, trail maps/descriptions, and a small flashlight.

CELL PHONE

Please be aware that cell phones may not work in all areas, and that includes the ability to receive/send text messages. We have experienced that firsthand. Please alert others to your plans prior to heading out, and have a contingency plan if you're traveling with a group, in case someone gets separated. Simply put, do not rely exclusively on your cell phone for communication.

FUN ITEMS

While experiencing the spectacular scenic beauty of these trails, a camera is a North Shore essential! If there's one bug we actually want you to be bitten by, it's the shutterbug! Compact binoculars are also fun to have for identifying birds and butterflies. A small pocket notebook and pen are also nice for recording memories or thoughts.

DAYPACKS

Backpacks or waist packs are suggested and needed when carrying water or more than one pound of gear. Models with pockets especially for water bottles are convenient. The kind of pack you need depends on the type of hiking you'll be doing, how much gear you plan to carry, and its comfort and functionality.

CONCLUSION

When out on the trail away from modern conveniences, an ounce of prevention is worth more than a pound of cure. Some say it's worth a pound of gold! Implementing the above suggestions may take a little initial planning and organizing, but you'll be glad you did.

Foot Note:

Bug Beaters: For more information about protecting yourself against bug bites, please consult the Center for Disease Control's website: wwwnc.cdc.gov/travel/yellowbook/2018/the-pre-travel-consultation/protection-against-mosquitoes-ticks-other-arthropods

AUTHORS' CORNER

To help maximize your experience, we've created a series of "best of" lists. While subjective, we hope that you will agree with our selections, and we invite you to learn more about them through reading their individual descriptions throughout this guide. Trails, Almost Hikes, and Scenic Locales are listed in order under each category as they appear on the map starting from Duluth. For photos and supplemental information, please visit our website at www.d.umn.edu/~ltornabe/gh/

Now we encourage you to create your own "best of" categories!

Note: Trails/Almost Hikes marked with asterisks indicate hikes that incorporate a portion of a larger trail system.

> **Part of the Gitchi-Gami State Trail (GGST)
>
> ***Part of the Superior Hiking Trail Association (SHT)

Note: These lists are organized geographically, from south (in or near Duluth) to the Canadian border.

FLATTEST TRAILS AND FLATTEST ALMOST HIKES

Enger Park *(Almost Hike) (pg. 148)*
Bayfront Festival Park *(pg. 26)*
Canal Park Lighthouse Stroll *(Almost Hike) (pg. 150)*
Lakewalk: Canal Wall to Bayfront Festival Park*** *(pg. 28)*
Lakewalk: Canal Wall to Fitger's*** *(pg. 32)*
Leif Erikson Rose Garden *(Almost Hike) (pg. 151)*
Lester Park Trail *(pg. 52)*
Two Rivers, Three Views *(Almost Hike) (pg. 152)*
McQuade Small Craft Harbor
    (Breakwater Loop) (Almost Hike) (pg. 153)
Bear Trail *(Almost Hike) (pg. 154)*
Agate Bay Breakwater *(Almost Hike) (pg. 155)*

Leif Erikson Rose Garden
photo by Lisa Vogelsang

Caribou Falls
photo by Lisa Vogelsang

Tofte Park
photo by Lisa Vogelsang

Shovel Point Trail
photo by Lisa Vogelsang

BEST WATERFALLS

BEST VISTAS

BEST WOODED TRAILS

BEST HARBOR VIEWS

BEST BOAT WATCHING

Oberg Mountain and Lake in Autumn
photo by Lisa Vogelsang

BEST RIVER VIEWS

Lester Park Trail *(pg. 52)*
Plaza Overlook Loop *(pg. 66)*
Gooseberry River Loop *(pg. 74)*
High Falls at Tettegouche *(pg. 100)*
Caribou Falls*** *(pg. 108)*
Temperance River Lower Loop *(pg. 114)*
Temperance River Gorge Trail *(pg. 116)*
Kadunce River*** *(pg. 134)*
Brule River Loop *(pg. 140)*

The High Falls at Tettegouche
photo by Lisa Vogelsang

FOR HISTORY BUFFS

Lakewalk: Canal Wall to Fitger's*** *(pg. 32)*
Buchanan Historical Marker *(pg. 168)*
Agate Bay Trail: Lighthouse Loop to Paul Van Hoven Park *(pg. 54)*
Plaza Overlook Loop *(pg. 66)*
Little Two Harbors Trail *(fee portion) (pg. 84)*
Split Rock: Tour de Park *(pg. 86)*
Sugarloaf Cove Trail *(pg. 110)*
Tofte Park *(pg. 159)*
Old Dog Trail *(pg. 178)*
Grand Portage National Monument Picnic Area *(pg. 189)*
High Falls at Grand Portage *(pg. 144)*
Webster-Ashburton Trail and Picnic Area *(pg. 142)*
High Falls at Grand Portage *(pg. 144)*

The High Falls at Grand Portage
photo courtesy of Shutterstock

FOR ART VIEWING

The following feature one or more pieces of art. For more detailed descriptions of such artwork, please visit our website at www.d.umn.edu/~ltornabe/gh/

Bayfront Festival Park *(the stage is a work of art!) (pg. 26)*
Lakewalk: Canal Wall to Bayfront Festival Park *(small replica of an incredibly famous statue) (pg. 28)*
Lakewalk: Canal Wall to Fitger's, including Lake Place *(mural & sculpture). (pg. 32)*
Bear Trail *(Almost Hike) whimsical, fun cutouts make for great photo ops!) (pg. 154)*
Tofte Park *(very intriguing sculpture) (pg. 159)*
Harbor Park/Bear Tree Park *(Almost Hike) (sculpture) (pg. 162)*
Gooseberry Falls *(nature art column located outside visitor center) (pg. 64)*
Tettegouche State Park Visitor Center *(art exhibits) (pp. 90-100)*
High Falls at Grand Portage *(exhibit paintings and tile art) (pg. 144)*

HIKES WITH KID-FRIENDLY FEATURES

Hiking is an excellent way to introduce children to the natural world. While we provide our take on the best kid-friendly hikes, our disclaimer is that we have seen smiling kids and parents on nearly every trail within our book. Therefore, our best advice is to refer to individual descriptions for safety concerns and other details before bringing children on any trail.

With that said, our best kid-friendly recommendations begin with all of our picnic areas, waysides, and scenic locales, because they are typically level and provide nearby parking and restrooms. We also suggest all paved trails, and Flattest Trails and Flattest Almost Hikes in Authors' Corner.

Locale	Kid-friendly Feature
Enger Park (pg. 148)	Paved path to Tower climb and spacious grounds. Note: Tower lookouts are open-air but have higher walls topped with rails for additional safety. Resting platforms on each level.
Bayfront Festival Park (pg. 26)	Paved path featuring Playfront Park, a "gem" for kids! Find out more at bayfrontfestivalpark.com/playfront-park/
	Also, check our trail Foot Note for website of happenings in Bayfront Festival Park, as some festivals have activities specifically for children. If you're visiting near Thanksgiving/Christmas, Bentleyville "Tour of Lights" is an absolute must! www.bentleyvilleusa.org
Lakewalk: Canal Wall to Bayfront Park (pg. 28)	Paved path featuring Maritime Museum and prime boat watching (free admission, lsmma.com), harbor cruises (Vista Fleet, www.vistafleet.com), ore boat tours (decc.org/william-a-irvin/).
	Great Lakes Aquarium (glaquarium.org) and much more adventure in Canal Park (www.canalparkduluth.com) and miles of beaches at nearby Park Point (www.parkpointbeach.org). All sections of the Lakewalk are paved, non-motorized, multiuse, and tobacco free!
Lakewalk: Canal Wall to Fitger's (pg. 32)	Paved path featuring Maritime Museum and prime boat watching (free admission, lsmma.com), horse and buggy rides (www.facebook.com/TopHatCarriages/), surrey bicycle rentals (wheelfunrentals.com/mn/duluth/canal-park/), pebble beach for stone skipping, Hi-Spy Viewing machines (in Sister Cities Park near Lake Place).
Lakewalk: Rose Garden to Fitger's (pg. 36)	Leif Erikson Park has an open stage and two stone towers, plus a large field hosts numerous events. Movie night in summer is a big draw for families. downtownduluth.com/calendar
Leif Erikson Rose Garden (pg. 151)	Thousands of roses to delight little noses! Spectacular Lake Superior views.
Bagley Nature Area (pg. 44)	Located on the University of Minnesota Duluth (UMD) campus, this area features wood-chipped paths. While not stroller-friendly, there is Rock Pond for viewing ducks and other wildlife. Walk-in, tent-only open-field campground surrounded by trees and trails, with parking and portable toilet nearby. Great opportunity for families new to camping, as UMD rents all equipment needed (d.umn.edu/recreational-sports-outdoor-program/programs/rental-center/bagley-nature-area-campground). Summer bonus: A Bagley Park Ranger provides nature-education programs and activities on weekends.

To further assist in showcasing trails with kid-friendly features, such as playgrounds, a campus campground (Bagley Nature Area at the University of Minnesota Duluth, complete with gear rental), hikes with cultural features, interpretive signs/centers, and seasonal events (e.g., movies in Leif Erikson Park!), we have created the following chart. Our list also includes functional features, such as fairly level paths (many paved for stroller accommodation) and bathrooms for when you inevitably hear, "I have to go potty—NOW!" The chart below lists the locale, page number, kid-friendly highlight, bathroom type/location, trail surface, and any safety concerns.

As you might expect, we are quite conservative when it comes to safety. Yet because any outdoor activity poses different degrees of risk, an attentive on-site parent/guardian is always our best "kid-friendly feature" recommendation!

Note: These lists are organized geographically, from south (in or near Duluth) to the Canadian border.

Restroom Type & Location	Safety Alert
Flush; centrally located.	Enger Park is surrounded by slopes and drop-offs.
Flush; centrally located with portables added for events.	
Flush toilets inside Maritime Museum, Vista Fleet gift shop, and Aquarium.	
Flush toilets inside Maritime Museum, near Endion Station, and in Fitger's complex.	
Flush toilets.	
Portable toilet near Rock Pond and campground.	

Locale	Kid-friendly Feature
Rock Knob—Hartley Pond & Tischer Creek Loop *(pp. 48, 50)*	Not stroller friendly, but . . . the view from Rock Knob is amazing and Hartley Pond is home to summer fun. Both trails are located at Hartley Park, which hosts summer camps and other kid-oriented outdoor activities. hartleynature.org
Lester Park Trail *(pg. 52)*	Nice playground and covered picnic area at trailhead. Beautiful hike above river.
McQuade Small Craft Harbor (Breakwater Loop) *(pg. 153)*	Paved path leads to several fishing piers.
Bear Trail Almost Hike *(pg. 154)*	Wood-chipped path, but irresistible bear-face cutouts for fun family photo ops. And did we mention the candy store on the premises where third- and fourth-generation candymakers honor 100 years of tradition when making treats the old-fashioned way? Sweet!
Agate Bay Trail: Burlington Bay to First Street *(pg. 58)*	Beach near trailhead. Paved trail along Lake Superior with playground across the street at 0.1 mile (Lakeview Park).
Plaza Overlook Loop *(pg. 66)*	Paved trail to Gooseberry Falls (Middle and Upper falls). Both spectacular waterfalls. Plaza Overlook Loop has paved access, and many kiosks display interesting information. Must-see exhibits at visitor center.
Split Rock River Beach *(pg. 156)*	Pebble Beach access via tunnel under Highway 61. Also, the paved multi-use Gitchi-Gami State Trail (GGST) literally passes right outside this tunnel, providing easy access for bicycles. To see all GGST sections along the North Shore, visit www.ggta.org
Little Two Harbors Trail & Pebble Beach *(pg. 80)*	Crushed limestone surface with Pebble Beach access and great family picnic areas. Iconic photo ops of Split Rock Lighthouse. Nearby Minnesota Historical Society offers Lighthouse tours. www.mnhs.org/splitrock
Triple Overlook Loop *(pg. 90)*	This paved, wide path strings together three overlooks with guardrails on the last two (the first is not very close to the lake nor is it perched on a cliff). Visitor center houses a spectacular interpretive exhibit.
Taconite Harbor Public Water Access and Safe Harbor *(pg. 173)*	Paved access to mining artifacts makes for fun photo ops/exploration with an educational twist.
Poplar River Overlook *(pg. 124)*	Short hike leads to wonderful overlook of river, and en route are a plethora of activities at Lutsen Mountain that may be appealing to kids of all ages! (www.lutsen.com)
Harbor Park/Bear Tree Park *(pg. 162)*	Direct pebble beach access with some paved and hard-packed dirt surfaces. Ample benches to supervise stone skipping.
Sugarloaf Cove Trail *(pg. 110)*	Interpretive trail. Center offers nature-oriented activities and learning opportunities for families. Explore pebble beach to search for rocks polished by Lake Superior (sugarloafnorthshore.org/about-sugarloaf/)
Grand Portage National Monument Picnic Area *(pg. 189)*	Visit the Heritage Center that houses exhibit galleries about Ojibwe culture. Junior Ranger program in summer. www.nps.gov/grpo/index.htm
High Falls at Grand Portage *(pg. 144)*	Paved access to spectacular view of highest falls along the Minnesota and Canada border. Welcome center exhibit is a must-see.

Restroom Type & Location	Safety Alert
Flush toilets inside Hartley Nature Center. Portable toilet in parking lot.	
Portable toilets in parking lot.	Steep cliffs, some without guardrails.
Flush toilets near boat launch.	
Vault toilet at nearby rest area (see trail description).	
Flush toilets at Lakeview Park.	
Flush toilets at visitor center.	Lots of steep places with no guardrails.
None.	GGST can be very hilly in sections.
Flush toilets at picnic shelter; vault toilet near Pebble Beach.	
Flush toilets at visitor center.	
Portable toilets near boat launch.	
Portable restrooms at nearby Boulder Park (see pg. 176).	
Flush toilets at interpretive center.	
Flush toilets.	
Flush toilets at welcome center.	

▼⁄⁄◢ Venue Name:*

The trail profile starts with the official name of the trails, Almost Hikes, waysides and scenic locales, and picnic areas. However, if an asterisk appears, the trail has been given a *Gentle Hikes* name because either no name previously existed or it is part of another trail.

In smaller print and listed directly under the venue name, we provide the following when applicable:
—Venue's location (e.g., in Duluth, within a State Park, or part of the SHT or GGST)
—Entry point to the venue (e.g., on or off Highway 61)
—Approximate mileage from Duluth

- **Highlights: Showcases the primary features of or other pertinent information about this venue.**

DIRECTIONS:

These are given from either I-35 or from Highway 61. If from Highway 61, we use the mile markers provided therein, which are in whole numbers (e.g., 58) and are green with white numbering. For improved accuracy, we list them in tenths of a mile (e.g., 58.5). **Note:** Mile marker 26 in Two Harbors is not posted, and there may be others missing due to road construction.

FYI: All state park entrances are on Highway 61, with the exception of George H. Crosby Manitou State Park. Most sections of the SHT are off various county roads that intersect Highway 61. For venues in Duluth, directions are given from the southwest end of Duluth on I-35.

CONTACT:

A phone/website is provided for trails only (not for other scenic locales) as a means to obtain more information about the trail.

TOTAL TRAIL LENGTH, SURFACE, & WIDTH:

Trail length is round-trip distance to the nearest tenth of a mile. Trail surface varies from paved, gravel, and hard-packed dirt to rock and root. When rock and root are present, they are reported in three categories: minimum, moderate, and significant. **Please note:** With the exception of Duluth's Lakewalk, paved trails are not plowed or de-iced during the snow season. However, even though the Lakewalk is plowed, it can still be icy, as can be entry ramps.

INCLINES & ALERTS:

Although inclines can be reported as a percentage grade, we chose to use degrees (for conversion table, see page 211). The number of inclines exceeding 10° (18 percent grade), their degree ranges, the steepest incline (its length and location), and the longest incline (exceeding 30) is listed for every trail. Alerts include potential safety hazards or other matters of concern.

TRAILHEAD FACILITIES & FEES/AMENITIES:

Unless otherwise noted, facilities are mentioned only if they are at trailhead parking area or on the trail. Fees pertain to parking and entrance. **Note:** There is no fee to park at Gooseberry Falls Visitor Center (two-hour limit, but parking may be challenging during high traffic), Tettegouche Visitor Center (four-hour limit), highway access to Temperance River & Cascade Falls (no overnight, out by 10 p.m.), and Grand Portage State Park (four-hour limit). However, if vehicles are driven to or parked at other areas within the park, a day-use or annual permit is required and available at state park offices.

MILEAGE & DESCRIPTION/NARRATIVE

0.0   For all trails, we include a step-by-step description of what to expect on the trail, reported in increments of 0.1 mile. While not every tenth of a mile on the trail is described, we do note locations of steps, inclines, benches, bridges, safety alerts, wayfinding elements, and of course, spectacular scenery, otherwise known as photo ops! For Almost Hikes, a general narrative is provided.

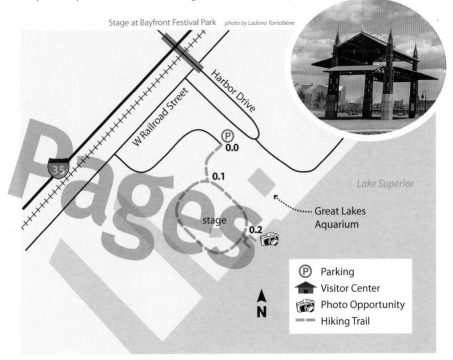

Stage at Bayfront Festival Park   *photo by Ladona Tornabene*

OTHER ITEMS YOU'LL FIND:

 Foot Note:

Information that may be of interest to our readers, typically about a trail/scenic locale, its history, or a nearby sight to see. These are listed near the specific trails, Almost Hikes, waysides, and picnic areas to which they pertain.

 Says Who?

Professional information from research-based sources related to health. These are scattered throughout the book.

Two Harbors

Duluth

Canadian Border

Grand Marais

Little Marais

The Trails

- ◉ Duluth to Two Harbors
- ○ Beyond Two Harbors to Little Marais
- ◉ Beyond Little Marais to Grand Marais
- ○ Beyond Grand Marais to the Canadian Border

How to Use This Section

TRAIL RATING:

To accommodate hikers of all levels, each trail follows a rating system. The rating system is governed by a set of criteria (see below) and offers three levels. Trails range from the **Lighter Side of Gentle**, which includes all paved trails (and more), to the **Rugged Side of Gentle**, which offers more challenge to those who desire it. The **Moderate Side of Gentle**, as you might expect, falls somewhere in between. All trails are less than 3 miles in total length.

Regardless of the rating, each trail will always state the trail surface and width, the number of inclines more than 10 degrees, the steepest and longest incline, safety concerns, and all step and bench locations.

Our trail descriptions are very detailed and correspond to the trail in increments of tenths of a mile. We have made every attempt to locate and note trail aspects that may challenge (e.g., inclines, rocks, roots, steps, etc.) as well as features that may be helpful (e.g., benches, hand railings, paved trails, etc.). With this information, our readers can make an informed decision based on their abilities/circumstances as to how far to go on a certain trail or whether to choose another altogether.

ICONS:

The following icons represent our trail-rating system.

LIGHTER

The **Lighter Side of Gentle** must meet all of the following criteria (excluding options):

INCLINES: 10–12° (or less)
ROCK/ROOT: Minimal (intermittent moderate sections)
TOTAL NUMBER OF STEPS ENCOUNTERED THROUGHOUT THE TRAIL: <25
TRAIL SURFACE: Even (intermittent uneven sections)

MODERATE

The **Moderate Side of Gentle** meets ONE or more of the following criteria:

INCLINES: 14–16° (or no more than 2 inclines between 18–22°, not exceeding 35' in length)
ROCK/ROOT: Moderate
TOTAL NUMBER OF STEPS ENCOUNTERED THROUGHOUT THE TRAIL: <175
TRAIL SURFACE: Even or uneven

RUGGED

The **Rugged Side of Gentle** meets ONE or more of the following criteria:

INCLINES: 18–22°
ROCK/ROOT: Moderate to significant
TOTAL NUMBER OF STEPS ENCOUNTERED THROUGHOUT THE TRAIL: <325
TRAIL SURFACE: Even or uneven, laid-log paths possible.

ICONS IN THE DESCRIPTIONS:

These icons, embedded in the trail description and mileage section for each trail, allow you to quickly see what's ahead on the trail.

INCLINE
DECLINE   Indicates the location of the steepest incline or decline on the trail.

STEPS   We note in the description if they ascend/descend, their composition, and if they have handrails or not. "Non-continuous" indicates a brief resting area between sets of steps.

BENCH   Indicates the location of benches on the trail.

PHOTO   On our trails, we have chosen places where we thought the views were photo-worthy. Some are obvious, others are purely subjective; we hope you will be pleased with our suggestions. We have found it to be a great way of preserving and sharing memories for years to come, as well as a whole lot of fun taking them.

MAPS:

Provided for each trail, maps show mileage markers that correspond to selected trail descriptions. Not all mileage markers are shown on the maps—only those that will help you locate your position on the trail.

Duluth to Two Harbors

Herb Garden within the Duluth Rose Garden *photo by Ladona Tornabene*

▰▰▰ Bayfront Festival Park

Bayfront Park • Duluth, MN

- **Commanding views of the Aerial Lift Bridge and a great boat watching location.**
- **Home to several music festivals and events (see Foot Note).**
- **Playfront on the Bayfront designed with little ones in mind.**

TRAILHEAD DIRECTIONS:

I-35 North to Lake Avenue South exit, turn right. Take another right at the first intersection (traffic light) onto Railroad Street and follow for 0.5 mile. After passing under Harbor Drive, look left for the entrance to the parking lot. Trailhead begins near playground area. Parking fees may apply during events, but parking is free for up to 2 hours for Playfront Park use only. For helpful parking info, visit: bayfrontfestivalpark.com/parking/

CONTACT:

Duluth Parks and Recreation: 218-730-4300 or www.duluthmn.gov/parks/

TOTAL TRAIL LENGTH, SURFACE, & WIDTH:

0.5 mile; asphalt, brick, and concrete; average 8–15' wide.

INCLINES & ALERTS:

No inclines. This is a multiuse, non-motorized path. During special events, other regulations may apply. Trail is not plowed during snow season. In addition, no smoking is allowed at Bayfront Festival Park or in the parking areas.

TRAILHEAD FACILITIES & FEES:

Seasonal flush toilets and water fountain. No parking fees, except during special events.

MILEAGE & DESCRIPTION

0.0
BENCH
PHOTO
Trailhead begins on asphalt near the Playfront, then changes to a herringbone-pattern brick as you enter Bayfront Festival Park. Directly ahead is the welcoming artistic arch framing the Bayfront stage, a work of art in and of itself!

0.1
BENCH
PHOTO
Turn left and begin walking toward the harbor on asphalt path. In 400', you will arrive at an intersection with another part of the Lakewalk entering from the left. Turn right, choosing either the asphalt or the concrete walkway; both run parallel and lead to the same place.

0.2
BENCH
PHOTO
Stroll out to the deck overlooking the Duluth Harbor for a commanding view of the Aerial Lift Bridge. This is also a great place for boat watching. Take some time to read the informational display about the slip's history. This area is also a popular kayaking and sailing location as well as the summer home to many species of waterfowl. Geese are especially prevalent here.

0.3
BENCH
Continue walking the asphalt pathway along the back of the Bayfront stage. The path does continue over to the Silos Restaurant and Pier B Resort, but to complete this hike, remain on the path until you come full-circle to the brick surface and Playfront again.

0.5 Trailhead and parking area.

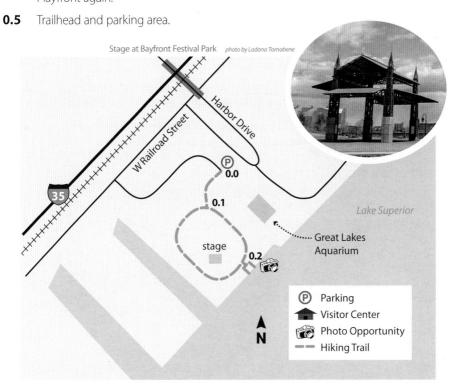

Stage at Bayfront Festival Park *photo by Ladona Tornabene*

Lake Superior

Great Lakes Aquarium

stage

Ⓟ Parking
🏛 Visitor Center
📷 Photo Opportunity
— — Hiking Trail

N

👣 **Foot Note:**

Bayfront Festival Park hosts an array of activities, including concerts and festivals (bayfrontfestivalpark.com). In winter, the park houses an outdoor ice rink and a holiday favorite—the Bentleyville "Tour of Lights" (www.bentleyvilleusa.org).

Lakewalk:
Canal Wall to Bayfront Festival Park*

Canal Park • Duluth, MN
*Superior Hiking Trail section: MN/WI Border to Duluth (flat and paved)

- **Premier location for boat watching! It just does not get much better than this (see Foot Notes for schedules).**
- **Peruse the Maritime Visitor Center: There's no admission fee and there are programs/exhibits on maritime history (see Foot Notes).**
- **Walk under the Aerial Lift Bridge, Duluth's best-known landmark, which raises 138' in 55 seconds.**

TRAILHEAD DIRECTIONS & PARKING:
I-35 North to Lake Avenue South exit, turn right. Continue straight onto Canal Park Drive. Trailhead begins at the end of Canal Park Drive in front of Lake Superior Maritime Visitor Center. Most parking is fee-based (May 15–Oct. 26) and enforced 24/7. For helpful parking info, visit: canalpark.com/parking-transportation/

CONTACT:
Duluth Parks and Recreation: 218-730-4300 or www.duluthmn.gov/parks/

TOTAL TRAIL LENGTH, SURFACE, & WIDTH:
1.2 miles; concrete and asphalt; average 8–10' wide; sidewalk sections average 4–5' wide.

INCLINES & ALERTS:
No inclines except a gentle ramp access located in front of the Maritime Center. The first 0.2 mile of this trail is with signage informing visitors that they need to use at their own risk. If windy, waves can crest the structure or flood the area. This is a multiuse, non-motorized path. Some sidewalk sections are uneven along Harbor Drive behind the Duluth Entertainment and Convention Center (DECC). The entire Lakewalk is tobacco free.

TRAILHEAD FACILITIES & FEES:
Flush toilets and water fountain at Lake Superior Maritime Visitor Center, which offers several free exhibits/programs on maritime history. For hours of operation and more, visit www.lsmma.com/visitors-center/. No fees for trail use.

MILEAGE & DESCRIPTION

0.0
BENCH
PHOTO
The trailhead begins on the paved walkway down the very wide gentle grade near the doorway to the Lake Superior Maritime Visitor Center. This center is operated by the U.S. Army Corps of Engineers and houses some fine exhibits and programs. Admission is free. There are ample benches in this area for boat watching.

At the canal wall, when facing the shipping canal, turn right and walk under Duluth's most famous landmark—the spectacular Aerial Lift Bridge. As you walk under this bridge, notice how its deck is not solid, but an open pattern to allow water to drain. This section of trail offers a fantastic boat-watching vantage point, since boats can be observed arriving and leaving under the bridge (see Foot Notes for schedules). The excitement they bring is simply invigorating! The path soon rounds the corner and continues as it parallels the harbor affording impressive and unobstructed views.

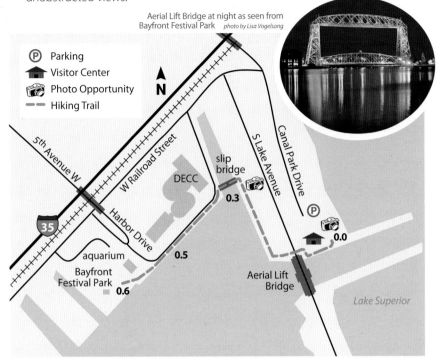

Aerial Lift Bridge at night as seen from Bayfront Festival Park   *photo by Lisa Vogelsang*

0.3
BENCH
PHOTO

Look straight ahead for the Minnesota Slip Bridge, as the trail will pass over it. Beyond this bridge sits the "proud flagship of U.S. Steel's Great Lakes Fleet," the *William A. Irvin*, which offers tours (see Foot Notes). Another commonly observed sight are boats from the Vista Fleet, which offer fully narrated cruises on the harbor and Lake Superior from phenomenal viewpoints. Their office and bountiful gift shop are just across the slip bridge (see Foot Notes). The trail becomes less defined after the slip bridge, but stay to the left and follow the patchwork of sidewalks that parallel the beautiful harbor basin as well as Harbor Drive. **Alert:** The sidewalk is slightly slanted/uneven in many places. Continue for another 0.2 mile (that huge structure to the right is the Duluth Entertainment Convention Center) until a boardwalk begins.

0.5
PHOTO

A few yards before the wide section of boardwalk (uneven in places) and prior to the road curving, look to the right across Harbor Drive. There stands a small replica of the Statue of Liberty! As you continue down the boardwalk, the path passes behind the Great Lakes Aquarium, a place where kids of all ages will enjoy interactivity and various exhibits (see Foot Notes). Also in this location facing the water are interpretive signs that inform about the harbor and Aerial Lift Bridge.

0.6
PHOTO
The next interpretative sign informs about the Bayfront Festival Park (see Foot Notes). The trail continues (see pg. 26 for Bayfront Festival Park); however, to complete this section of the Lakewalk, turn around and retrace the path to the trailhead.

1.2 Trailhead.

 Foot Notes:

Waiting for your ship to come in? This trail is absolutely prime for boat watching! Visit: duluthshippingnews.com. You can also check ship status in real-time at ais.boatnerd.com

"Knot" getting enough Maritime history? See the trail highlight for the Lake Superior Maritime Museum: www.lsmma.com/visitors-center/

Want a shipshape tour? The *William A. Irvin* is at your service. Visit: decc.org/william-a-irvin/

Which cruise to choose? Vista Fleet offers many narrated Lake Superior/harbor tours. Visit: www.vistafleet.com

Yearning for "deeper" learning? Explore Great Lakes Aquarium. Visit: www.glaquarium.org

Duluth Lighthouse view from trailhead near the Lake Superior Maritime Visitor Center   *photo by Ladona Tornabene*

Lakewalk: Canal Wall to Fitger's*

Canal Park • Duluth, MN • Superior Hiking Trail section: MN/WI Border to Duluth (flat and paved except for gentle ramp access to Lake Place)

- **See nonstop, gorgeous vistas of Lake Superior and stunning, iconic views of the Aerial Lift Bridge and lighthouses!**
- **Feel Canal Park's pulse as the trail parallels lodging, eateries, local breweries, and specialty shops (see Foot Note).**
- **Visit Lake Place, Sister Cities Park, and the open-air Korean Veterans Memorial and Northland Vietnam Veterans Memorial.**

TRAILHEAD DIRECTIONS:

From I-35 North, take the Lake Avenue South exit, turn right. Continue straight onto Canal Park Drive. Trailhead begins at the end of Canal Park Drive in front of Lake Superior Maritime Visitor Center. Most parking is fee-based (May 15–Oct. 26) and enforced 24/7. For helpful parking info, visit: canalpark.com/parking-transportation/

CONTACT:

Duluth Parks and Recreation: 218-730-4300 or www.duluthmn.gov/parks/

TOTAL TRAIL LENGTH, SURFACE, & WIDTH:

2.0 miles; concrete; boardwalk and blacktop run parallel to each other; average 5–8' wide.

INCLINES & ALERTS:

No inclines more than 10°. No bikes or in-line skates allowed on boardwalk. Blacktop, which runs parallel to boardwalk, is a multiuse, non-motorized path. During colder seasons, frost/ice on boardwalk may create slick conditions. The entire Lakewalk is tobacco free.

TRAILHEAD FACILITIES & FEES:

Flush toilets and water fountain at Lake Superior Maritime Visitor Center, which offers several exhibits/programs on maritime history. Admission is free. For hours of operation and more, visit www.lsmma.com/visitors-center/. Additional restrooms with flush toilets and seasonal water fountains near base of Lake Place Park steps. No fees for trail use.

MILEAGE & DESCRIPTION

0.0
BENCH
PHOTO

Trailhead begins at canal wall near Lake Superior Maritime Visitor Center, which merits a stop. Admission is free. When facing the city, to the right is the lighthouse and shipping canal. To the left is a very close look at the Aerial Lift Bridge. This is a fantastic location for viewing ships entering and leaving the harbor, with ample benches for your viewing pleasure. Adding to this photo op–rich location is the *Bayfield* (a now land-based U.S. Army Corps of Engineers tugboat), an imaginative sculpture of the Aerial Lift Bridge (to lift your spirits!), a retired fishing vessel transformed into a food stand, and a repurposed ship pilot house that houses bicycle rentals.

Numerous larger-than-life shipping artifacts and panoramic vistas of the lake welcome you as this trail soon divides into boardwalk, blacktop, and a gravel path where all three parallel each other.

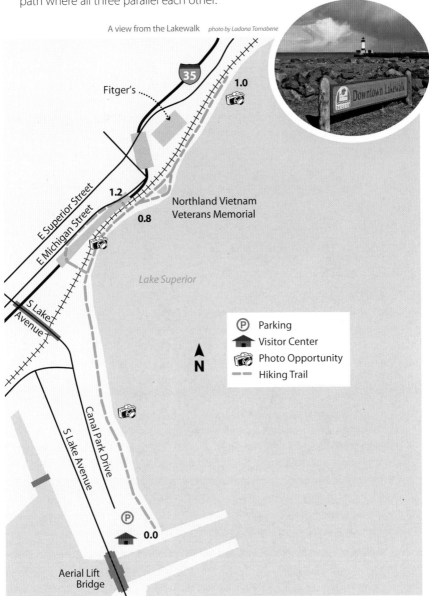

A view from the Lakewalk   *photo by Ladona Tornabene*

Fitger's

35

1.0

1.2

0.8

Northland Vietnam
Veterans Memorial

E Superior Street

E Michigan Street

Lake Superior

S Lake
Avenue

N

Ⓟ Parking

🏠 Visitor Center

📷 Photo Opportunity

– – – Hiking Trail

Canal Park Drive

S Lake Avenue

Ⓟ

0.0

Aerial Lift
Bridge

0.1
BENCH
PHOTO
To the left are sights and sounds of Canal Park, where much action takes place in the summer. Horse-drawn buggies leisurely stroll along a gravel path as local musicians periodically showcase their talents. This section of the trail passes behind several lodging and eating establishments as well as local breweries.

Interpretive signs line the boardwalk with facts about a shipwreck, Lake Superior, the Lakewalk, and shipping history, while strategically placed benches afford marvelous views of the lake and lighthouse—all ideally positioned for boat watching or just soaking in the extraordinary views. As beautiful as the lake is, surprisingly it wasn't a place of urban development for Duluth. The path you now stand on wasn't created until 1986.

0.2
BENCH
PHOTO
By now you may have noticed an odd-looking structure in the lake. The interpretative sign nearby reveals the truth and the fascinating history behind The Cribs, informally known as "Uncle Harvey's Mausoleum," a remnant of efforts to take advantage of the planned, but never built, Outer Harbor Breakwater of the late 1800s. A must-read for history aficionados!

0.5
PHOTO
There is a modern restroom (year-round) and water fountain (seasonal) just before the numerous steps leading up to Lake Place and Sister Cities Parks. Instead of taking these steps, we advise continuing on the walk as we recommend entering via the ramp farther along the Lakewalk.

As the path curves to the right, it parallels an amazing Image Wall, which extends nearly 600'! This mural was created by Duluth artist Mark Marino and is composed of several million ceramic tiles depicting chronological scenes of sunken ships. The views change as you move along. Be sure to read the interpretative panels here.

0.8
BENCH
PHOTO
As you meander along, the views of Lake Superior continue to deliver. As the boardwalk and blacktop sections temporarily part, two memorials are featured here. The Korean Veterans Memorial honors a highly decorated group of local soldiers, most of whom served in combat. Illuminated, it is especially poignant at night. The Northland Vietnam Veterans Memorial is crafted in the style of the Washington, D.C., Vietnam Memorial and depicts local heroes. The bunker and its strategic placement of sidelights merit spending some time in this area.

1.0
BENCH
PHOTO
Soon you will come to two sets of stairs. The first leads to the Fitger's Brewery Complex (filled with specialty shops, restaurants, and a hotel). The second set of stairs leads to the PortLand Malt Shoppe and more specialty shops. Many benches near the stair entrance provide exceptional views of the Aerial Lift Bridge and shipping canal as well as the unsurpassed beauty of Superior's shoreline.

This second set of stairs signals the end of the boardwalk. The blacktop portion of the Lakewalk continues (see "Rose Garden to Fitger's," pg. 36); however, to complete this section, turn around and retrace the path to trailhead.

1.2
BENCH
PHOTO
On the return, as you pass the Vietnam and Korean Memorials on the left, begin looking to the right across the railroad tracks for a generous ramp entrance that will bring you to Lake Place Park. After crossing the tracks, turn left to enter this 3-acre addition with vistas of the lake, Aerial Lift Bridge, shipping lane, lighthouse, pebble beach, and rugged rocky shore! Benches abound and you will find a partially enclosed windbreak for wave watching in November. Lake Place also showcases sculptures by various artists and provides easy access to downtown Duluth, where shopping, lodging, and multiple eateries await. However, while up here, take time to visit Sister Cities Park, which is located 0.1 mile southwest of Lake Place.

1.3
BENCH
PHOTO
Sister Cities Park has views similar to Lake Place, but the addition of the complimentary Hi-Spy viewing machines take boat watching to a completely new level. Exploring this park entails a walk of about 0.3 mile around the entire perimeter; benches abound and the surface is half paved and half boardwalk.

You can return to the main trail the same way you came up or take the steps or the switchback ramp (located between Lake Place and Sister Cities Parks) that will lead back down to the Lakewalk. Then retrace your steps toward the Lake Superior Maritime Visitor Center, where you began your adventure. The return walk is just as beautiful as the initial one, while viewing Lake Superior from a slightly different perspective. Allow yourself time, as there is so much to see and do in the Canal Park area (see Foot Note).

2.0
BENCH
PHOTO
Trailhead. While you're here, take the "Canal Park Lighthouse Stroll Almost Hike" (pg. 150) to the lighthouse, and save some time to peruse the Lake Superior Maritime Visitor Center, which offers several exhibits and programs on maritime history.

Foot Notes:

For more information about Canal Park, including attractions, eateries, shopping, parking, lodging, and more, visit: www.canalparkduluth.com

For more information on the arts in Duluth or along the North Shore, visit www.duluth.com/attractions or www.northshorevisitor.com/attractions/the-arts/

Says Who?

Beer for what "ales"?

Having a beer—emphasis on the "a"—with dinner can be as healthy as having a glass of wine, because their antioxidant content is similar

Nutrition, Metabolism and Cardiovascular Diseases[32]

Art for the heart!

Did you know that participation in arts-based activities can decrease stress and increase positive well-being?

American Journal of Public Health[37]

Lakewalk: Rose Garden to Fitger's

Duluth, MN • Superior Hiking Trail section: MN/WI Border to Duluth

- **Commanding views of the Aerial Lift Bridge and, of course, the lake.**
- **Access point to this section of the Lakewalk is home to thousands of roses and a peony garden!**

TRAILHEAD DIRECTIONS:

Take I-35 North to Lake Avenue North exit, and turn left. Turn right at the first traffic light onto Superior Street. At 10th Avenue E, turn right onto London Road (this is where London Road begins and then runs parallel to Superior Street). Drive to the paved parking lot on right side of the street between S 13th Avenue E and S 14th Avenue E.

CONTACT:

Duluth Parks and Recreation: 218-730-4300 or www.duluthmn.gov/parks/

TOTAL TRAIL LENGTH, SURFACE, & WIDTH:

1.4 miles; cobblestone and asphalt; average 8–10' wide.

INCLINES & ALERTS:

No inclines greater than 10°. This section is a multiuse, non-motorized path and may be used by in-line skaters and cyclists. Although pets are welcome on the Lakewalk, they are not allowed in the rose garden. Please use the sidewalk next to London Road and follow it around to the access ramp if you are walking your pet.

TRAILHEAD FACILITIES & FEES:

Seasonal flush toilets and water fountain available near parking lot. Grocery and eateries nearby. Portable toilet available in winter. No fees for trail use.

MILEAGE & DESCRIPTION

0.0 The trailhead begins on a concrete land bridge (paved, double handrail) located at the far end of the rose garden (see Leif Erikson Rose Garden Almost Hike, pg. 151). This bridge is part of an access ramp leading down to the Lakewalk. As you cross the bridge, the Lakewalk and railroad are directly beneath you.

PHOTO Pause and look left while crossing the bridge for a stunning view of small rock jetties lining the shore of Lake Superior. As you descend the ramp switchbacks, watch for in-line skaters, cyclists, and dogs on leashes.

0.1 At the end of ramp, continue straight onto an asphalt trail, which brings you into
BENCH Leif Erikson Park. This can be a busy "intersection" of the multiuse Lakewalk, so
PHOTO please be mindful of others entering (sometimes swiftly) from the left and right.

Several benches are scattered along the trail at various intervals. As you continue along this path, the open-air amphitheater will be to your left. This park is used during all times of the year for various activities and is a favorite open-field play area. Take some time to explore this beautiful area, as seasonal gardens abound. Look for the "Angel of Hope" just off the main path to the right, a memorial for parents who have lost a child. Inviting florals and a gentle gravel path lead to this statue.

0.5
BENCH
PHOTO
Pause for a great photo op of the Aerial Lift Bridge and shipping canal from the perfectly placed benches.

0.7
Soon you will encounter a set of steps to the right that lead to the PortLand Malt Shoppe and other eateries. Shortly thereafter, the second set leads to Fitger's Complex, which hosts many specialty shops and restaurants.

The Lakewalk continues into Canal Park (see Canal Wall to Fitger's, pg. 32); however, to complete this section, turn around and retrace path to trailhead.

1.4
Trailhead.

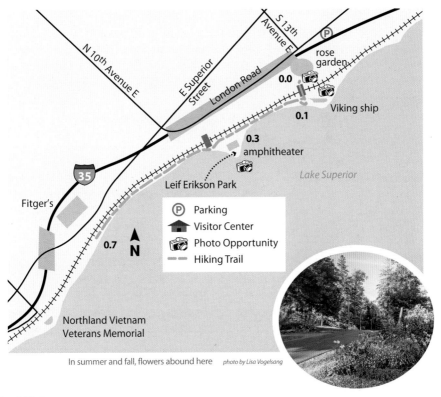

In summer and fall, flowers abound here   *photo by Lisa Vogelsang*

Foot Note:

Can't wait to get here? Have a sneak peek via the Parks & Recreation virtual tour! Visit: www.duluthmn.gov/parks/parks-listing/rose-garden/

Lakewalk East:
Rose Garden to Water Street

Duluth, MN

- **Access point to this section of the Lakewalk is home to thousands of roses and a peony garden!**
- **Experience some of Superior's most scenic, rugged shoreline— especially beautiful when waves are crashing.**

TRAILHEAD DIRECTIONS:

Take I-35 North to Lake Avenue North exit, turn left. Turn right at the first traffic light onto Superior Street. At 10th Avenue E, turn right onto London Road (this is where London Road begins and then runs parallel to Superior Street). Drive to the paved parking lot on right side of street between S 13th Avenue E and S 14th Avenue E.

CONTACT:

Duluth Parks and Recreation: 218-730-4300 or www.duluthmn.gov/parks/

TOTAL TRAIL LENGTH, SURFACE, & WIDTH:

1.8 miles; cobblestone and asphalt; average 8–10' wide.

INCLINES & ALERTS:

No inclines greater than 10°. This section is a multiuse, non-motorized path. Although pets are welcome on the Lakewalk, they are not allowed in the Rose Garden. Please use the sidewalk next to London Road and follow around to the access ramp if you are walking your pet. Street crossing is necessary if you continue through the optional interrupted section of the Lakewalk.

TRAILHEAD FACILITIES & FEES:

Seasonal flush toilets and water fountain available near parking lot. Grocery and eateries nearby. Portable toilet available on Lakewalk East. No fees for trail use.

MILEAGE & DESCRIPTION

0.0 Trailhead begins on a concrete land bridge (paved, double handrail) located at the far end of the rose garden (see Leif Erikson Rose Garden Almost Hike, pg. 151). This bridge is part of an access ramp leading down to the Lakewalk. As you cross the bridge, the Lakewalk and railroad are directly beneath you.

PHOTO Pause and look left while crossing the bridge for a stunning view of small rock jetties lining the shore of Lake Superior. As you descend the ramp switchbacks, watch for in-line skaters, cyclists, and dogs on leashes.

0.1 At end of ramp, turn right and follow Lakewalk as you head northeast along
BENCH Duluth's rugged yet beautiful lakeshore. **Alert:** This can be a busy "intersection"
PHOTO of the multiuse Lakewalk, so please be mindful of others entering (sometimes swiftly) from the left and right. Several benches abound throughout this entire trail, offering sweeping vistas of Lake Superior and her rugged shoreline as well as the Aerial Lift Bridge.

0.2
BENCH
PHOTO

Soon you will come to a picnic table set amid summer wildflowers on the left. To the right is an optional spur trail (gravel and hard-packed dirt) that leads through a brief semi-wooded area, then down to the lake and onto rocky outcrops (uneven footing there).

This path rejoins the Lakewalk via 6 uneven steps (stone, no handrail).

0.3
BENCH
PHOTO

More picnic tables await and views of the lake are continuous, uninterrupted, and best of all—spectacular!

Soon you will see a building on the left that, from a distance, is easy to mistake for a restroom, but it is not. It is a sewer lift station.

0.6 The huge structure to the left is an overpass over I-35, with paved switchbacks that lead to 17th Avenue E. Continue straight along the main path.

0.9 When you see an open gate, seasonal portable toilets, cul-de-sac, and a parking lot to the left, this signals the end of this section. However, the Lakewalk does continue (see pg. 40, London Road to Water Street). To complete this section, turn around and retrace path to trailhead.

1.8 Trailhead.

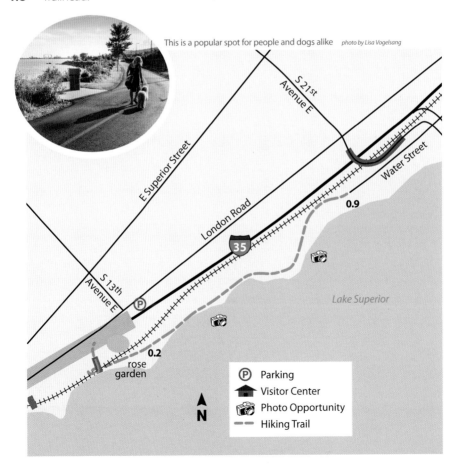

This is a popular spot for people and dogs alike   *photo by Lisa Vogelsang*

S 21st Avenue E

E Superior Street

Water Street

London Road

0.9

35

Lake Superior

S 13th Avenue E

0.2
rose
garden

N

(P) Parking
Visitor Center
Photo Opportunity
- - - Hiking Trail

Lakewalk East Extension*: London Road to Water Street

Duluth, MN • *Gentle Hikes* name

- **The "road less traveled" describes this section of the Lakewalk, which features a more rugged shoreline, including small cliff views.**
- **More trees, fewer lake views; this combination gives a remote feeling to this city hike.**

TRAILHEAD DIRECTIONS:
Travel on I-35 North until it ends at London Road (do not turn right to follow the North Shore). Cross London Road and begin up 26th Avenue E, turning right onto Alexander Street (the first street after the gas station). Follow to the paved parking area.

CONTACT:
Duluth Parks and Recreation: 218-730-4300 or www.duluthmn.gov/parks/

TOTAL TRAIL LENGTH, SURFACE, & WIDTH:
1.6 miles; asphalt; average 6–8' wide.

INCLINES & ALERTS:
No inclines greater than 10°. This section is a multiuse, non-motorized path. The trail crosses the railroad tracks at the base of a long, gradual decline after leaving the parking lot. Street crossing is necessary if you continue through the optional interrupted section of the Lakewalk.

TRAILHEAD FACILITIES & FEES:
Seasonal portable toilet. Convenience store near parking lot. No fees for trail use.

MILEAGE & DESCRIPTION

0.0
PHOTO
There is a sweeping vista of Lake Superior from the parking lot, with a small rose garden in the foreground. The trailhead begins near a sign indicating a wheelchair-accessible parking place on a 10-foot-wide paved path down a gradual decline. In 100', trail splits; stay straight (if you want to go left, see pg. 42). Walk down the gentle decline, cross railroad tracks, and the trail continues parallel to them through a tunnel (there is a very tall fence between you and the tracks).

0.2 At the first intersection is a stop sign. Watch for bicycles and in-line skaters. The Lakewalk continues to the left and to the right. For now, turn right (at mile 1.0 we will take you to the left).

0.3 A bench is situated here, with partial Lake Superior views.
BENCH
0.4 Shortly there will be a huge structure to your right that is an overpass with paved switchbacks providing access across I-35 to restaurants, lodging, and specialty shops. Here's your opportunity to grab a sandwich and enjoy lakeview dining on the picnic tables provided.

To the left, there is also an optional spur trail of hard-packed gravel, which parallels Lake Superior's glorious shoreline. It will lead to the same intersection as the paved portion of the trail, only in a much more scenic manner.

If you continue along the paved portion of the Lakewalk, it parallels I-35 and you will lose the lake view.

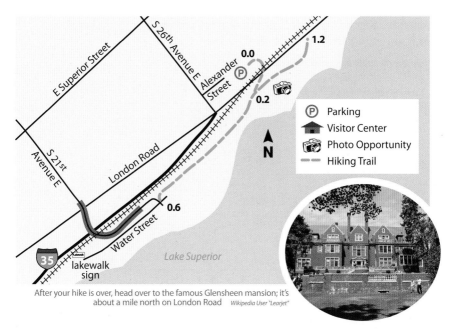

After your hike is over, head over to the famous Glensheen mansion; it's about a mile north on London Road *Wikipedia User "Learjet"*

0.6 The Lakewalk does continue to the right of Water Street (see pg. 38, "Rose Garden to Water Street"); however, to complete this section, turn around at the intersection of S 21st Avenue E and Water Street. Then retrace your path toward the first intersection at the stop sign (see 0.2 in the notes above).

1.0 Back at the stop sign, do not return to the parking lot but continue straight (this would have been a left at mile 0.2). Soon you'll travel through a nice stand of aspen, then experience some surprisingly rugged beauty.

1.2 Look at the cliff views here. They aren't the tallest, but they're a sweet surprise right
PHOTO in the middle of the city. They are especially striking when waves are crashing.

The London Road sidewalk signals the end of the Lakewalk. Turn around and retrace the path back to the stop sign at the intersection, where you will turn right and head back via the path that parallels and crosses the railroad tracks before the gentle incline to the parking area.

1.5 Just before reaching the parking area, the Lakewalk does continue to the right (see pg. 42 for details).

1.6 Trailhead.

Lakewalk East Extension:
S 26th Ave E to N 40th Ave E
(i.e., Duluth East High School)*

Duluth, MN • *Gentle Hikes* name

- **Spacious footbridge offers photo-worthy views of Tischer Creek as it meanders through a modest ravine.**
- **Lovely wooded serene path.**

TRAILHEAD DIRECTIONS:
Follow I-35 North until it ends at London Road (do not turn right to follow the North Shore). Cross London Road and begin up 26th Avenue E, turning right onto Alexander Street (first street after the gas station). Follow to the paved parking area.

CONTACT:
Duluth Parks and Recreation: 218-730-4300 or www.duluthmn.gov/parks/

TOTAL TRAIL LENGTH, SURFACE, & WIDTH:
2.6 miles; asphalt; average 9–10' wide.

INCLINES & ALERTS:
No inclines greater than 10°. This section is a multiuse, non-motorized path and may be used by in-line skaters and cyclists. There are two street crossings, and vehicles have the right-of-way. The entire trail borders a residential section (please be respectful of private property) and a railway, with fence between the tracks and the trail.

TRAILHEAD FACILITIES & FEES:
Seasonal portable toilet. Convenience store near parking lot. No fees for trail use.

MILEAGE & DESCRIPTION

0.0
PHOTO
There is a sweeping vista of Lake Superior from the parking lot, with a small rose garden in the foreground. The trailhead begins near a sign indicating wheelchair accessible parking place on 10-foot-wide paved path. In 100', the trail splits; veer left (if you want to continue straight, see pg. 40). Trail continues through a lovely partially wooded/residential section with the railroad tracks to your right. Keep your camera handy in case you get a glimpse of the steam train. A magnificent sight!

0.5
BENCH
PHOTO
This path continues through a street crossing where vehicles have the right-of-way. In 300', find a 9-foot-wide wooden bridge (double handrail) that crosses a huge ravine. This is a very picturesque location over Tischer Creek. A bench at the end of the bridge provides views of the nearby wooded areas. You'll also find an informational marker about the creek.

0.8
Another street crossing. Vehicles have the right-of-way.

0.9
BENCH
Enter a lovely wooded area ablaze with wildflowers during spring, but beautiful at any time of year.

1.3 The next street you encounter will be N 40th Avenue E (the location of Duluth East High School), which marks the turnaround point that completes this section of the trail. However, the Lakewalk does continue approximately another 4 miles to Brighton Beach, as it passes through residential areas and parallels multiple shops/stores and eateries on Superior Street, then skirts Lester Park before heading into a tunnel that emerges at Brighton Beach (see pg. 182).

2.6 Trailhead.

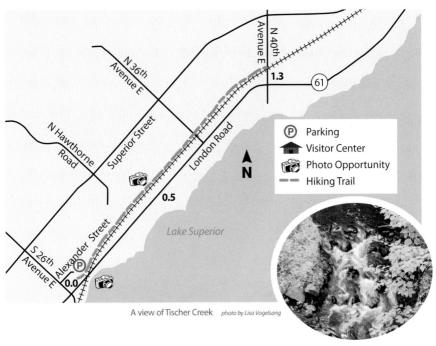

A view of Tischer Creek   photo by Lisa Vogelsang

🦉 Says Who?

Decrease your chances of getting a stroke by getting in stride!

Walking briskly for about 30 minutes a day can reduce the risk of stroke by about 20–27 percent.

CDC Stroke Fact Sheet[16]

Bagley Nature Area
University of Minnesota Duluth • Duluth, MN

- **A beautiful wooded hike rich in maple and oak featuring Rock Hill, Rock Pond, and Tischer Creek—all nestled amid 55 acres on the University of Minnesota Duluth's campus.**

- **Photo ops abound and range from the plethora of wildflowers in spring and the blazing colors of fall to the sweeping vistas from Rock Hill, including Lake Superior, Duluth Harbor, Park Point, portions of Wisconsin, and UMD campus.**

- **The trail parallels Bagley's tent-only walk-in campground.**

TRAILHEAD DIRECTIONS:
Take I-35 North to exit 258 (watch for sign indicating University of Minnesota Duluth), and turn left at the end of exit ramp. Continue up 21st Avenue E until it ends at Woodland Avenue. Turn right and follow for 0.9 mile to St. Marie Street (there's a traffic light and gas stations at corner). Turn left and follow for 0.5 mile to one block beyond Montrose Avenue. Turn right into a paved parking lot (watch for a sign indicating Bagley Nature Area), and look for the limited metered (and monitored) parking. Additional parking is available in a pay lot just off the intersection of St. Marie Street and University Drive across from the campus stadium and track. Free parallel parking may be obtained along St. Marie Street, but it is hard to find when classes are in session, unless you arrive very early in the morning.

CONTACT:
UMD Recreational Sports Outdoor Program: (218) 726-7128 or visit http://d.umn.edu/recreational-sports-outdoor-program/

TOTAL TRAIL LENGTH, SURFACE, & WIDTH:
1.6 miles; grass and mulched trail; average 5' wide.

INCLINES & ALERTS:
There are three inclines ranging from 12° to 16°. The steepest is 16° for 25' at 0.4 mile. Parking is limited to the few meters in this lot near the trailhead. Additional parking in pay lot located just off intersection of St. Marie Street and University Drive across from the campus stadium and track. Bagley is a beautiful maze of various trails with many intersections and footpaths. If the trail description sounds confusing, no need for alarm. It is impossible to get "lost" since the trail is bordered by roads. As long as you don't cross any roads, you can explore these paths at your leisure until you recognize a familiar sight. The entire trail system is less than 3 miles total.

TRAILHEAD FACILITIES & FEES:
Portable toilet at trailhead. Picnic table near Rock Pond. Bagley walk-in tent campground. No fees for trail use, but fee for camping.

MILEAGE & DESCRIPTION

0.0 Trailhead begins near metered parking area and kiosk map display. Enter trail by the yellow gate and immediately experience the tranquility of Rock Pond, which borders the trail to the left. To the right is UMD's Bagley Outdoor Classroom, which is committed to sustainability practices.

0.1 Continue beside Rock Pond until you encounter a "T" intersection. At this intersec-
BENCH tion, turn right and proceed up a slight incline, passing a bench and then behind the Bagley Outdoor Classroom. Over the next 0.2 mile, you will encounter two more intersections. Continue straight on the path.

0.3 Look to the right to spot the walk-in Bagley Nature Area campground located a few yards from the path. Tent camping is welcome right here on UMD's campus, with complete gear rental packages offered (see Foot Note). Shortly after passing the campground, you will come to another intersection. There, turn left (if you arrive at the baseball field, turn around, as you've gone too far).

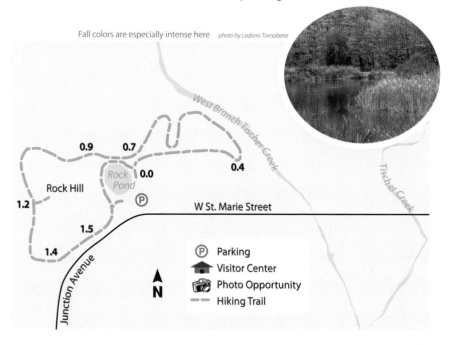

Fall colors are especially intense here   *photo by Ladona Tornabene*

0.4 In a few yards, there will be another trail intersection. Turn left as trail parallels
INCLINE West Branch Tischer Creek for another 0.1 mile. As a point of wayfinding, beyond the creek are homes and beyond those homes is Arrowhead Road. Continuing along the path, the trail will turn away from the creek as you encounter the area of steepest incline (16° for 25') in this section. Ignore the spur trails, and continue for approximately 0.1 mile, where you will veer right at that intersection. In just a few yards, another right leads down a path, which loops back to the main trail in about 0.2 mile. You have the option to take it or stay on the main trail that passes behind Bagley Outdoor Classroom. While this can sound very confusing, remember as long

as you don't cross any roads, you will not get lost, as these trails will eventually bring you to a location you recognize or to a student who can help you find your vehicle!

0.7
INCLINE
BENCH
PHOTO
Assuming you took the loop, you should now be back on the main trail passing behind Bagley's Outdoor Classroom and will descend the decline that leads to Rock Pond. Continue straight on the trail that will soon parallel the top of Rock Pond and walk until you see a trail to the right. Take it, and shortly you will cross a quaint wooden bridge (double handrail) that is irresistibly photo-worthy in fall. Stay on this trail (ignore trail spurs) and in about another 0.1 mile there will be a bench just before you will cross another quaint wooden bridge (double handrail) that is also irresistibly photo-worthy in fall!

0.9
After crossing that second wooden bridge, you will encounter another intersection. Turn right.

1.0
INCLINE
As the path continues to climb, there may be areas of erosion. Soon you will encounter two areas of incline, with the first being the steepest in this section (12° for 40'). At the first intersection, turn right and continue climbing the trail. While there may be several very narrow trails to the left, keep ascending the main path, and very shortly you will reach a definitive intersection. Look left for a fairly wide gravel path. Turn left onto it and then continue left to follow it up the hill. This portion of trail is actually an old road that led to the top of Rock Hill.

If you visit in fall, don't forget your camera!   *photo by Ladona Tornabene*

1.2
PHOTO

In a few yards you will reach the top of Rock Hill. Once there, the location is very spacious. Look right to find an observation deck (guardrails). From this deck you can see a panorama of Duluth Harbor, Park Point, Wisconsin, Lake Superior, and the UMD campus. If you are fortunate enough to visit in the fall, the trees can be ablaze with color.

Retrace your path back down the hill and turn right on that previous gravel path. Turn right on mulched trail, then right again in about 50'. At the next intersection, turn right once more. You will come to an area of decline (14° for 50').

1.4

At the next intersection, turn left. This brings you into a nice stand of maple and birch. Soon you will come to another intersection; turn left and encounter another area of decline (14° for 60'). Turn right at the next intersection.

1.5
PHOTO

This section returns you to a clearing. Turn right, then right again at the next intersection. Next you will come to another clearing. At a "Y" in the trail, take the path to the left. It will bring you to the parking area. **(Note**: Depending on trail maintenance, the hike may not loop completely around the pond.) Rock Pond itself is a wonderful reflecting pool for the fall colors that surround it, affording nearly perfect photo ops during sunny autumn late afternoons.

1.6

Parking area and trailhead.

Foot Note:

UMD's Recreational Sports Outdoor Program offers complete gear rental packages for camping and other equipment, as well as a variety of year-round programs. Visit http://d.umn.edu/recreational-sports-outdoor-program

This trail overlooks UMD campus, which offers a variety of undergraduate and graduate degrees and so much more! Check it out at www.d.umn.edu

Rock Knob

Duluth, MN • Superior Hiking Trail section: Rose Garden to
Hartley Nature Center

- **See an awesome panoramic view of Hartley Park, including a portion
  of Lake Superior from Rock Knob overview!**
- **View beautiful Hartley Pond en route to Rock Knob.**
- **Visit the Hartley Nature Center, which houses wonderful exhibits and
  more to delight any age.**

TRAILHEAD DIRECTIONS:

Take I-35 North to exit 258. Turn left onto 21st Avenue E and follow it uphill for 0.7 mile
to Woodlawn Avenue. Turn right onto Woodlawn Avenue, and follow for 2.5 miles to
entrance of Hartley Park, which will be on the left side. Drive 0.3 mile to paved parking
area. Wheelchair-accessible parking available.

CONTACT:

Hartley Nature Center: 218-724-6735

TOTAL TRAIL LENGTH, SURFACE, & WIDTH:

1.1 miles; gravel and hard-packed dirt; average 2–4' wide. Moderate rock in one section,
minimum roots.

INCLINES & ALERTS:

There are two inclines ranging from 13–15° en route to Rock Knob. Rock Knob itself is an
incline ranging from 13–20°.

TRAILHEAD FACILITIES & FEES:

Flush toilets, water fountain, small gift shop, interactive displays, and exhibits all available
in Nature Center.

MILEAGE & DESCRIPTION

0.0 The trailhead begins from parking area near Nature Center kiosk on 8-foot-wide
brick path. Follow path toward Nature Center, and veer left onto 4-foot-wide gravel
path. Continue around the Nature Center, veering right on the path. Note Superior
Hiking Trail (SHT) sign on a post, turn left, and continue over two small sections of
boardwalk. The nature center has a large exclosure to keep deer and other foraging
animals out of the play area maintained for its Nature Preschool. Veer left at the
exclosure gate and continue over several additional sections of boardwalk, passing
the exclosure. Continue following the SHT signs.

0.2
PHOTO A gentle slope takes you to a dam crossing. Continue to follow the SHT sign, crossing the dam (the grate with chain-link fence guardrails). Beautiful Hartley Pond is on
the right, and it is also a great spot to catch sunsets.

0.3 At the intersection, follow the SHT sign that reads "Overlook," turning right.
Continue to look for SHT markers on trees, which will now be white, indicating a

spur trail. The trail becomes more rocky and uneven. Continue straight on this trail all the way to Rock Knob.

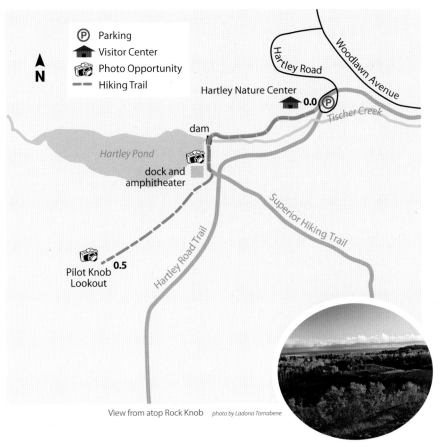

View from atop Rock Knob   *photo by Ladona Tornabene*

0.4
INCLINE

Incline 15° for 50' followed by another incline of 15° for 13' past an intersection with a small sign for Rock Knob on the right side; continue straight.

0.5
INCLINE
PHOTO

Rock Knob! The path just left of Rock Knob is easier to ascend. The incline is gradual and levels off in places. Expect inclines from 14–20° as you scramble over the rock to the top. Rock may be slippery if wet—use caution. At the top, it levels off to a wide expanse with awesome panoramic views of Hartley Park and a small sectional view of Lake Superior. A few homes are peppered throughout, but overall it's a great natural view. When ready, retrace path to the trailhead.

1.1   Trailhead.

Foot Note:

Hartley Nature Center offers hands-on environmental education classes for all ages and houses interactive displays. Visit hartleynature.org

Hartley Pond & Tischer Creek Loop*

Duluth, MN • Superior Hiking Trail section: Rose Garden to Hartley Nature Center
Gentle Hikes name

- **View beautiful Hartley Pond, which is a great place to see sunsets over the water.**
- **Lovely view of Tischer Creek from a small bridge.**
- **Visit the Hartley Nature Center, which houses wonderful exhibits and more to delight any age.**

TRAILHEAD DIRECTIONS:
Take I-35 North to exit 258. Turn left onto 21st Avenue E and follow up hill for 0.7 mile to Woodlawn Avenue. Turn right onto Woodlawn Avenue, and follow for 2.5 miles to entrance of Hartley Park, which will be on the left side. Drive 0.3 mile to paved parking area. Wheelchair-accessible parking available.

CONTACT:
Hartley Nature Center: 218-724-6735 or hartleynature.org

TOTAL TRAIL LENGTH, SURFACE, & WIDTH:
0.6 mile; gravel and hard-packed dirt; average 2–4' wide

INCLINES & ALERTS:
There are no inclines more than 10°.

TRAILHEAD FACILITIES & FEES:
Flush toilets, water fountain, small gift shop, interactive displays, exhibits all available in Nature Center.

MILEAGE & DESCRIPTION

0.0 The trailhead begins from the parking area near the Nature Center kiosk on an 8-foot-wide brick path. Follow the path toward the Nature Center and veer left onto 4-foot-wide gravel path. Continue around Nature Center, veering right on path. Note the Superior Hiking Trail (SHT) sign on post, turn left, and continue over two small sections of boardwalk. Veer left at the exclosure gate and continue over several more sections of boardwalk, passing exclosure. Continue following the SHT signs.

0.2
PHOTO
A gentle slope takes you to the dam crossing. Continue to follow the SHT sign and cross the dam (grate with chain-link fence guardrails). Beautiful Hartley Pond is on the right, and is also a great spot to catch sunsets.

0.3 At the intersection, follow the SHT sign, turning left on Tunnel Trail. In 70', locate blue SHT paint markers on trees as you cross Hartley Road Trail. Enter the forest path on two small sections of boardwalk. Roots abound. Follow the blue paint on trees. This is a lovely, gentle, wooded section of the SHT.

0.4   As you intersect the 8-foot-wide ski trail, turn left. You will leave the SHT, but there is still a lot of beauty in this area. Continue to next intersection and veer left, heading toward bridge. Cross Hartley Road Trail and head to the bridge that crosses picturesque Tischer Creek.

0.5   Veer right at intersection and follow the gravel trail to parking area.

0.6   Trailhead.

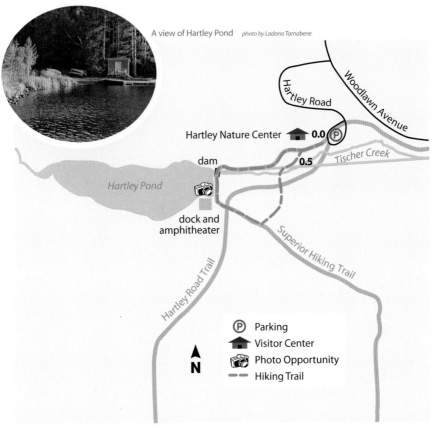

A view of Hartley Pond   *photo by Ladona Tornabene*

Foot Note:

In addition to many other offerings, Hartley Nature Center's signature events include: Wine in the Woods; Spring Youth Outdoor Expo; Howl-o-ween; and Candlelight Ski, Skate & Snowshoe. Visit hartleynature.org

Lester Park Trail

Lester Park • Duluth, MN

- **A lovely wooded hike along Lester River and Amity Creek, both of which range from a gentle rumble to roaring rapids!**
- **A quaint gazebo offers views of small waterfalls; one of the cobblestone bridges from the historic Seven Bridges Road can be seen nearby.**
- **There's a nice playground and picnic area at the beginning of this trail.**

TRAILHEAD DIRECTIONS:

Take I-35 North until it ends; at the split, veer left (do not follow North Shore). Cross London Road and begin up 26th Avenue E, turning right onto Superior Street. Continue for 3.5 miles, then turn left onto Lester River Road. The paved parking lot is immediately on the left.

CONTACT:

Duluth Parks and Recreation: 218-730-4300 or www.duluthmn.gov/parks/

TOTAL TRAIL LENGTH, SURFACE, & WIDTH:

0.8 mile; concrete, hard-packed dirt and gravel; average 3–4' wide. Minimum rock and root.

INCLINES & ALERTS:

No inclines greater than 10°. Steep cliffs; some have rails. Wooden bridges can be very slippery when wet.

TRAILHEAD FACILITIES & FEES:

Flush toilets (seasonal, not wheelchair accessible), covered picnic tables, playground. No fees for trail use.

MILEAGE & DESCRIPTION

0.0
BENCH
PHOTO
The trailhead begins from the parking lot at the wide paved bridge over the Lester River. This bridge is very scenic and provides photo ops up- and downriver.

If you brought the kids, they'll love what's next! A nice playground for them and a couple of benches for you with lots of green space to enjoy. All of this and picnic tables too (including an open-sided shelter) spell great family fun.

Continue to follow the sidewalk around the playground area until it ends. Then head onto the 6-foot-wide gravel path and go toward the bridge (wood, double handrail). Pause and take in the view of Amity Creek. Immediately after crossing the bridge, turn right at the trail intersection (do not continue up the steps).

0.1
PHOTO
As you enter the wooded section of this trail, you'll cross another bridge (wood, single handrail). You will also be traveling on a ridge overlooking the waters.

0.2 Cross another bridge (wood, single handrail). At the "Y," continue straight following the river.

0.3 At the next "Y," veer left; stay on the trail and head toward the gazebo.

0.4
BENCH
PHOTO
Gazebo and bench. After enjoying the views, cross over the bridge (cobblestone, double handrail). Look to the left for historic Seven Bridges Road. At trail intersection, turn right.

0.5
PHOTO
Here you'll find two more bridges (wood, handrails); look between the trees for a waterfall view. Depending on conditions, this one can be striking!

0.6
The trail merges with another hiking trail from the left. Continue straight on the wide path. Follow the trail to playground, then to the parking lot.

0.8
Trailhead.

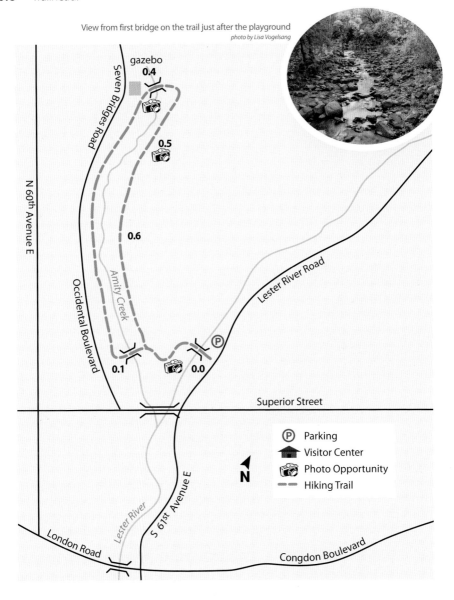

View from first bridge on the trail just after the playground
photo by Lisa Vogelsang

gazebo
0.4

0.5

0.6

Seven Bridges Road

N 60th Avenue E

Occidental Boulevard

Amity Creek

Lester River Road

0.1

0.0

Superior Street

S 61st Avenue E

Lester River

London Road

Congdon Boulevard

N

Ⓟ Parking
🏠 Visitor Center
📷 Photo Opportunity
-- Hiking Trail

LIGHTER

Agate Bay Trail: Lighthouse Loop to Paul Van Hoven Park

Two Harbors, MN • Off Highway 61, 26 miles from Duluth

- **One of the best photo ops of the Original Two Harbors Lighthouse— Minnesota's oldest in operation—is from the parking area.**

- **An excellent vantage point for boat watching/harbor docking, with sweeping views of Agate Bay and Lake Superior.**

- **Here you'll see the former sites of Whiskey Row (where rail workers once let off steam), a coal facility, a fishing village, and the first permanent buildings in Two Harbors.**

TRAILHEAD DIRECTIONS:

From Highway 61 at mile marker 26 (**Note:** you will not find an actual mile marker—use your odometer reading from marker 25), turn right onto Waterfront Drive (at the corner of Dairy Queen and Black Woods Grill and Bar) and follow for 0.5 mile to South Avenue. Turn left and follow for 0.3 mile to 3rd Street; turn right and follow for 0.2 mile to a paved parking area. However, if you prefer to first visit Paul Van Hoven Park via vehicle, drive past South Avenue, cross railroad tracks, and in less than 0.1 miles, arrive at the Park.

CONTACT:

Two Harbors Area Chamber of Commerce: 218-834-2600 or www.twoharborschamber.com/visitors-information/

TOTAL TRAIL LENGTH, SURFACE, & WIDTH:

1.3 miles; gravel/hard-packed dirt, paved; average 6–8' wide. Minimal rocks and roots.

INCLINES & ALERTS:

Two 12° declines; the longest is 12° for 40' at 0.4 mile.

TRAILHEAD FACILITIES & FEES:

Vault toilet. No fees for trail use.

MILEAGE & DESCRIPTION

0.0
BENCH
PHOTO
The trailhead begins to the right of the Lighthouse near Lake Superior under the "Spirit of Two Harbors" archway on a 6- to 8-foot-wide dirt/gravel path. The first 0.4 mile of this semi-wooded trail affords partial lake views and foliage-dependent lake access. Photo ops abound where there is lake access, and there are also several benches, but please use caution as erosion and overgrowth may impede those spur trails.

0.2
PHOTO
Look left for the restored pilot house recovered from the ore boat Frontenac and the original Two Harbors Lighthouse, which was first lit on Lake Superior in 1892. It continues today, making it the oldest operating lighthouse in Minnesota.

0.4
At the trail intersection, veer left and continue through the wooded section. Soon you will encounter the area of steepest decline (12° for 40').

0.5 As trail intersects with an asphalt path, turn left onto the asphalt path, and in a few yards, cross the road where you entered the Lake Superior Agate Bay Public Water Access (pg. 168). Continue straight onto the unpaved path directly ahead. If strolling along a pebble beach sounds appealing, begin looking left for a fairly level spur trail that leads to it. There are other spurs a bit farther on, but they are steeper.

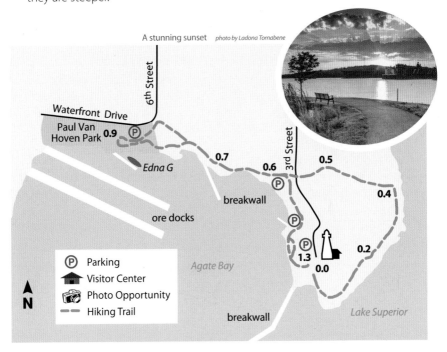

A stunning sunset *photo by Ladona Tornabene*

Waterfront Drive
6th Street
Paul Van Hoven Park **0.9** Ⓟ
Edna G
3rd Street
0.7
0.6
0.5
breakwall
0.4
ore docks
Ⓟ
0.2
Ⓟ
1.3
0.0
Agate Bay

Ⓟ Parking
🏠 Visitor Center
📷 Photo Opportunity
– – Hiking Trail

N

breakwall
Lake Superior

0.6 A bench affords amazing views of Agate Bay, Lake Superior, and the ore docks. Did
BENCH PHOTO you know that ships that only travel within the Great Lakes are called Lakers, while ships that pass through the St. Lawrence Seaway to the Atlantic Ocean and beyond are called Salties? If you thirst for historical knowledge, then check out the interpretative sign because you are now standing on what was formerly known in 1883 as "Whiskey Row," where 7 of the 8 to 10 houses standing at the time were saloons. Vintage photos are displayed on the sign as well.

0.7 Begin looking to the right for an odd-shaped structure. This marks the ruins of an 1888 facility that once held up to 3 million tons of coal to meet the railroad's demand for it. A corresponding interpretive sign containing historical photos can be found a bit farther down the path. Soon, you'll encounter a trail intersection; both paths lead to Paul Van Hoven Park.

0.9 Arrive at Paul Van Hoven Park, where you can obtain the closest view of the 1896
BENCH PHOTO historic tug, the *Edna G*, which was the last steam-driven tugboat on the Great Lakes. Read more about her at the interpretative sign under the gazebo, where you can also learn more about the Agate Bay Light Station and Two Harbors Iron

Ore Docks. Another informational marker about the park's history is located in the middle of the paved parking lot. Several strategically placed picnic tables and benches beckon a stay.

From there, return to the parking area of Lake Superior Agate Bay Public Water Access, access and retrace the path that the street crossing mentioned in section 0.5; however, instead of crossing the road, turn right onto the sidewalk.

1.1
BENCH
PHOTO
From here on out, continue along the sidewalk, which skirts the parking area, offering continuous and fantastic views of Agate Bay, Lake Superior, and ore docks. Soon, you will notice a huge 10-ton bronze propeller from the *Eugene W. Pargny*, along with an informational marker. In a few yards, watch for a small "hidden" pond on the left that is home to many ducks.

1.3
BENCH
PHOTO
An interpretive sign here marks the vestiges of the once bustling commercial fishing at Agate Bay and displays information about it, including the 1938 sea lamprey invasion, which destroyed commercial fishing throughout the entire Great Lakes in just two decades.

This brings us full-circle and we highly recommend concluding with the Agate Bay Breakwater Almost Hike (pg. 155) for some sweeping views of Lake Superior and the shoreline.

 Foot Note:

Tour or stay in the Original Two Harbors Lighthouse—Minnesota's oldest in operation (since 1892). Visit lighthousebb.org/lighthouse-history

Two Harbors Lighthouse   *photo by Ladona Tornabene*

Agate Bay Trail:
Burlington Bay to First Street

Two Harbors, MN • Off Highway 61, 26 miles from Duluth

- **Paved trail with a beautiful shaded forest of towering pine, spruce, fir, and birch on one side and Lake Superior on the other—right in the heart of Two Harbors.**

TRAILHEAD DIRECTIONS:
From Highway 61 at mile marker 25, set your odometer to zero, and 1.4 miles later, after passing through the main area of town, watch for a sign indicating Burlington Bay Campground, and turn right onto 1st Street. Follow for 0.1 mile to find parking in a gravel lot.

CONTACT:
Two Harbors Area Chamber of Commerce: www.twoharborschamber.com/visitors-information/

TOTAL TRAIL LENGTH, SURFACE, & WIDTH:
0.7 mile; paved; approximately 8' wide.

INCLINES & ALERTS:
No inclines greater than 10°. Some spur trails may have drop-offs; no guardrails.

TRAILHEAD FACILITIES & FEES:
No facilities at trailhead; however, flush toilets (seasonal) available in picnic area across 1st Street at 0.1 mile. No fees for trail use.

MILEAGE & DESCRIPTION

0.0
BENCH PHOTO
Trailhead begins uphill from parking area (approximately 400') at a sign indicating "No Unauthorized Vehicles in Park." A forest of spruce, pine, and birch welcomes you. A turn in the trail gives way to the first of many benches placed in honor or memory of loved ones. Several spur trails throughout the remainder of this trail lead you to rest and soak up the sights, sounds, and sweeping vistas of Lake Superior.

0.1 This section takes you past a small picnic area; a larger picnic area is located across 1st Street and is complete with playground equipment, a shelter, and seasonal flush toilets.

0.2
BENCH PHOTO
At the "Y" in the trail, notice a sign indicating restrooms (those described above). Farther down the trail, additional benches and a scenic overlook await you.

0.3 When you reach the intersection with 1st Street (at the sidewalk), we suggest you turn around here and retrace the path to trailhead. If you turn left and continue, you will eventually arrive at a parking area near the old lighthouse.

0.7 Trailhead.

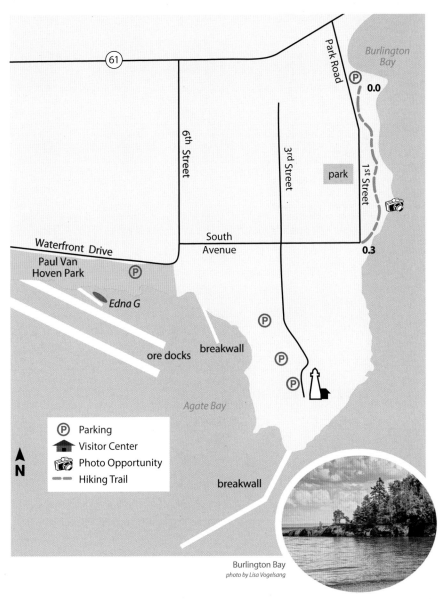

61

Burlington Bay

Park Road

0.0

6th Street

3rd Street

park

1st Street

0.3

Waterfront Drive

South Avenue

Paul Van Hoven Park

Ⓟ

Edna G

Ⓟ

ore docks

breakwall

Ⓟ

Ⓟ

Ⓟ

Agate Bay

Ⓟ Parking

Visitor Center

Photo Opportunity

Hiking Trail

N

breakwall

Burlington Bay
photo by Lisa Vogelsang

Foot Note:

For more information on what to see and do in the Two Harbors area, visit the Two Harbors Area Chamber of Commerce at www.twoharborschamber.com/visitors-information/

Beyond Two Harbors to Little Marais

Split Rock Lighthouse   photo by Ladona Tornabene

Silver Creek Cliff Trail*

Gitchi-Gami State Trail section: Silver Creek Cliff Segment • On Highway 61, approximately 31 miles from Duluth • *Gentle Hikes* name

- **5,000 feet of nonstop photo ops featuring spectacular Lake Superior vistas.**

- **This site is home to the longest continuous segment of Lake Superior visible to the public throughout the entire North Shore.**

- **Built on the former roadbed of Highway 61; the replicas of old barriers for cars and a facsimile of the 1900s Silver Creek Gateway Arch drive the imagination. Before the construction of the tunnel, this high precipice was once a nerve-wracking drive.**

TRAILHEAD DIRECTIONS:
On Highway 61 at mile marker 31, look for blue "Scenic Overlook" sign. Turn right into the paved parking area. Wheelchair-accessible parking; there are potential RV spots, due to five consecutive parallel parking spots

CONTACT:
Gitchi-Gami State Trail: www.ggta.org/contact.php

TOTAL TRAIL LENGTH, SURFACE, & WIDTH:
1.1 mile; paved; 10' wide.

INCLINES & ALERTS:
No inclines greater than 10°; however, it is not flat. Gentle grade. Trail follows cliff; potential for falling rock. While there are steep drop-offs with no guardrails, the trail is wide and located a safe distance from them. Keep children in hand. This is a multiuse, non-motorized path frequented by bicycles.

TRAILHEAD FACILITIES & FEES:
No facilities. No fees for trail use.

MILEAGE & DESCRIPTION

0.0
PHOTO
Trailhead leads toward the cliff on 10-foot-wide paved path near "scenic overlook" sign. In 350', cross a 10-foot-wide bridge (wood, double handrail). Potential traffic noise until trail goes around the Silver Creek Tunnel.

0.1
PHOTO
Bridge ends. Look behind you for a terrific photo op of Lake Superior's rugged shoreline. The journey down memory lane commences as you trace the historic roadbed of Highway 61. Boulders that line the path are replicas of barriers used on the old road to protect vehicles from the cliff edges.

0.2
PHOTO
Interpretative signs abound, including images of the old road and the 1994 Silver Creek Tunnel grand opening.

0.3
BENCH
PHOTO
Savor those fabulous Lake Superior views from this prime bench location; the trail there is paved.

0.4
BENCH
PHOTO
A photo-worthy bench? Indeed. Beautifully crafted from marble and other rock—it's worth a sit on a warm day just to experience the feel. There are views of a private pebble beach and quaint cliffs.

0.5
PHOTO
Soon you'll walk under the exquisite replica of the 1900s Silver Creek Gateway Arch that stood to welcome travelers.

0.6
PHOTO
Trail's end; retrace path to trailhead.

1.1
Trailhead.

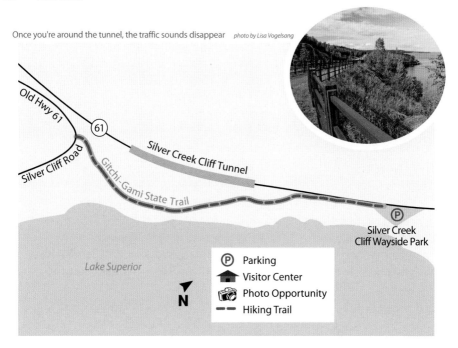

Once you're around the tunnel, the traffic sounds disappear *photo by Lisa Vogelsang*

Old Hwy 61

61

Silver Cliff Road

Silver Creek Cliff Tunnel

Gitchi-Gami State Trail

Ⓟ
Silver Creek
Cliff Wayside Park

Lake Superior

N

Ⓟ Parking
🏠 Visitor Center
📷 Photo Opportunity
▬ ▬ Hiking Trail

Says Who?

Get Your Daily Dose

Exercise may be as effective as medications in treating heart disease and diabetes.

Time[38]

Gooseberry Falls

Gooseberry Falls State Park • On Highway 61, 39 miles from Duluth

- **Experience the magic of the North Shore's most visited waterfall!**
- **See Gooseberry Falls from exceptional vantage points, as a paved trail leads to the Upper and Lower Falls.**

TRAILHEAD DIRECTIONS:
On Highway 61 at mile marker 38.9, turn right into Gooseberry Falls State Park and follow signs to the paved parking area.

CONTACT:
Gooseberry Falls State Park: (218) 595-7100 or www.dnr.state.mn.us/state_parks/gooseberry_falls/index.html

TOTAL TRAIL LENGTH, SURFACE, & WIDTH:
0.7 mile; paved; average 6' wide (**Note:** all benches have pavement extended to them). The park states that this trail meets the standards for Universal Design.

INCLINES & ALERTS:
No inclines greater than 10°. Steep cliffs, no guardrails. Potential wet areas. Only the trail to Middle Falls is cleared via snowblower in winter, but it may have ice.

TRAILHEAD FACILITIES & FEES:
There is a spectacular visitor center which houses a gift shop, interpretive center, and 24/7 access to flush toilets, water, and vending machines. There is no fee to park at Gooseberry Falls Visitor Center (two-hour limit, but parking may be challenging during high traffic). However, if vehicles are driven to or parked at other areas within the park, a day-use or annual permit is required; these are available at the park office.

MILEAGE & DESCRIPTION

0.0 Trailhead begins at the far end of the visitor center on asphalt, then splits shortly. Continue straight, following the sign indicating falls area.

0.1
BENCH
At the "Y" in trail, veer right, following the sign noting the "Middle & Lower Falls." In 70' find a bench to the left. You have the option of steps or switchback ramp to reach the Middle Falls. We took the ramp, which has 3 more benches 100' apart.

0.2
PHOTO
Excellent view of Middle Falls! The water levels fluctuate dramatically, ranging from raging torrents during spring runoff to mere ribbons of water during a dry summer season. From this area you can also hike to Lower Falls; however, the trail is not paved and there are steps.

To continue to Upper Falls, you have two choices. The 60 steps (concrete, double handrail, non-continuous) that you see on your return from Middle Falls will take you there, or you can retrace your steps back to the intersection and then turn right following the sign indicating the Middle & Lower Falls.

0.4
PHOTO
If you took the stairs, turn right as soon as you reach the paved path; along it you will find views of the Gooseberry River as it topples over Middle Falls. **Alert:** Please heed the warning sign to stay on the trail—erosion is a serious problem on the surrounding steep hills. Keep young children in hand.

0.5
PHOTO
Here you'll find a dramatic view of the Upper Falls! **Alert:** There is a steep drop-off here and no guardrail. This is a very popular photo op, and many family pictures have been taken here. An interpretive sign details the area's former Civilian Conservation Corps (CCC) camp, which was located close by.

The paved portion of the trail ends here, which concludes this hike. Turn around and follow the paved path back to the visitor center. However, if you want to continue on this trail, please see our description for Gooseberry River Loop (pg. 74).

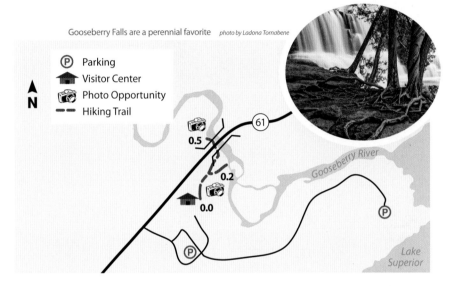

Gooseberry Falls are a perennial favorite   *photo by Ladona Tornabene*

0.6
BENCH
On your return to the visitor center, there will be a statue of a CCC worker, honoring the dedication and spirit of the 3 million men who were active in the CCC in the country; 86,000 young men participated in Minnesota. You'll also find two benches here. Interpretive signs contain vintage photos and showcase amazing nearby structures that still remain today. Notice the stonework, which was cut by hand in the 1930s!

0.7   Visitor center and trailhead.

Foot Notes:

Can't wait to get here? Have a sneak peek via the Gooseberry Falls State Park virtual tour! Visit: www.dnr.state.mn.us/state_parks/virtual_tour/gooseberry_falls/dialup.html

Gooseberry Falls State Park has a phenomenal nature store, gift shop, and a plethora of amazing books! Proceeds from items purchased at all park gift shops help fund resource management and interpretive projects.

▟▖ Plaza Overlook Loop

Gooseberry Falls State Park • On Highway 61, 39 miles from Duluth

- **This is a history buff's paradise! From historical facts about the park to the formation of Lake Superior's basin, it's all here and more.**

- **See "Castle in the Park"—a CCC wonder, and a remnant of the original bridge.**

- **One of the best vantage points for viewing the Upper Falls, with a beautiful vista of Gooseberry River—all from a paved trail.**

TRAILHEAD DIRECTIONS:

On Highway 61 at mile marker 38.9, turn right into Gooseberry Falls State Park, and follow signs to paved parking area.

CONTACT:

Gooseberry Falls State Park: (218) 595-7100 or www.dnr.state.mn.us/state_parks/gooseberry_falls/index.html

TOTAL TRAIL LENGTH, SURFACE, & WIDTH:

0.6 mile; paved; average 6–8' wide (**Note:** all benches have pavement extended to them). The park states that this trail meets the standards for Universal Design.

INCLINES & ALERTS:

No inclines greater than 10°. Trail is not cleared in winter. Information boards are covered in winter.

TRAILHEAD FACILITIES & FEES:

There is a spectacular visitor center that houses a gift shop, interpretive center, and 24/7 access to flush toilets, water, and vending machines.

There is no fee to park at Gooseberry Falls Visitor Center (two-hour limit, but parking may be challenging during high traffic). However, if vehicles are driven to or parked at other areas within the park, a day-use or annual permit is required; these are available at the park office.

MILEAGE & DESCRIPTION

0.0 The trailhead begins at the far end of the visitor center on a blacktop path. In 80', trail splits; veer left following sign toward the Plaza and Bridge Overlook. Pass through a stand of cedar and aspen.

0.1 A bench is on the left side. The huge wall to the left is the Plaza Wall; it borders the
PHOTO Plaza Overlook. The Plaza Wall is more than 300' long.

In 100', find another bench on the right and a third one just before the steps. The ramp to the Plaza is to the left; however, continue straight on blacktop for now. We will access the Plaza Overlook via a different route, as famous views of Upper Falls and Gooseberry River await.

After crossing under Highway 61, turn right onto a wide concrete bridge (iron guardrails) located directly below Highway 61.

0.2
PHOTO
It is definitely worth spending some time here. This bridge offers an exceptional vantage point for viewing the Upper Falls and the Gooseberry River—beautiful views on either side of bridge.

At the end of the bridge, turn right and follow pavement as the trail parallels Highway 61. Cross the river on the pedestrian path on the highway bridge.

0.3
PHOTO
Spend a little time as you cross this bridge (double guardrail) and enjoy a charming sight: Gooseberry River creates an interesting scene as it negotiates rocks and boulders—it's worth the traffic noise for this view! Lake Superior provides a splendid backdrop.

The interpretive sign reveals that Lake Superior is home to two types of salmon—Chinook and Coho—and four types of trout—Brook, Brown, Lake, and Rainbow.

At the end of the bridge, turn left onto the Plaza Overlook. The signs along the way give history and trivia about this area.

0.4
As you leave Plaza Overlook, you can read more about the "Castle in the Park." Have more fun discovering North Shore trivia via the interpretive signs.

0.5
At intersection, turn right and follow signs to the visitor center.

0.6
Visitor center and trailhead.

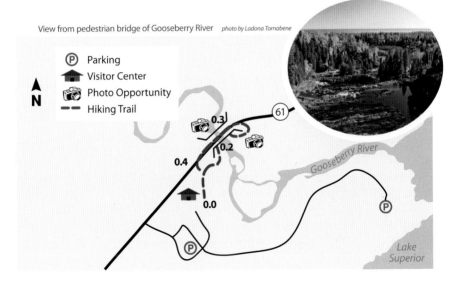

View from pedestrian bridge of Gooseberry River   *photo by Ladona Tornabene*

Ⓟ Parking
🏠 Visitor Center
📷 Photo Opportunity
▬ ▬ Hiking Trail

N

River View Trail

Gooseberry Falls State Park • On Highway 61, 39 miles from Duluth

- **Depending on the time of year and foliage, you might have constant views of Gooseberry River.**
- **An impressive, but distant, view of Gooseberry Falls.**
- **Depending on weather conditions, the trail's end is a great place to watch waves crash on Lake Superior's rugged shoreline or observe the Gooseberry River as it merges with the lake.**

TRAILHEAD DIRECTIONS:

From Highway 61 at mile marker 38.9, turn right into Gooseberry Falls State Park, and follow signs to main paved parking area.

CONTACT:

Gooseberry Falls State Park: (218) 595-7100 or www.dnr.state.mn.us/state_parks/gooseberry_falls/index.html

TOTAL TRAIL LENGTH, SURFACE, & WIDTH:

1.5 miles; hard-packed dirt and gravel; average 3–4' wide. Minimal rocks and roots.

INCLINES & ALERTS:

There are two inclines at 20° within 200' of each other and measure 20' and 15'; both occur around 1.0 mile in. Steep cliffs with no guardrail. The basalt rock may be slippery when wet.

TRAILHEAD FACILITIES & FEES:

There is a spectacular visitor center that houses a gift shop, interpretive center, and 24/7 access to flush toilets, water, and vending machines.

There is no fee to park at Gooseberry Falls Visitor Center (two-hour limit, but parking may be challenging during high traffic). However, if vehicles are driven to or parked at other areas within the park, a day-use or annual permit is required; these are available at the park office.

MILEAGE & DESCRIPTION

0.0
BENCH
From the northeast corner of the main parking lot, follow the paved path toward the visitor center; just before you reach it, look for the "Y" intersection where the path you are on merges with another paved path near a big rock with a plaque inscription that reads "Joseph Alexander Visitor Center." Turn right (away from the visitor center) and follow that paved path. In a few yards, find a bench on the right with a wooded view. Shortly on the left, another bench is located slightly off the paved path and offers stunning views of Gooseberry River. Continue along the paved path until the next intersection in 0.1 mile. Turning right returns you to the parking area, so veer left onto the dirt trail, which is also the ski trail.

0.1
Watch for a sign indicating campground. Listen for falls; there are nice views (depending on the foliage) to the left.

0.2
STEPS
PHOTO
At the next intersection, turn left and descend 20 steps (wood, no handrail, non-continuous); then turn right. Here there's a great view of Middle Falls in the distance (the view of Lower Falls is foliage dependent).

0.3
STEPS
BENCH
Ascend 7 uneven steps (stone, no handrail), and then continue straight. Do NOT take the next set of stone steps leading right. Further along the trail, you'll cross a short portion of boardwalk and find a bench that affords great river views.

0.6
In this section are two steep declines within 200' of each other. These are the inclines you will encounter at 1.0 mile on the return trail.

0.7
PHOTO
At the "Y," continue straight on trail to quaint log picnic tables and great views of Lake Superior. The trail to the left leads to a pebbled beach area that is used as a kayak campsite. Continue on the trail to the overlook above the mouth of Gooseberry River, and watch the river and lake as they blend. It's almost hypnotic.

0.8
STEPS
PHOTO
You have the option to continue onward to the picnic shelter and more dramatic views of Superior's rugged shore by ascending the 20 steps (quarried rock, handrail) at the trail's end. Photo ops abound in this area. Have fun exploring.

There is a vault toilet near the parking-side entrance of the picnic shelter. Flush toilets (seasonal) are available at the back of the shelter. This shelter can also be reached by car. See Gooseberry Falls Picnic Areas (pg. 183).

After you've finished exploring this area, return to main trail and retrace your path to the trailhead.

1.0
INCLINE
This section contains the areas of steepest incline, as mentioned in 0.6 above. The first incline is 20° for 20', with a trail surface of hard-packed gravel. The second is 20° for 15', with trail surface of solid rock. **Alert:** Slippery when wet or icy.

1.5
Trailhead.

Where the Gooseberry River meets Lake Superior   *photo by Ladona Tornabene*

P   Parking
🏠   Visitor Center
📷   Photo Opportunity
- - -   Hiking Trail

N

RUGGED
//▲ Gitchi Gummi

Gooseberry Falls State Park • On Highway 61, 39 miles from Duluth

- **Spectacular vistas of Lake Superior crashing (or lapping) its rugged shoreline!**

- **Dynamic views of Gooseberry River as it flows into Lake Superior.**

- **An outstanding vantage point for viewing the Upper Falls is en route to the official trailhead.**

TRAILHEAD DIRECTIONS:
On Highway 61 at mile marker 38.9, turn right into Gooseberry Falls State Park and follow signs to paved parking area.

CONTACT:
Gooseberry Falls State Park: (218) 595-7100 or www.dnr.state.mn.us/state_parks/ gooseberry_falls/index.html

TOTAL TRAIL LENGTH, SURFACE, & WIDTH:
2.0 miles; paved first 0.2 mile; average 8' wide. Hard-packed dirt and gravel; average 1–2' wide. Minimal root and rock (moderate at times).

INCLINES & ALERTS:
There are five inclines, ranging from 12–18°. The steepest is 18° for 45' at 1.0 mile. The longest is 16° for 75' at 1.2 miles. Steep cliffs and loose gravel with no guardrails and eroding soil beneath. (This includes vista overlooks.) Vegetation overgrowth may be problematic in summer.

TRAILHEAD FACILITIES & FEES:
There is a spectacular visitor center that houses a gift shop, interpretive center, and 24/7 access to flush toilets, water, and vending machines. There is no fee to park at Gooseberry Falls Visitor Center (two-hour limit, but parking may be challenging during high traffic). However, if vehicles are driven to or parked at other areas within the park, a day-use or annual permit is required; these are available at the park office.

MILEAGE & DESCRIPTION

0.0   The official trailhead actually begins at 0.3 mile; however, the best route is to start at the far end of the visitor center on the blacktop path. This distance is included in the total trail length. In 80' trail splits; veer left following a sign toward the Plaza and Bridge Overlook.

0.1
BENCH   There is a bench on the left side. The huge wall to the left is the Plaza Wall, which borders the Plaza Overlook. In 100', find another bench on the right and a third one just before the stairs. Continue on the blacktop (do not go up or down any stairs). Views of Gooseberry River and Upper Falls begin.

After passing under Highway 61, turn right onto a wide concrete bridge (iron rails) located directly below Highway 61.

0.2
PHOTO

It's definitely worth spending some time here! This bridge offers an exceptional vantage point for viewing the Upper Falls and the Gooseberry River. There are breathtaking views on either side of the bridge.

At the end of the bridge, follow the sign to the Gitchi Gummi Trail by turning right. Continue on the concrete path, taking the second trail on the right marked by a blue Hiking Club sign. Follow the sign to Gitchi Gummi Trail, as the surface changes to hard-packed dirt and gravel. **Alert:** Do not take the trail with stairs that is located directly above the river.

0.3
STEPS

At a "Y" in the trail, veer left. Follow the sign to the Gitchi Gummi Trail. Traverse a few sections of boardwalk en route to a very nice stand of birch. Over the next 200', ascend two sets of steps—11 and 7 respectively (stone, wood, no handrail—then find the bench.

0.4

At the next "Y" in the trail, find sign stating "Hazardous. Keep children in hand" and a trail map. A bench offers a view of Lake Superior (depending on foliage). Continue straight (the trail to the left eventually returns to this point). Traverse more boardwalk en route to an incredible vista farther up the path!

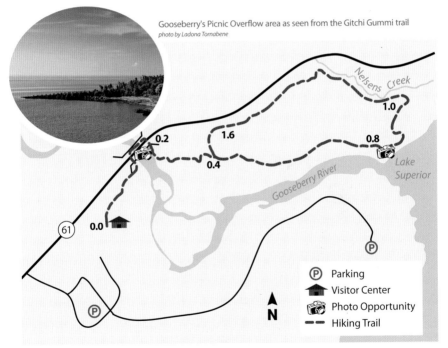

Gooseberry's Picnic Overflow area as seen from the Gitchi Gummi trail
photo by Ladona Tornabene

0.8
BENCH
PHOTO

The introduction to this spectacular overlook is a rustic stone shelter (benches are inside) that not only serves as a resting place, but provides great framing for photos. In this section are two spectacular overlooks of Lake Superior. Three steps (wood, no handrail) lead up to each overlook; each has benches and guardrails.

0.9 In 200' find a 18° decline with surface of hard-packed dirt and gravel.

1.0
INCLINE
This section contains the area of steepest incline on the trail (18° for 45') followed shortly by another 18° decline. Nelsens Creek is just yards away.

1.2 A gradual incline takes you closer to Highway 61. Over the next 0.3 mile, the trail splits twice. At the first split you will see a deer fence with a less-groomed trail beside it. DO NOT take this one. Take the trail toward the right. At the second split, follow the trail toward the left.

1.6
BENCH
Another trail shelter with benches inside signals a return (in 150') to the previously mentioned hazardous warning sign at 0.4. At trail intersection, turn right and retrace the path to trailhead.

2.0 Trailhead and visitor center.

 Says Who?

Want to get smart? Work out the heart!

Walking improves the functioning of the brain.

BC Medical Journal[2]

Sunrise on Lake Superior   *photo by Lisa Vogelsang*

MODERATE

// Gooseberry River Loop*

Gooseberry Falls State Park • On Highway 61, 39 miles from Duluth •
Gentle Hikes name

- **Dramatic views of Upper Gooseberry Falls!**
- **Hike along the delightful Gooseberry River through a mixed forest,
  then onto a section of the Superior Hiking Trail.**

TRAILHEAD DIRECTIONS:
On Highway 61 at mile marker 38.9, turn right into Gooseberry Falls State Park and
follow the signs to the paved parking area.

CONTACT:
Gooseberry Falls State Park: (218) 595-7100 or www.dnr.state.mn.us/state_parks/
gooseberry_falls/index.html

TOTAL TRAIL LENGTH, SURFACE, & WIDTH:
1.2 miles; hard-packed dirt and gravel; average 3–4' wide. Minimum rock, moderate in
sections; moderate roots. Second half of trail is primarily boardwalk.

INCLINES & ALERTS:
No inclines greater than 10°. Steep cliffs near Upper Falls (no guardrails at times).
Potential wet areas. No swimming allowed in river.

TRAILHEAD FACILITIES & FEES:
There is a spectacular visitor center that houses a gift shop, interpretive center, and
24/7 access to flush toilets, water, and vending machines. There is no fee to park at
Gooseberry Falls Visitor Center (two-hour limit, but parking may be challenging during
high traffic). However, if vehicles are driven to or parked at other areas within the park, a
day-use or annual permit is required; these are available at the park office.

MILEAGE & DESCRIPTION

0.0 Trailhead begins at the far end of the visitor center on asphalt, then splits shortly;
continue straight following the sign toward the falls area.

0.1 In this section you will find a statue of a Civilian Conservation Corps (CCC) worker
BENCH that honors the dedication and spirit of the 3 million men across the country
(and 86,000 young men in Minnesota) who worked for the CCC. Interpretive
signs contain vintage photos and showcase amazing nearby structures that
still remain today. Another interpretive sign features information about the
various North Shore rivers that carve their way through rock as they travel
toward Lake Superior.

0.2 Enjoy the dramatic view of Upper Falls! (**Alert:** Steep drop-off with no guardrail.)
PHOTO This is a very popular photo op and many family pictures have been taken
here. Another interpretive sign details the CCC camp, which was located close
by. Vintage photos offer a rare glimpse into the CCC workers' lives. There's also
a bench.

The paved trail ends and rock/root surface begins (significant, but the flat bedrock is easily negotiable). Stay on the trail near the river. In 200', you will find a stone monument and a warning sign. The trail surface changes to hard-packed gravel. At the trail intersection, turn right.

0.5
PHOTO

At the next trail intersection, turn right and cross the wide bridge (wood, double steel railing). You'll find great photo ops up- and downriver. Immediately after crossing the bridge, turn right onto the boardwalk. This 0.3-mile section is part of the Superior Hiking Trail and will follow along above the Gooseberry River.

0.6
STEPS

In this section you will encounter steps in the following series: Descend 6 steps (wood, no handrail, non-continuous); in 400' ascend 16 steps (wood, no handrail, non-continuous).

0.7
STEPS
PHOTO

Look right for a photo op upriver. In this section, you will encounter the following series: Ascend 4 steps (wood, no handrail, non-continuous); 5 steps, cross a small wooden bridge, then ascend 9 steps (wood, no handrail).

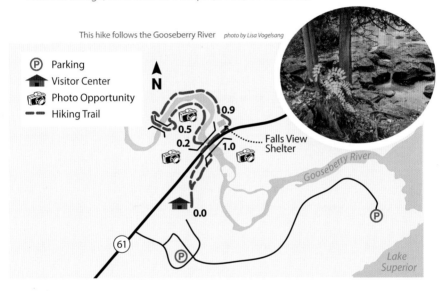

This hike follows the Gooseberry River   *photo by Lisa Vogelsang*

- (P) Parking
- Visitor Center
- Photo Opportunity
- Hiking Trail

N

0.9
0.5
0.2   1.0   Falls View Shelter
0.0
Gooseberry River
61
(P)
Lake Superior

0.8
STEPS

Continue on the boardwalk, then descend 13 steps (wood), cross a bridge (wood, double handrail), then ascend 4 steps (wood).

0.9

At the big pine surrounded by birch and spruce, look left to see the SHT sign and follow until you see a building to your right. Then look for the sign to the visitor center. Falls View Shelter was the last CCC structure built at Gooseberry and showcases another interpretive CCC sign.

1.0
PHOTO

Back on the asphalt, turn right at the bridge that runs under Highway 61. It's definitely worth spending some time here! This bridge offers an exceptional vantage point for viewing Upper Falls and Gooseberry River. There are breathtaking views on either side of bridge. At the trail intersection, turn left and cross under the highway.

1.1 Pass the stairs on the right and left, with a bench at the base of the plaza steps;
BENCH   continue straight. At a "Y" in the trail, follow sign to visitor center. In 200', find a
bench to your left. Another 100' farther will be a bench to your right.

1.2 Visitor center and trailhead.

Says Who?

Want to reduce your risk of getting cancer?

Physical activity, such as walking, may reduce the risk for lung and colon cancer as well
as 12 other cancers.

Cancer.net[12]

Gooseberry River   *photo by Ladona Tornabene*

Iona's Beach

On Highway 61, 42 miles from Duluth • Gitchi-Gami State Trail section:
Twin Points Beach to Split Rock Lighthouse State Park

- **See Iona's Beach, a rare pink rhyolite pebble beach formed as rock eroded from nearby cliffs. Listen. . . if waves hit just right, the beach's "music" serenades (source: DNR).**

- **The GGST bridge is the only vantage point from which to enjoy an "aerial" view of Iona's Beach coupled with the stunning rhyolite cliffs that formed it.**

- **Breathtaking stands of towering pine and beautiful birch, along with sweeping vistas of Lake Superior, augment the dramatic scenery.**

DIRECTIONS:
On Highway 61 at mile marker 42, turn right into the paved parking area.

TOTAL TRAIL LENGTH & SURFACE:
This hike has two parts: The 1.0-mile section of GGST is paved. The other 0.2-mile section, which varies in length depending on how much you explore, leads directly to Iona's Beach and the surrounding area. It is partially paved, yielding to either hard-packed dirt or grass and has rhyolite pebbles at the beach.

INCLINES & ALERTS:
There are no inclines more than 10°, but the trail is not flat throughout. Depending on how you explore the area around Iona's Beach proper, you may encounter steep cliffs and severe overgrowth in places. The rhyolite beach itself can be challenging to walk on, as pebbles are very loose and uneven. The non-motorized multiuse Gitchi-Gami State Trail runs through the paved portion of this hike.

AMENITIES & FEES:
Small craft harbor; portable toilet may be available seasonally. No fees for parking or trail use.

MILEAGE & DESCRIPTION

0.0 Trailhead begins on paved 10-foot-wide GGST trail at the northwest end of parking area near a marvelous stand of pine, balsam fir, birch, and alder. This area is especially scenic closer to sunset, as the towering pine trunks are brightened by the retiring sun's golden light.

0.1
PHOTO
To continue onto bridge for an "aerial" view of Iona's Beach, stay on the paved GGST. To proceed directly to Iona's Beach and explore that area, take the dirt path straight ahead near the bicycle rack. A few yards into a glorious wooded stroll, find an intersection with an informational display about Iona's Beach. From that display, various spur trails beckon: Left leads to the stunning pink rhyolite pebble beach, otherwise known as Iona's Beach; the middle to a rocky promontory; the right to a large, rocky picturesque cove. The remainder of this trail account is written as if you had stayed on the paved trail.

0.2   The paved path begins to curve through a beautiful stand of birch before it runs parallel to Highway 61. While traffic noise is noticeable, there is ample vegetation between the path and highway for safety.

0.3   Here commanding vistas of Lake Superior emerge as you head toward the bridge.

0.5
PHOTO   This spacious bridge (wood/steel, double guardrail) has more than ample room to wander and wonder. Stop here and notice the stunning rhyolite cliff, which is the "founding father" of this beach. This cliff is specially photo-worthy in late afternoon, as sunlight illuminates the beautiful pink rhyolite, which is complemented by the deep blue hues of Lake Superior. This is the only vantage point from which to enjoy "aerial" views of Iona's Beach to the south. This bridge also marks the turn-around point as you retrace the path to the trailhead.

1.0   Trailhead and parking lot.

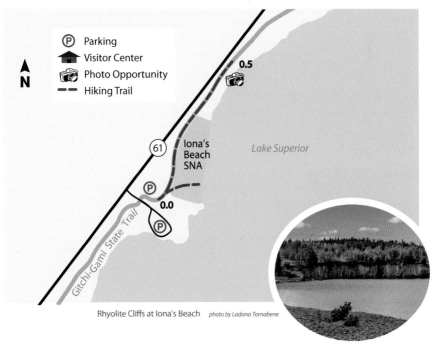

Rhyolite Cliffs at Iona's Beach   *photo by Ladona Tornabene*

Foot Note:

Iona's Beach was "named after Iona Lind, former owner of Twin Points Resort, which previously occupied the current parking area" (DNR, 2001). That fact and more information about this Minnesota Scientific and Natural Area can be found at www.dnr.state.mn.us/snas/detail.html?id=sna01000

LIGHTER

Little Two Harbors Trail & Pebble Beach

Split Rock Lighthouse State Park • On Highway 61, 46 miles from Duluth

- **Extraordinary, classic views of Split Rock Lighthouse, Ellingsen Island, and of course, Lake Superior!**
- **Several picnic tables nearby with superb views of the lake, woods, or Ellingsen Island.**
- **Remnants of an early fishing village may be visible beneath Superior's surface.**

TRAILHEAD DIRECTIONS:

On Highway 61 at mile marker 45.9, turn right into Split Rock Lighthouse State Park. Follow past the park office, turning right onto the first street you encounter. Follow for 0.5 mile to a paved parking lot near sign indicating Pebble Beach Picnic Area.

CONTACT:

Split Rock Lighthouse State Park: 218-595-ROCK (7625) or www.dnr.state.mn.us/state_parks/split_rock_lighthouse/index.html

TOTAL TRAIL LENGTH, SURFACE, & WIDTH:

0.8 mile; crushed limestone, gravel/dirt; average 8' wide.

INCLINES & ALERTS:

No inclines greater than 10°.

TRAILHEAD FACILITIES & FEES:

A vault toilet is available at the trailhead. Flush toilets and water are at the Trail Center. An annual or day-use state park permit is required; they are available at the park office.

MILEAGE & DESCRIPTION

0.0
BENCH
PHOTO

Trailhead begins at the southwest corner of the parking area on a gravel/dirt path near a vault toilet. In about 100', there is an intersection. A right leads to the pebble beach and a left leads to the Little Two Harbors Trail. The trail leading to the pebble beach has extraordinary, classic views of Split Rock Lighthouse and remnants of an early fishing village, which may be visible beneath Superior's surface if the water is still and clear. In 0.2 miles, views of Ellingsen Island (a bird sanctuary) become more prominent as the trail curves into the campground, making an ideal turnaround point.

0.4
BENCH
PHOTO

The Little Two Harbors Trail section's surface is crushed limestone and has several picnic tables scattered about with superb views of Ellingsen Island, woods, and the lake. One picnic site very close to the lake is wheelchair accessible. The Little Two Harbors Trail ceases its crushed limestone surface as it continues up to the Visitor Center; however, there is a fee area en route (see pg. 84 for details). To complete this trail as we wrote it, turn around at the picnic shelter and Trail Center (which houses flush toilets and water). It is 0.2 mile from this point back to the trailhead.

0.8   Trailhead.

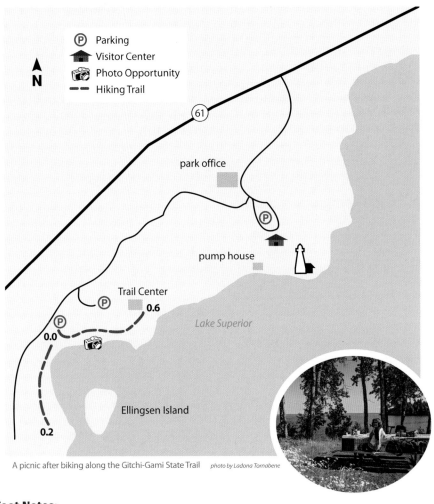

A picnic after biking along the Gitchi-Gami State Trail   *photo by Ladona Tornabene*

Foot Notes:

Birch trees are beautiful, but on their trunks, please leave no mark,
For those glorious birches can die, when stripped of their bark.

Can't wait to get here? Have a sneak peek via the Split Rock Lighthouse State Park virtual tour! Visit: www.dnr.state.mn.us/state_parks/virtual_tour/split_rock_lighthouse/dialup.html

 Split Rock: Birch to Beacon*

Split Rock Lighthouse State Park • On Highway 61, 46 miles from Duluth • Gitchi-Gami State Trail section: Twin Ports Public Access to Split Rock Lighthouse State Park • *Gentle Hikes* name

- **This paved trail winds through one of the most magnificent stands of birch on the North Shore; it is especially stunning in fall!**
- **Spectacular overlook of Split Rock Lighthouse from overlook (see pg. 170).**

TRAILHEAD DIRECTIONS:
From Highway 61 at mile marker 45.9, turn right into Split Rock Lighthouse State Park. Follow past the park office, turning right onto the first street you encounter. Follow for 0.4 mile and turn left at sign indicating Trail Center and picnic area.

CONTACT:
Split Rock Lighthouse State Park: 218-595-ROCK (7625) or www.dnr.state.mn.us/ state_parks/split_rock_lighthouse/index.html

TOTAL TRAIL LENGTH, SURFACE, & WIDTH:
1.3 mile; paved; 10' wide

INCLINES & ALERTS:
No inclines greater than 10°, but the trail is a steady uphill climb, which is why it earned a moderate rating. The trail crosses the state park road.

TRAILHEAD FACILITIES & FEES:
Flush toilets and water are available at the trailhead. There are enclosed and open picnic areas. An annual or day-use state park permit is required; they are available at the park office.

MILEAGE & DESCRIPTION

0.0 The trailhead begins at the east side of the parking lot on the 10-foot-wide paved Gitchi-Gami State Trail. In a few yards, there will be a building to the right that houses restrooms, water, and covered picnic shelters. At the paved intersection, turn left. Immediately you'll be treated to stunning views of birch, which continue throughout the trail. Follow the path toward the park road.

0.1 **Alert:** State park road crossing. Please use caution and continue straight. For the next 0.5 mile, trail switchbacks create nearly panoramic views of spectacular birch stands. Dazzling in fall!

0.6
PHOTO
When the trail begins to parallel the Highway 61 pull-through, turn right into the parking area (shared with vehicles) and soon find the iconic overlook of a distant, yet photo-worthy, view of Split Rock Lighthouse. Then retrace the path to the trailhead.

1.3 Trailhead

Foot Note:

The concept of Split Rock Lighthouse began in 1905 when a fierce November gale wrecked some thirty ships. The Lighthouse was completed in 1910, and its beacon ranged 22 miles. Although decommissioned in 1969, it still stands as a North Shore icon and one of the state's most photographed sights. We acknowledge the Minnesota Historical Society for providing this information. They also offer tours of the lighthouse and grounds. Visit: www.mnhs.org/splitrock/activities/lighthouse

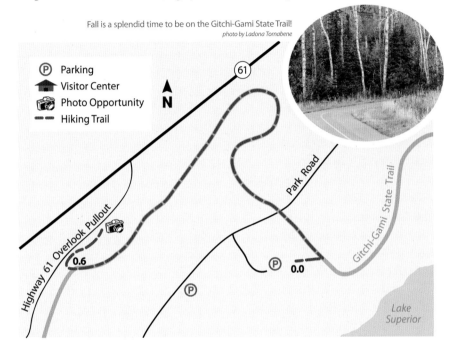

Fall is a splendid time to be on the Gitchi-Gami State Trail!
photo by Ladona Tornabene

/⚑ Little Two Harbors Trail

Split Rock Lighthouse State Park • On Highway 61, 46 miles from Duluth

- **A birch-lovers' paradise! Hike through this stunning forest that leads to Split Rock Lighthouse.**
- **Several spur trails lead to dramatic lighthouse views.**
- **This trail also leads to historic sites that are located in a fee area. Please see Foot Note.**

TRAILHEAD DIRECTIONS:

From Highway 61 at mile marker 45.9, turn right into Split Rock Lighthouse State Park. Follow past the park center, turning right onto the first street you encounter. Follow for 0.4 mile and turn left at sign indicating Trail Center and picnic area.

CONTACT:

Split Rock Lighthouse State Park: 218-595-ROCK (7625) or www.dnr.state.mn.us/state_parks/split_rock_lighthouse/index.html

TOTAL TRAIL LENGTH, SURFACE, & WIDTH:

0.8 mile; gravel and hard-packed dirt; average 6–8' wide.

INCLINES & ALERTS:

There is one incline of 14° for 25' at 0.2 mile. Optional spur trails may lead to rocky and uneven surfaces.

TRAILHEAD FACILITIES & FEES:

Flush toilets and water are available in the enclosed shelter. An annual or a day-use state park permit is required; they are available at the park office. There is a fee for trail use beginning at 0.3 miles, where spurs lead to the pump house, dock site, and old tramway. Pay for admission at the visitor center via the Minnesota Historical Society. See Foot Note for contact info.

MILEAGE & DESCRIPTION

0.0
PHOTO

Trailhead begins off the pavement at the back of the enclosed picnic shelter (south corner) near a sign for Little Two Harbors Trail and Lighthouse. Various spur trails lead you to dramatic lighthouse views and historical sights on the rocky shore of Lake Superior.

Enter what we consider the most stunning stand of birch among our hikes! Complemented by spruce, this trail is gorgeous every season of the year. Next you will cross a bridge (wood, double handrails).

0.2
INCLINE

In this section you will encounter the steepest incline (14° for 25'), as you continue to hike through this striking forest of birch, spruce, and fir.

0.3
BENCH

There is a bench to your left and an intersection. **Alert:** This marks the beginning of the fee area. With paid admission, you can continue up the trail and/or take the spurs to the right that lead to the lake, pump house, dock site, and old tramway (used 1916–1934).

0.4 Back on the main trail, pavement begins. If you continue another 200', you will arrive at the visitor center and an amazing gift/book shop (there is also a small gift shop at the park office). Seasonal tours of the lighthouse are available (see Foot Note). To complete this trail, turn around and retrace the path to trailhead.

0.8 Trailhead.

Split Rock Lighthouse as seen from a spur trail *photo by Ladona Tornabene*

Foot Note:

Seasonal tours of Split Rock Lighthouse, completed in 1910, are offered by the Minnesota Historical Society. Since part of this trail provides access to historical sites, an admission fee for such part, which includes Lighthouse tour/other amenities, is required when the site is open (call ahead or head online for times) and can be purchased in the visitor center. Visit www.mnhs.org/splitrock or call 218-226-6372.

Split Rock: Tour de Park*

Split Rock Lighthouse State Park • On Highway 61, 46 miles from Duluth • Gitchi-Gami State Trail section: Split Rock Lighthouse State Park to Beaver Bay • *Gentle Hikes* name

- **A lovely wooded hike through Split Rock Lighthouse State Park on a paved path.**

TRAILHEAD DIRECTIONS:

On Highway 61 at mile marker 45.9, turn right into Split Rock Lighthouse State Park. Follow past the park office, turning right onto the first street you encounter. Follow for 0.4 mile and turn left at sign indicating the Trail Center and picnic area.

CONTACT:

Split Rock Lighthouse State Park: 218-595-ROCK (7625) or www.dnr.state.mn.us/state_parks/split_rock_lighthouse/index.html

TOTAL TRAIL LENGTH, SURFACE, & WIDTH:

1.6 miles; paved; average 10' wide

INCLINES & ALERTS:

No inclines greater than 10°, but trail is not flat.

TRAILHEAD FACILITIES & FEES:

Flush toilets and water are available at trailhead, as are enclosed and open picnic areas. Annual or day-use state park permit is required; they are available at the park office.

MILEAGE & DESCRIPTION

0.0 The trailhead begins at the east side of the parking lot on the 10-foot-wide paved Gitchi-Gami State Trail. In a few yards, you'll see a building to the right that houses restrooms, water, and covered picnic shelters. At paved intersection, turn right following the sign to "Beaver Bay." Stay on the paved trail as various unpaved paths lead to the Little Two Harbors Trail (see pg. 84).

0.2 Cross the bridge (wood, double handrail) over the creek. Continue on the paved trail after the bridge crossing.

0.4 The trail parallels the park road for the next 0.1 mile but has ample vegetation separating it from the lanes. Just prior to approaching a beautiful stand of birch, pause and look right for a nice view of Lake Superior and her picturesque shoreline.

0.6
STEPS You'll encounter an intersection. From this point, you can simply turn around and retrace your path to the trailhead to complete this hike. If you cross the park road and continue straight, the GGST eventually leads to Beaver Bay in 6 miles and that distance clearly exceeds our Gentle Hikes criteria. If you turn left, the path goes to a small park office and gift shop. However, if you turn right, it leads to the Historical Society's stellar visitor center and museum store that exceeds our expectations every . . . single . . . time. This store is also accessible by vehicle via the park road. But if you are already on foot, another 0.2 mile will bring you to the door where you

can also purchase tickets to tour the Lighthouse! En route there is a quaint artistic bicycle rack that is truly one of a kind—we deem it photo-worthy. Just beyond it are 7 steps (wood/dirt, no handrail) to descend before reaching the visitor center. Flush toilets and a water fountain are available when the store is open.

0.8 From the visitor center, if you purchased a tour ticket, you are allowed to take the Little Two Harbors Trail (pg. 84) back to the parking area. Otherwise, please retrace your path to trailhead.

1.6 Trailhead.

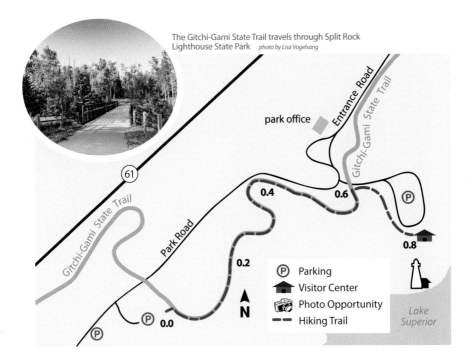

The Gitchi-Gami State Trail travels through Split Rock Lighthouse State Park *photo by Lisa Vogelsang*

 Says Who?

Want to reduce your risk of osteoporosis?

Walk briskly! People who perform moderate exercise have a lower risk of developing osteoporosis.

National Health Service UK[39]

Northshore Scenic Overlooks and Trails

Off Highway 61, approximately 54 miles from Duluth

- **Each of these three easy trails leads through a forest to a different overlook: Silver Bay highlights, a sweeping vista of Lake Superior, or an inland forest. See one or see them all!**
- **Find out about mining, Lake Superior, and her shipwrecks, as well as the city of Silver Bay.**

TRAILHEAD DIRECTIONS:

On Highway 61 at mile marker 54.3 in Silver Bay (**Note:** there is a sign indicating "Scenic Overlook" preceding the marker), turn left onto Outer Drive (at traffic light). Follow for 0.6 mile, watching for a sign on the right indicating Scenic Overlook. Turn left toward the solid waste recycling station (there is no street sign). Follow the Scenic Overlook sign 0.3 mile to a paved parking area. A lower lot provides RV parking.

CONTACT:

Silver Bay Visitor Center (seasonal): 218-226-3143 (Open Memorial Day weekend through mid-October.)

TOTAL TRAIL LENGTH, SURFACE, & WIDTH:

0.5 mile total for all three trails; gravel; average 5–6' wide. Minimally rocky to moderate in sections.

INCLINES & ALERTS:

There are two inclines of 12°. Longest is 15' at 0.3 mile. Some washout may be present.

TRAILHEAD FACILITIES & FEES:

No facilities available. No fees for trail use.

MILEAGE & DESCRIPTION

0.0
PHOTO
The trailhead begins in a parking lot at a sign indicating Plant View #1. It is about 90' to the first overlook of Lake Superior and the Northshore Mining plant with an informative interpretive display showing the various steps involved in taconite pellet production.

0.1
PHOTO
The trail to Lake View #2 begins at the far left corner of the parking lot with a sign indicating Views #2 & #3. At the trail intersection, find the sign indicating Lake View; turn right. From the overlook, you can see Palisade Head, and beyond that, Shovel Point at Tettegouche State Park. There is interesting historical information about the shipwrecks of the *Hesper* and *Madeira*, both of which sank in 1905. Please note the information board for other points of interest.

0.2 Back at the intersection, take a right and follow the sign indicating City View #3.

0.3 This overlook provides you with a panorama of the city of Silver Bay. See the infor-
INCLINE
PHOTO mation board for various points of interest. Return to the trail, and turn right at the
intersection toward the parking lot. The area of steepest incline (12° for 15') is in this
section. Washout and overgrowth may be present.

0.5 Parking lot and trailhead.

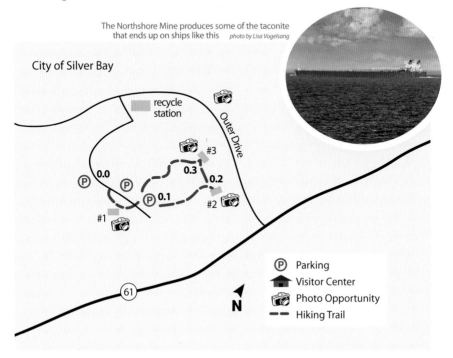

The Northshore Mine produces some of the taconite
that ends up on ships like this   *photo by Lisa Vogelsang*

City of Silver Bay

recycle
station

Outer Drive

#3

0.3

0.2

0.0

0.1

#2

#1

61

N

Ⓟ Parking

🏠 Visitor Center

📷 Photo Opportunity

‑ ‑ Hiking Trail

Foot Note:

To find more information about all there is to do and see in Silver Bay,
visit www.silverbay.com

Triple Overlook Loop*

Tettegouche State Park • On Highway 61, 58 miles from Duluth •
Gentle Hikes name

- **Three distinct overlooks on a very level and flat path, with views of Palisade Head, a towering 320' rhyolite cliff; a Lake Superior vista; and an incredibly picturesque lookout to Shovel Point framed by the rugged shoreline.**
- **This trail meets Universal Design Standards criteria.**

TRAILHEAD DIRECTIONS:

From Highway 61 at mile marker 58.6, turn right into Tettegouche State Park. There is paved parking for cars to the right, and for RVs to the left. The parking is wheelchair accessible.

CONTACT:

Tettegouche State Park: (218) 353-8800 or www.dnr.state.mn.us/state_parks/tettegouche/index.html

TOTAL TRAIL LENGTH, SURFACE, & WIDTH:

0.5 mile; paved; average 6' wide.

INCLINES & ALERTS:

None.

TRAILHEAD FACILITIES & FEES:

The visitor center offers a snack counter serving coffee/light refreshments (vending machines accessible 24/7), a gift shop, interpretive exhibits, flush toilets, and a water fountain. An amphitheater is also on-site as is a massive indoor fireplace, and an enormous outdoor stone fireplace, which is available for public use with purchase of wood. The area also has covered and open picnic areas (see Tettegouche General Picnic Areas pg. 185).

The visitor center houses the wayside rest area, which is open 24/7. There is no fee to park at Tettegouche Visitor Center (four-hour limit). However, if vehicles are driven to or parked at other areas within the park, a day-use or annual permit is required; these are available at the park office.

MILEAGE & DESCRIPTION

0.0
BENCH
PHOTO

The trailhead begins near the covered picnic shelter at the northeast corner of the visitor center on a 10-foot-wide paved path. Follow the sign indicating the "Shovel Point and Baptism River Trail," although this hike will not venture to either of these. Just past the visitor center there is a lovely area that houses a massive outdoor fireplace, which we'll revisit later. For now, continue straight ahead to Overlook #1, where a view of Lake Superior and a bench await. While there are no guardrails per se, it is not very close to the lake nor is it perched on a cliff. To see the second overlook, when facing the lake, turn left onto the paved path and head toward the Shovel Point Trail (pg. 94).

0.1
BENCH
PHOTO
Overlook #2 hosts a marvelous view of Palisade Head (pg. 172) with the rugged shoreline of Lake Superior in the distance. Break out the camera. A bench is perched on the wooden surface of the overlook (guardrails). To reach Overlook #3, retrace your steps back to the first overlook and continue straight on the path past two more benches.

0.2
The paved path transitions to boardwalk for a few yards before it changes back to blacktop, but the transition is virtually seamless. Stay on the paved path until it ends at Overlook #3.

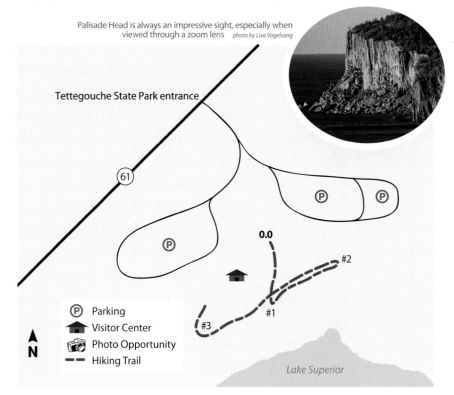

Palisade Head is always an impressive sight, especially when viewed through a zoom lens   *photo by Lisa Vogelsang*

0.3
BENCH
PHOTO
Overlook #3 is a beauty! A magnificent and incredibly picturesque overlook of Shovel Point and the nearby rocky outcrop make this a near-perfect photo op. Another bench can be found on the wooden surface of this overlook (guardrails).

You can choose to return the same way or complete the loop. As you retrace your path to the trailhead, we will unpack the features encountered en route to these overlooks. The hard-packed dirt trail accompanied by a wooden rail just prior to overlook #3 leads to the Baptism River Loop Trail (pg. 98). Directly behind the visitor center is the beautiful, massive stone fireplace that is available for public use when one purchases wood from the park. Behind the fireplace is an amphitheater. The visitor center houses another phenomenal colossal fireplace, a gift shop, and interpretive exhibits sure to intrigue and delight all who enter. To complete the loop, choose one of the paved paths on the left that go through a picnic area towards the west side of the rear of the visitor center. You can get to the parking lot on either the west or east side of the visitor center or through the visitor center during open hours.

0.5 Trailhead and parking area.

 Foot Note:

Tettegouche State Park has an amazing gift shop that has many awesome books. Proceeds from items purchased at all state park gift shops help fund resource management and interpretive projects.

Shovel Point as seen from overlook #3   *photo by Ladona Tornabene*

RUGGED

//◢ Shovel Point Trail

Tettegouche State Park • On Highway 61, 58 miles from Duluth

- **This hike is on a peninsula and provides breathtaking views of Palisade Head, rugged cliff faces, and Lake Superior, all of which are not to be missed.**

TRAILHEAD DIRECTIONS:

From Highway 61 at mile marker 58.6, turn right into Tettegouche State Park. There is paved parking for cars to the right, and for RVs to the left. The parking is wheelchair accessible.

CONTACT:

Tettegouche State Park: (218) 353-8800 or www.dnr.state.mn.us/state_parks/tettegouche/index.html

TOTAL TRAIL LENGTH, SURFACE, & WIDTH:

1.2 miles; asphalt, mostly boardwalk, some gravel and hard-packed dirt; average 2–4' wide. Minimal roots and rocks.

INCLINES & ALERTS:

There are five inclines ranging from 12–20°. The steepest is 20° for 20' at 0.8 mile. There are steep cliffs—no guardrails. Keep children in hand.

TRAILHEAD FACILITIES & FEES:

The visitor center offers a snack counter serving coffee/light refreshments (vending machines accessible 24/7), a gift shop, interpretive exhibits, flush toilets, and a water fountain. An amphitheater is also on-site, as is a massive indoor fireplace, and an enormous outdoor stone fireplace, which is available for public use with purchase of wood. The area also has covered and open picnic areas (see Tettegouche General Picnic Areas pg. 185).

The visitor center houses the wayside rest area, which is open 24/7. There is no fee to park at Tettegouche Visitor Center (four-hour limit). However, if vehicles are driven to or parked at other areas within the park, a day-use or annual permit is required; these are available at the park office.

MILEAGE & DESCRIPTION

0.0
STEPS

The route to the trailhead begins on a paved path that's far left of the visitor center and behind the picnic pavilion. Just past the visitor center to the right are several tables and chairs, as well as a beautiful outdoor fireplace. To the left is an amphitheater. After passing the amphitheater, turn left and follow the path to an overlook (guardrails) with views of Palisade Head. Find a sign indicating the Hiking Club Trail and follow the boardwalk. Shortly, descend 24 steps (wood, single handrail, non-continuous) onto a dirt path. At the intersection, a left leads back to the RV parking area, so continue straight. Descend 31 steps (wood, no handrail, non-continuous), and follow the sign to Shovel Point. Note: The trail to the right leads to the beach area and contains 112 steps (wood, with/without handrail, non-continuous).

0.1
STEPS
BENCH
PHOTO

An overlook platform (guardrail and bench) affords commanding views of distant Palisade Head (to visit it, see Palisade Head Overlook on pg. 172. Descend 5 steps (wood, double handrail). Shortly after, descend 15 steps (wood, single handrail, non-continuous), and cross the wooden bridge (double handrail). Immediately ascend 16 steps (wood, single handrail, non-continuous).

0.2
STEPS
BENCH
PHOTO

Take the spur trail to the right and descend 6 steps (wood, no handrail, non-continuous); these lead to an overlook of a sea stack—the remains of the North Shore's only sea arch, which collapsed in 2010 (Kelleher, 2010[i]). Return to the trail and ascend 169 platform-like steps (wood, no handrail, non-continuous). This section has several level places to rest if needed and most steps are single with sufficient platforms in between. These may best be thought of like a boardwalk with frequent "step-ups."

0.4
STEPS
BENCH
PHOTO

Ascend 43 steps (wood, no handrail, non-continuous) for a spectacular distant view of Palisade Head with Lake Superior shoreline. The sights from these cliffs are some of the most photographed and are often found on postcards. This view is especially stunning in fall! Rock climbers also frequent this area.

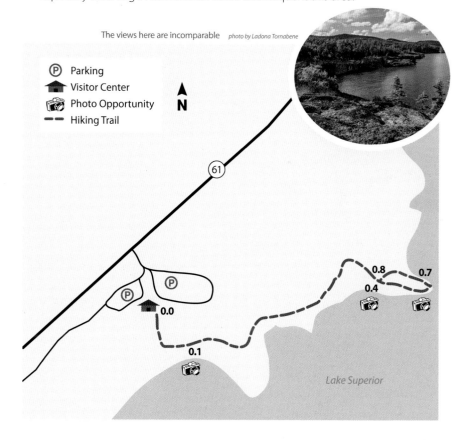

The views here are incomparable   *photo by Ladona Tornabene*

Parking
Visitor Center
Photo Opportunity
Hiking Trail

N

61

0.8   0.7
0.4

0.0

0.1

Lake Superior

[i]Kelleher, B. 2010. Visitors come to see what's left of Tettegouche arch. Retrieved July 17, 2017, from www.mprnews.org/story/2010/08/22/tettegouche-arch-collapses

0.5
DECLINE
STEPS
PHOTO

Take the boardwalk from the overlook, cross the rock surface, and then go down 2 steps (wood, no handrail, non-continuous). This section is home to the steepest incline (16° for 35'), moderate roots, and at time of this writing, some washout. You will also find 3 spur trails leading to more glorious views similar to those at the overlook in section 0.4. **Alert:** There are no guardrails at the end of these spurs and the cliffs are dangerously steep. These spur trails have platform steps (wood, no handrail, non-continuous) and are in the following order: The first spur descends 6 steps; the second and third spurs descend 15 steps at each. Back on the trail, there is one very short section of boardwalk. Shortly, descend 5 steps (wood, no handrail).

Two additional overlooks (no guardrail) lead to the cliff edge and many photo ops. This trail section has the steepest decline (16° for 35'), and shortly after it, you can take the spur trail to the right and descend a set of 16 steps (wood, no handrail). This once again leads to the cliff edge (no guardrail). After returning to the trail, find two sections of boardwalk, then descend 5 steps (wood, no handrail).

0.7
STEPS
BENCH
PHOTO

A set of 26 steps (wood, double handrail) leads to a platform overlook (bench, guardrail) with stunning views of the rocky shoreline and popular sights along Lake Superior's north shore. However, these pinkish cliffs are rhyolite, and on a sunny day, when juxtaposed against the aqua-blue water, they reveal a beautiful photo-worthy sight.

Back at the top of the steps, go straight, continuing across the rocky surface, as the trail meanders around the tip of the "shovel." Reenter the wooded area and hike through pine and cedar. **Alert:** This is a steep cliff with no guardrail.

0.8
INCLINE

This section takes you up two areas of incline, which includes the area of steepest incline (20° for 20'), then brings you back to the main trail near the cliffs. Retrace the path to trailhead.

1.2 Trailhead.

 Foot Note:

Can't wait to get here? Have a sneak peek via the Tettegouche State Park virtual tour! Visit: www.dnr.state.mn.us/state_parks/virtual_tour/tettegouche/dialup.html

Soft light, calm winds, and photographic technique combined to pop the colors within Shovel Point Trail's rugged cliffs   *photo by Ladona Tornabene*

Baptism River Loop*

Tettegouche State Park • On Highway 61, 58 miles from Duluth •
Gentle Hikes name

- **Access to Baptism River mouth as it flows alongside picturesque rocky bluffs en route to Lake Superior.**
- **A dramatic view of Shovel Point and rugged shoreline.**

TRAILHEAD DIRECTIONS:
From Highway 61 at mile marker 58.6, turn right into Tettegouche State Park. There is paved parking for cars to the right, and for RVs to the left. The parking is wheelchair accessible.

CONTACT:
Tettegouche State Park: (218) 353-8800 or www.dnr.state.mn.us/state_parks/tettegouche/index.html

TOTAL TRAIL LENGTH, SURFACE, & WIDTH:
0.5 mile; asphalt, gravel, and hard-packed dirt; average 3–4' wide. Minimal rocks and roots.

INCLINES & ALERTS:
No inclines greater than 10°. No guardrails on some overlooks and trail sections.

TRAILHEAD FACILITIES & FEES:
The visitor center offers a snack counter serving coffee/light refreshments (vending machines accessible 24/7), a gift shop, interpretive exhibits, flush toilets, and a water fountain. An amphitheater is also on-site as is a massive indoor fireplace, and an enormous outdoor stone fireplace, which is available for public use with purchase of wood. The area also has covered and open picnic areas (see Tettegouche General Picnic Areas pg. 185).

There is no fee to park at Tettegouche Visitor Center (four-hour limit). However, if vehicles are driven to or parked at other areas within the park, a day-use or annual permit is required; these are available at the park office.

MILEAGE & DESCRIPTION

0.0 Trailhead begins at the southeast end of the visitor center on a 6-foot-wide paved path at the sign indicating "Shovel Point and Baptism River Trails." In a few feet, take the path to the right past several picnic tables (paved to the bench and underneath). Continue veering right toward a short boardwalk section before the paved path resumes.

0.1
STEPS
BENCH
PHOTO
Soon you will see a 3-foot-wide dirt path to the right, with a wooden railing on one side; however, before taking it, we highly recommend continuing on the paved path for a few more feet to an overlook (guardrails and bench) with a dramatic view of Shovel Point and the nearby rocky outcrops. After returning to the dirt path, it will lead to 45 steps that descend (wood, single handrail, non-continuous).

0.2
STEPS
BENCH
PHOTO

A lone bench offers partial views of Lake Superior before the path descends 19 more steps (wood, single handrail, non-continuous) to an intersection. A spur trail to the left and down 11 steps (wood, single handrail) leads to overlook (two benches, no guardrail) with views of Baptism River mouth, Lake Superior's rugged shoreline, and Shovel Point. Back on the trail, descend 21 steps (wood, handrail). To the left and up 4 steps (wood, handrail), find a bench with a different view of the river mouth.

Next, descend 7 steps (wood, no handrail) to a platform path. A spur down 15 steps (wood, no handrail) leads to the sandbar at the beach. Return to the main trail and turn left at the kayakers' information board.

Soon there will be two optional spur trails—one leads down 45 steps (wood, double handrail) to the water's edge; the other leads to benches and an overlook (guardrails) with lovely views up- and downriver.

0.3
STEPS

Continuing on the trail, ascend 3 steps to cross a wooden bridge (double handrails) and then ascend 49 steps (wood, single handrail, non-continuous) that lead to the park entry road. Turn right and follow the paved walking lane along the right side of the road back to the parking area and visitor center.

0.5 Trailhead.

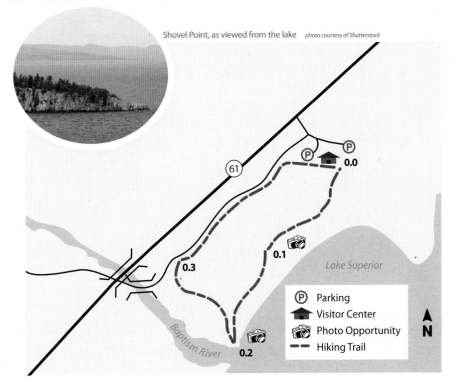

Shovel Point, as viewed from the lake *photo courtesy of Shutterstock*

Lake Superior

Baptism River

P Parking
Visitor Center
Photo Opportunity
--- Hiking Trail

N

MODERATE

High Falls At Tettegouche

Tettegouche State Park • On Highway 61, 58 miles from Duluth

- **Breathtaking views of the 80' High Falls. Bring your best camera.**
- **Phenomenal views of the Baptism River.**

TRAILHEAD DIRECTIONS:

From Highway 61 at mile marker 58.6, turn right into Tettegouche State Park, and immediately take another right. After you get a visitor pass at the visitor center, keep driving, and soon you will drive over a bridge. Continue on this curvy road, and in approximately 1.2 miles, there will be an intersection. Do NOT turn right as that leads to the camping area; instead, follow signs to Trail Center, where a paved/gravel parking lot is located.

CONTACT:

Tettegouche State Park: (218) 353-8800, www.dnr.state.mn.us/state_parks/tettegouche/index.html

TOTAL TRAIL LENGTH, SURFACE, & WIDTH:

1.6 miles; hard-packed dirt and gravel; 3–4' wide. Minimal rocks and roots.

INCLINES & ALERTS:

There are four inclines of 12–16°. The steepest and longest is 16° for 45' at 1.2 miles. The suspension-bridge crossing permits no more than five persons at a time. There are steep cliffs with no guardrails, and there is erosion in places.

TRAILHEAD FACILITIES & FEES:

A vault toilet and picnic area (see High Falls Picnic Area pg. 186) are nearby; an annual or day-use state park permit is required; these are available at the park office.

MILEAGE & DESCRIPTION

0.0 The trailhead begins from the parking area at a sign indicating "High Falls." A portion of this trail is a Superior Hiking Trail spur. On the trail, a forest of cedars scattered with alder greets you as you gradually ascend a 10° grade on a wide path for the first 0.1 mile. Expect some erosion.

0.1 The trail becomes rockier, but there's still a good walking surface. Pines now join the forest here.

0.2
DECLINE
At the trail intersection, find the sign indicating the Superior Hiking Trail. Turn right and follow the signs to High Falls (0.5 mile ahead). This is where the trail joins the SHT spur. The next 0.4 mile travels through several beautifully wooded areas. The section at 0.4 miles contains the steepest decline (16° for 45'). Soon a couple sections of boardwalk follow.

0.6
STEPS
BENCH
PHOTO
Encounter a wooden platform where a bench marks the trail intersection, and steps descend in both directions. Turn left and descend 67 steps (wood, no handrail, non-continuous) that lead to an overlook (guardrails and benches) with a foliage-dependent view of High Falls.

After the overlook, ascend 4 steps, and continue on the boardwalk, then descend 39 platform-type steps (wood, no handrail, non-continuous) and find a spur to the right equipped with boardwalk leading to an overlook (guardrail). This provides a dramatic view of the falls from a vantage point directly above them.

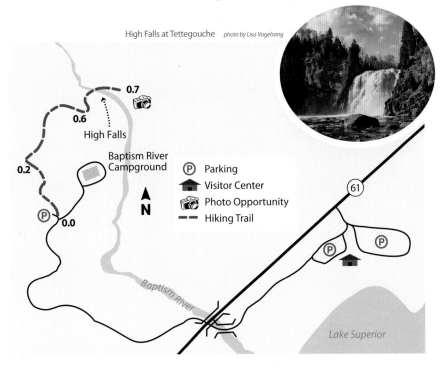

High Falls at Tettegouche   *photo by Lisa Vogelsang*

0.7
STEPS
PHOTO
Back on the trail, descend 37 steps (wood, no handrail) to the platform (wood, double-steel guardrail), then down 5 steps. Continue on and across a small bridge (wood, double handrail). Soon, ascend 10 steps (wood, double handrail) before approaching the suspension bridge; only 5 people are allowed to be on the bridge at one time. From there you can enjoy impressive views up- and downriver.

Once across the suspension bridge, find the following series of wood steps (no handrail unless otherwise noted): ascend 12 (double handrail); descend 12; ascend 10 (handrail). Continue on the boardwalk for the best view of High Falls thus far on the trail from a small viewing platform (guardrail). Officially we ended our portion of the trail here. However, there is an option* for a simply superb view of High Falls, one that we believe is worth the trek. Read on or retrace path to trailhead.

*Option: If you're up for the challenge of 180 steps (non-continuous), this option delivers a superlative view. Encounter the following series of steps (all wood, some handrail, non-continuous): ascend 28, descend 71 (with various rise and steepness), and find a timely positioned bench before descending the remaining 81 steps to the river's edge. The reward is a picture-perfect view of the entire falls. If you explore this area, please use caution, as it will necessitate travel over an uneven rocky surface upon leaving the last step. If photography excites you, spend some time scoping out the best shot. It's worth it!

1.2 The area of steepest incline (16° for 45').
INCLINE
1.6 Trailhead.

Says Who?

Feeling stressed out? Get out and about!

Walking 30 minutes 4–6 days per week at a moderate pace can prevent or reduce stress and anxiety.

APA Monitor on Psychology[23]

The High Falls from river level   *photo by Lisa Vogelsang*

Benson Lake Trail

George H. Crosby Manitou State Park • Off Highway 61, approximately 59 miles from Duluth

- **Hike beneath a rocky ridge in the shade of maple, birch, fir, and cedar along the shores of beautiful Benson Lake.**
- **Remoteness and tranquility characterize this pristine environment.**

TRAILHEAD DIRECTIONS:

From Highway 61 at mile marker 59.3, turn left onto Highway 1 and follow for 6.2 miles (you will travel through Finland). Turn right onto County Road 7, and follow for 7.6 miles. (**Note:** The road is paved for 1 mile, then turns to hard-packed dirt.) Turn right onto Benson Lake Road (also fire marker #7616) into George H. Crosby Manitou State Park, and follow for 0.5 mile to a gravel parking lot on the left.

CONTACT:

This park is managed by Tettegouche State Park: (218) 353-8800 or www.dnr.state.mn.us/state_parks/tettegouche/index.html

TOTAL TRAIL LENGTH, SURFACE, & WIDTH:

1.1 miles; gravel roadway; average 10' wide, for 0.1 mile. Boardwalk (2' wide) for almost the entire remainder of the trail.

INCLINES & ALERTS:

No inclines greater than 10°. Watch for vehicles while walking on roadway. Wet areas possible on trail. The section after Matt Willis Trail intersection can become impassable after heavy rains.

TRAILHEAD FACILITIES & FEES:

Vault toilets are available at the parking lot by informational signs, and at the picnic area (see Benson Lake Picnic Area on pg. 187). Water (seasonal) is available at park entrance. An annual or day-use state park permit is required. A pay box is available at the entrance.

MILEAGE & DESCRIPTION

0.0 The trailhead begins at the far end of the parking area at a sign on roadway indicating Benson Lake Trail. The road is shared with vehicles going to the picnic area at the lakeshore.

0.1 Enter the trail to the left side of the road preceding the picnic area, at a sign
STEPS
PHOTO indicating Benson Lake Trail. Soon descend 3 steps (wood, no handrail), then cross a small bridge (wood, no handrail), and head onto the boardwalk. The boardwalk continues almost entirely around the lake, with 37 platform-like steps (wood, no handrail, non-continuous) scattered throughout. Steps ascend and descend at various points.

Upon entering the first stand of fir, a sense of remoteness permeates the air. Soon you'll be treading alongside the pristine beauty of Benson Lake. This side of the lake hosts several pack-in campsites located atop the ridge to your left. Continue straight on the trail.

0.3
STEPS
As of this writing, a bubbling brook flowed from Benson Lake and under the boardwalk. Shortly, you will ascend 4 steps (wood, no handrail). In less than 200', the Beaver Bog Trail will intersect your path. A park map is located to your right. Continue walking along the lakeshore. Keep watch for a beaver dam.

0.6
The Matt Willis Trail intersects from the left; continue straight. A park map is located to your right. Note that the forest has opened to a more shrubby area. You will pass campsite #19.

0.7
A long section of boardwalk (about 1,250') brings you back into the forest. This newer boardwalk protects the forest floor and carries you over probable wet areas as well.

0.9
PHOTO
The boardwalk will eventually transport you to the wooded picnic area that you bypassed when starting this hike. Continue walking to the road and retrace your path to the trailhead.

1.1
Trailhead.

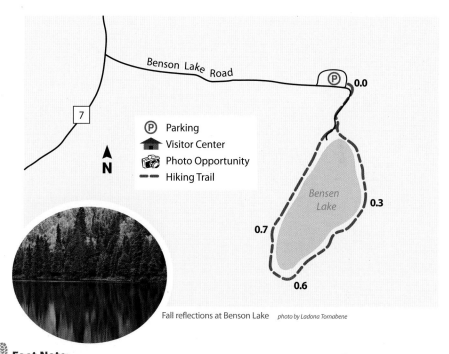

Fall reflections at Benson Lake   *photo by Ladona Tornabene*

Foot Note:

Can't wait to get here? Have a sneak peek via the Crosby Manitou State Park virtual tour! Visit: www.dnr.state.mn.us/state_parks/virtual_tour/george_crosby_manitou/dialup.html

Beyond Little Marais
to Grand Marais

Caribou Falls in autumn   *photo by Ladona Tornabene*

MODERATE

Caribou Falls

Off Highway 61, approximately 70 miles from Duluth •
Superior Hiking Trail section: Caribou River Wayside to Lutsen

- **Scenic sections along the Caribou River lead to the beautiful 35-foot-tall Caribou Falls—bring the tripod!**
- **Nice views of the Caribou River Gorge.**

TRAILHEAD DIRECTIONS:
From Highway 61 at mile marker 70.5, look for the Caribou River Falls Wayside sign. Turn left into the paved parking area.

CONTACT:
Superior Hiking Trail: 218-834-2700 or shta.org/trail-section/caribou-river-wayside-to-lutsen/

TOTAL TRAIL LENGTH, SURFACE, & WIDTH:
1.6 to 2 miles, depending on option taken; gravel and hard-packed dirt; average 4' wide. Minimum rocks and roots.

INCLINES & ALERTS:
There are four inclines of 12–15°. Most are of similar steepness and length. Steep cliffs, many without guardrails.

TRAILHEAD FACILITIES & FEES:
Vault toilet. No fees for parking or trail use.

MILEAGE & DESCRIPTION

0.0 The trailhead begins near a vault toilet where three flat, 5-foot-wide aggregate paths intersect. The paths to the far left and center lead to views of Caribou River, with the former being wheelchair accessible. Each one is less than 0.1 mile round-trip.

The path to the right eventually leads to Caribou Falls; however, the wheelchair-accessible gravel surface ends in 0.2 mile at a beautiful river view (see below). From that point, the trail becomes hard-packed dirt as it begins its ascent along the ridge before reaching the Falls.

0.2
INCLINE
BENCH
PHOTO
A picturesque cedar frames the rocky river flow, where a bench makes for a great place to pause before the trail turns to climb above the river. Here, the first incline of 10° for 20' is encountered.

0.3
INCLINE
There is a small section of moderate rock and incline of 12–15° for about 60'. Continue along this lovely wooded path for 0.3 mile until you reach an intersection. To view Caribou Falls, turn left.

0.6
STEPS
Descend 70 steps (wood, no handrail, non-continuous). This leads to another 28 descending steps (wood, handrail, non-continuous), which are steep in places and may be wet due to spray from the falls. However, several platforms provide various views of the falls.

0.7
STEPS
PHOTO

Descend 27 steps (wood, handrail, non-continuous) where a lone bench provides a view of Caribou Falls. It is only 28 more steps (wood/iron grate, handrail) down to the base of the Falls, where there is a small landing space (no guardrail) to accommodate one person comfortably. Please use extreme caution in this area if water is high, because it may crest the landing base, and nothing stands between you and the river. However, we think that the view from here is the best and is absolutely stunning! Look above Caribou Falls for a second smaller set of falls.

0.8
INCLINE
STEPS
PHOTO

Ascend the steps back to the trail intersection, where two options await. You can retrace your path back to the trailhead by turning right. Otherwise, you can continue upward by turning left, which after 0.2 mile leads to a very spacious viewing platform, with guardrails, that is above the falls and showcases partial views of Lake Superior and the river gorge. En route to this platform, there are two back-to-back inclines of 12–15° for approximately 50' each.

1.6
or
2.0

Trailhead (depending on the option you take when returning).

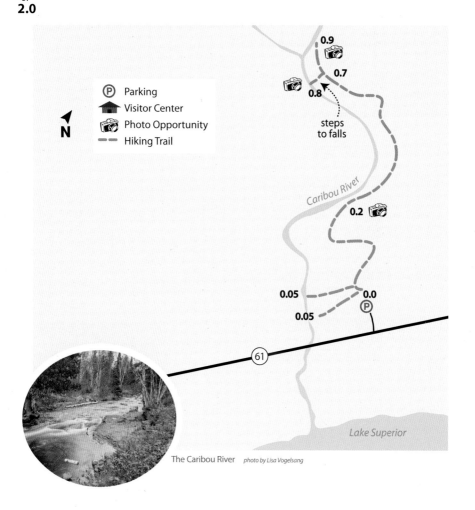

The Caribou River   photo by Lisa Vogelsang

Sugarloaf Cove Trail

On Highway 61, 73 miles from Duluth

- **There are many interesting features on this self-guided interpretive trail (guide booklets are available).**
- **This site was the former location of a pulpwood rafting operation (1943–1971).**
- **Sugarloaf Point and its cove beach are protected as a DNR Scientific and Natural Area.**

TRAILHEAD DIRECTIONS:

From Highway 61 at mile marker 73.2, locate the sign indicating "Sugarloaf Cove State Natural Area" (near fire marker #9096).Turn right and park in gravel lot.

CONTACT:

Sugarloaf Cove: 218-663-7679 or sugarloaf@boreal.org

TOTAL TRAIL LENGTH, SURFACE, & WIDTH:

1.0 mile; grass, gravel, and hard-packed dirt; average 5' wide.

INCLINES & ALERTS:

There is one incline (12° for 10'). Some sections of the trail have uneven surface; may be slippery in wet areas, especially on rocks. Please do not hike onto Sugarloaf Point itself, as the vegetation is very fragile.

TRAILHEAD FACILITIES & FEES:

A flush toilet and water are available at the interpretive center (summer hours: 9 a.m.– 4 p.m., 7 days a week). A seasonal portable toilet is located a short distance up the gravel road. No fees for parking or trail use. If wheelchair accessibility is needed, take the road on the south end of the parking lot. The interpretive center is the only part of this hike that is wheelchair accessible.

MILEAGE & DESCRIPTION

0.0
STEPS
BENCH

Although scenic and beautiful in its own right, this trail is best known for its interpretive features. To the left of the parking area information kiosk, descend 9 steps (stone, handrail). Follow the path toward the visitor center (gravel, hard-packed dirt, some roots) and down an additional set of 10 steps (wood, no handrail). Notice the signs on the tree and continue right to the visitor center. Cross a metal bridge (double handrail). Trail guides are available outside the building and will explain what you see at each interpretive signpost.

The trailhead starts at the visitor center. Walk back across the metal bridge to follow the other sign for Loop Trail. Soon you will enter a very dense stand of tall pine, where you can relax on the bench and enjoy the lovely shade.

0.1
STEPS

Descend 8 steps (wood, metal, handrail). You will encounter a somewhat rocky area, however the "Sugarloaf" can be viewed from this point.

0.3
BENCH
Find a bench nestled among spruce, pine, and birch.

0.4
STEPS
Minimum to moderate root in this area—watch your step! As you walk through the woods, look for lichen (called Old Man's Beard) hanging from spruce trees. Series of 9 steps (wood, handrail).

0.5
PHOTO
Can you locate the remains of the root cellar and part of the wellhead? Read the information signs before exploring the beach. Follow the shoreline about two-thirds of the way along the beach; watch for arrow on post to continue trail.

0.7
INCLINE
A boardwalk has been placed over the wetland area to make your hike more pleasant and help protect the vegetation. Once out of the wetland area, you will locate Sugarloaf Creek. The trail follows along the stream, then brings you to an area of incline (12° for 10').

0.9
STEPS
BENCH
Ascend 17 steps (wood, no handrail). When you reach the two benches, take a moment to pause and enjoy the shaded beauty of the pine plantation that was created by the paper company when they closed their rafting operation in 1971.

1.0
Return to parking area.

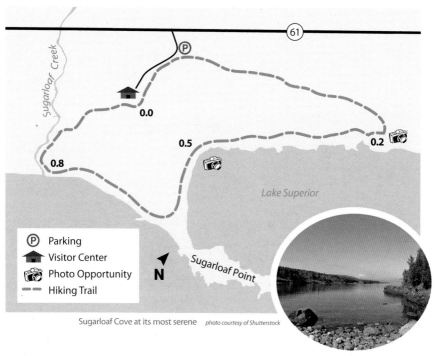

Sugarloaf Cove at its most serene   *photo courtesy of Shutterstock*

Foot Note:

Sugarloaf Cove Nature Center offers a breadth of nature-oriented activities and learning opportunities for families and individuals, including an Interpretive Center with exhibits. Visit sugarloafnorthshore.org/about-sugarloaf/

Dyers Creek

Off Highway 61, approximately 79 miles from Duluth • Superior Hiking Trail section: Cook County Road 1 to Temperance River State Park

- **A beautiful wooded hike with a short section that directly parallels Two Island River & Dyers Creek.**

TRAILHEAD DIRECTIONS:
From Highway 61 at mile marker 78.9 (across from Lamb's Resort and before Cross River Wayside), turn left on paved County Road 1 and follow for 3.6 miles (**Note:** the road eventually changes to gravel.) Look for a fire marker indicating "Cramer Road #843" on the right, and park in a gravel area for the Superior Hiking Trail.

CONTACT:
Superior Hiking Trail: 218-834-2700 or shta.org

TOTAL TRAIL LENGTH, SURFACE, & WIDTH:
2.6 miles; hard-packed dirt; average 2' wide. Minimum rocks and roots, changing to moderate amounts as trail continues.

INCLINES & ALERTS:
There are 3 inclines of 12–18°. The steepest and longest incline is 18° for 20' at 1.6 miles. There are two back-road crossings.

TRAILHEAD FACILITIES & FEES:
No facilities available. No fees for trail use.

MILEAGE & DESCRIPTION

0.0   The trailhead begins at the west end of the parking area near the Superior Hiking Trail sign indicating "Alfred's Pond" on a 4-foot-wide dirt/grass path. In just a few yards, cross a fairly wide concrete bridge (no handrail) as you hike through a mixed forest on this level path.

0.2   **Alert:** The turnoff for the SHT can be easy to miss. Once you see a gravel road in the distance, begin looking for the SHT sign on the right that indicates the trail will be to the left. Turn left onto the dirt trail and follow for about 0.4 mile. The trail leads down a drainage ditch to a road crossing (that same gravel road we mentioned at the beginning of this section) and up the opposite drainage ditch (dry at time of hiking). This is actually the same gravel road you drove in on. Once the trail enters back into the woods, it is simply a beautiful forest in which to hike. However, the path does take on more roots and rocks as it progresses.

0.4   Cross under a power line, as the trail opens before heading back into the woods.

0.7   At the intersection, turn left onto the gravel road and cross the inactive railroad tracks. Keep an eye to the left for a sign indicating Superior Hiking Trail, and take that path to reenter the woods.

0.9   Listen for sounds of the Island River as the path gradually descends. Views will
PHOTO   appear in another 0.3 mile.

1.1
INCLINE
STEPS
This section has two inclines (14–16° and 12–14°) for approximately 40' each. A decline of 18° for approximately 20' is located just prior to 47 uneven, laid-log wood/dirt steps (no handrail). **Alert:** At step 20, there is a steep rise.

1.2
STEPS
Follow a very short section of boardwalk, then up two steps (laid-log wood/dirt steps, no handrail), then over a couple tree roots. You'll see nice views of Two Island River for approximately the next 0.1 mile.

1.3
PHOTO
The bridge (wood, double handrail) that crosses Dyers Creek marks the turn-around point.

Retrace your path to trailhead.

1.6
INCLINE
Incline of 18° for approximately 20'.

2.6 Trailhead.

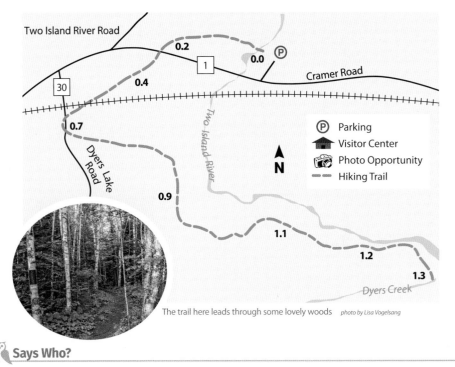

The trail here leads through some lovely woods   *photo by Lisa Vogelsang*

Says Who?

No time for physical activity?

Did you know that walking briskly for at least 10 minutes at a time can benefit your heart's health? Aim for a minimum of 150 minutes of brisk walking or other moderate exercise per week.

Medical Science In Sports and Exercise[8]

Temperance River Lower Loop*

Temperance River State Park • On Highway 61, 80 miles from Duluth •
Gentle Hikes name

- **This short trail is long on delivery: beautiful canyons and waterfalls!**
- **Photo ops of Lake Superior and Temperance River abound here in this unique setting.**

TRAILHEAD DIRECTIONS:

From Highway 61 at mile marker 80.2, pull into the paved parking area on either side of Temperance River or either side of the highway. The trailhead begins from the upper parking area on the lake side of highway.

CONTACT:

Temperance River State Park: 218-663-3100 or www.dnr.state.mn.us/state_parks/temperance_river/index.html

TOTAL TRAIL LENGTH, SURFACE, & WIDTH:

0.1 mile; gravel and hard-packed dirt; average 3' wide. Moderate rocks, minimal roots.

INCLINES & ALERTS:

No inclines greater than 10°. Steep cliff with no guardrails.

TRAILHEAD FACILITIES & FEES:

No facilities at trailhead; however, there are flush toilets (seasonal) and vault toilets in campground. Vault toilets are available only in the picnic area on the lake side of high-way. An annual or day-use state park permit is required to drive into the park; they are available at the park office. Otherwise, no permit is needed for the parking lots along either side of the highway.

MILEAGE & DESCRIPTION

0.0
STEPS
PHOTO

Trailhead begins from the lake side of parking area, very close to the bridge, near the kiosk. Descend 30 steps (cobblestone, no handrail), then descend 4 steps (wood/dirt, no handrail) onto a 4-foot-wide hard-packed dirt path. Continue straight toward the bridge. **Alert:** Uneven surfaces with moderate rock. At intersection, turn left and cross the bridge (wood, double handrail) over the highly scenic Temperance River. Photo ops abound on both sides, as the river rushes (or meanders) into Lake Superior. If you enjoy photography, plan on spending some time here, as the view of waters rushing through the gorge are spectacular!

The river rushing beneath this bridge is also a favorite spot for anglers.

After crossing the bridge, ascend the slight incline on a basalt rock surface for 40' with single handrail, then ascend 28 steps (wood, double & single handrail, non-continuous) to the bench. After you ascend 7 steps (wood, no handrail), signage offers information about the Temperance River Rain Garden and how it works. A left takes you back across the bridge on a paved path (with guardrails), which returns to the trailhead and parking area.

0.1   Trailhead.

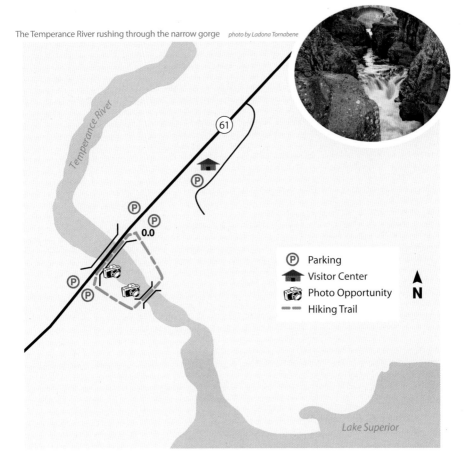

The Temperance River rushing through the narrow gorge   *photo by Ladona Tornabene*

Legend:
- **P** Parking
- Visitor Center
- Photo Opportunity
- – – Hiking Trail

N

▶▙▟▟▍ Temperance River Gorge Trail

Temperance River State Park • On Highway 61, 80 miles from Duluth

- **The shortest trail in this book that showcases seven overlooks.**
- **See powerful cascades rushing through beautifully carved canyon walls, rapids engulfing rugged rock faces, and exquisite kettle formations!**

TRAILHEAD DIRECTIONS:

From Highway 61 at mile marker 80.2, pull into the paved parking area on either side of the highway or either side of Temperance River. The trailhead begins on the side of the highway opposite the lake, at a kiosk on a paved path.

CONTACT:

Temperance River State Park: 218-663-3100 or www.dnr.state.mn.us/state_parks/temperance_river/index.html

TOTAL TRAIL LENGTH, SURFACE, & WIDTH:

0.7 miles; paved 230' to Hidden Falls viewing platform (wheelchair accessible).

INCLINES & ALERTS:

No inclines greater than 10°. Steep cliffs (no guardrail); rocks may be slippery when wet. Keep children close at hand when hiking this area. Some stone steps have uneven pitch heights with no railings.

TRAILHEAD FACILITIES & FEES:

No facilities at the trailhead; however, there are flush toilets (seasonal) and vault toilets in the campground. Vault toilets only are available in the picnic area on the lake side of the highway. An annual or day-use state park permit is required to drive into the park; they are available at the park office. Otherwise, no permit is needed for the parking lots along either side of the highway.

MILEAGE & DESCRIPTION

0.0
PHOTO

The trailhead begins on a paved 6-foot-wide path at a kiosk, which contains information about the Superior Hiking Trail. In 230', the paved path ends at the wooden viewing platform where Hidden Falls may be seen. The signage provides information about the ancient waterfall, the river, and the area's history and geography.

Shortly after, a trail surface on lava rock begins. The trail winds up the canyon of the Temperance River, which is wild and violent at times, prior to plunging into Lake Superior. At the trail intersection, a left takes you 40' to views of waterfalls and the Temperance River.

0.1
STEPS
PHOTO

Ascend a series of 40 uneven steps (rock/stone, no handrail, non-continuous). **Alert:** A few steps have a higher pitch height. That, coupled with their unevenness, can be a bit challenging on the return to the trailhead. At time of writing, there was a narrow path that circumvented some of the steps. At the trail intersection; veer left. Once you reach the open area, take time to explore the many different views and three additional overlooks in this part of the canyon. Interpretive signs may accompany some overlooks and stone landmarks help you find the trail.

0.2
STEPS
PHOTO
At the intersection, you will find the multiuse paved Gitchi-Gami State Trail (GGST), but please watch for cyclists. However, before crossing the trail, we encourage viewing the river gorge from the bridge (double handrail) on the left, which is also part of the GGST. Photo ops abound and we deem them tripod worthy.

Back on the trail, please follow the sign indicating Temperance River with the blue Hiking Club sign. In 50', descend 6 steep but fairly even steps (stone, no handrail). These lead you to the fifth and sixth overlooks. Continue through intermittent sections of rock and root. The trail is uneven in many places.

0.3
STEPS
PHOTO
In this section you will find a sign on the right indicating the last overlook (#7). Descend 23 steps (stone with rock wall, no handrail). **Alert:** This area frequently holds standing water. Still, the waterfalls and rushing rapids through wide canyon walls make this view worth the descent. When finished exploring, turn around and retrace path to trailhead.

0.7
Trailhead.

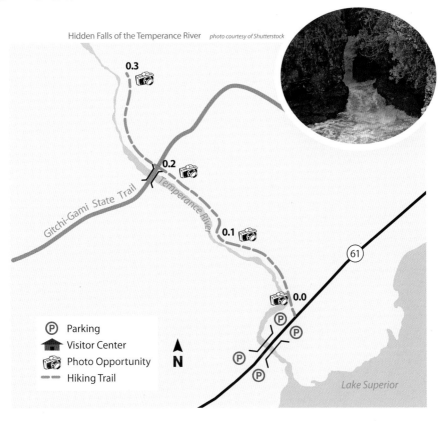

Hidden Falls of the Temperance River *photo courtesy of Shutterstock*

Foot Note:

Can't wait to get here? Have a sneak peek via the Temperance River State Park virtual tour! Visit: www.dnr.state.mn.us/state_parks/virtual_tour/temperance_river/dialup.html

Temperance River Gorge View*

Temperance River State Park • On Highway 61, 80 miles from Duluth • Gitchi-Gami State Trail: Temperance River Section • *Gentle Hikes* name

- **See powerful cascades rushing through beautifully carved canyon walls, rapids engulfing rugged rock faces, and exquisite kettle formations.**
- **If you really enjoy photography, the view is worth taking the tripod along.**

TRAILHEAD DIRECTIONS:

On Highway 61 at mile marker 80.5, turn right into Temperance River State Park. In 0.1 mile, get a park pass at the office, and then immediately look right for a small paved parking area that will be located within a circular drive. The trailhead begins on the sidewalk in front of the park office heading northeast.

CONTACT:

Temperance River State Park: 218-663-3100 or www.dnr.state.mn.us/state_parks/temperance_river/index.html

TOTAL TRAIL LENGTH, SURFACE, & WIDTH:

0.8 mile; paved.

INCLINES & ALERTS:

No inclines greater than 10°; however, trail is on a gentle but steady uphill grade after crossing Highway 61. Please use extreme caution when crossing the highway.

TRAILHEAD FACILITIES & FEES:

A vault toilet, the park office, and a small gift shop. Annual or day-use state park permit is required; they are available at the park office.

MILEAGE & DESCRIPTION

0.0   The trailhead begins on the sidewalk in front of the park office, heading northeast. Just beyond the park office, find the Gitchi-Gami State Trail (GGST), and turn left onto the 10-foot-wide paved path heading toward Highway 61.

0.1   Please use extreme caution when crossing Highway 61. Continue on the paved GGST up a steady, but gentle, uphill grade.

0.2   At the intersection, turn left and remain on the GGST, continuing up the gentle grade and through a lovely wooded area.

0.4   The wide wooden bridge (double handrail) affords phenomenal views upstream
PHOTO   and downstream of the astonishing Temperance River Gorge! Our hike ends here. Please retrace your path to the trailhead.

0.8   Trailhead.

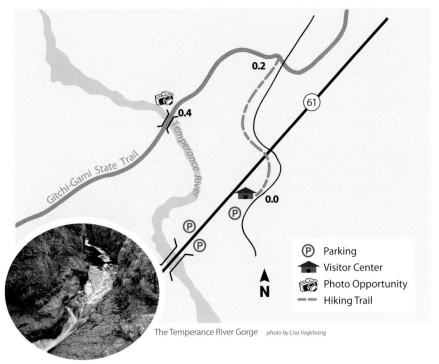

The Temperance River Gorge   *photo by Lisa Vogelsang*

Says Who?

In a bad mood? Stride toward a better attitude!

Walking 30 minutes four to six days per week at a moderate pace can improve personality, mood, self-esteem, and well-being.

APA Monitor on Psychology[23]

MODERATE

Oberg Mountain

Off Highway 61, approximately 87 miles from Duluth •
Superior Hiking Trail section: Oberg Mountain to Lutsen

- **Breathtaking vistas of Leveaux Mountain, Lake Superior, Carlton Peak, Moose Mountain, and Oberg Lake, amidst seven expansive overlooks throughout this loop hike.**
- **This trail segment was built in 1974–1975 on National Forest land.**

TRAILHEAD DIRECTIONS:
From Highway 61 at mile marker 87.5 (watch for the Superior Hiking Trail marker on the right side of highway preceding mile marker 88). **Note:** The turnoff from the highway may be easy to miss. Turn left onto Forest Road #336 (a.k.a. Onion River Road), and follow for 2.1 miles and park in the gravel SHT lot on the left side of road.

CONTACT:
Superior Hiking Trail: 218-834-2700

TOTAL TRAIL LENGTH, SURFACE, & WIDTH:
2.3 miles; gravel and hard-packed dirt; average 2–4' wide. Minimum to moderate rocks and roots.

INCLINES & ALERTS:
There are 12 inclines, ranging from 12–18°. The steepest incline is 18° for 15' at 1.0 mile. The longest is 16° for 60' at 1.2 miles. There are steep cliffs, many without guardrails. Depending on the season, there may be overgrowth on trail.

TRAILHEAD FACILITIES & FEES:
There is a vault toilet at the trailhead. There are no fees for parking or trail use.

MILEAGE & DESCRIPTION

0.0   The trailhead begins across Forest Road #336 at a sign for the Oberg Loop. Shortly thereafter, notice the sign about the Superior Hiking Trail. A gradual ascent eventually leads to the first intersection. Turn right following the sign to Oberg Trail (the trail to the left takes you on the main Superior Hiking Trail).

0.2   In this part of the trail, you will cross a small boardwalk, encounter occasional roots and rocks and continue on a gradual climb up the trail through a predominantly maple forest.

0.3   Depending on the foliage, there may be numerous open views of the lake and surrounding forest areas.

0.4   At the trail intersection, notice the sign indicating the parking area. Continue on the trail; do not turn left. You will return to this point on your way back. Shortly you will encounter sections of rocky surfaces as you begin to circle around the top of Oberg Mountain. You're on your way to the first breathtaking overlook of Leveaux Mountain.

0.6
BENCH
PHOTO
Here you'll see a sign for the first scenic overlook. This vantage point delivers one of the most stunning views on the trail! A flat rock surface leads to panoramic views and great photo ops of Lake Superior, Leveaux Mountain, and Carlton Peak to the southwest. The Superior National Forest below spreads like a beautiful quilt of maple, aspen, birch, cedar, and spruce. A picturesque log bench makes for photo ops or a great resting spot.

0.7
This is a relatively easy trail portion under the canopy of maples and birch. En route to next overlook, you'll cross several sections of boardwalk.

0.9
PHOTO
As you continue to go around Oberg Mountain, the second scenic overlook leads to a rustic log picnic table on an immense, flat rock surface, with views of Lake Superior and the forest below.

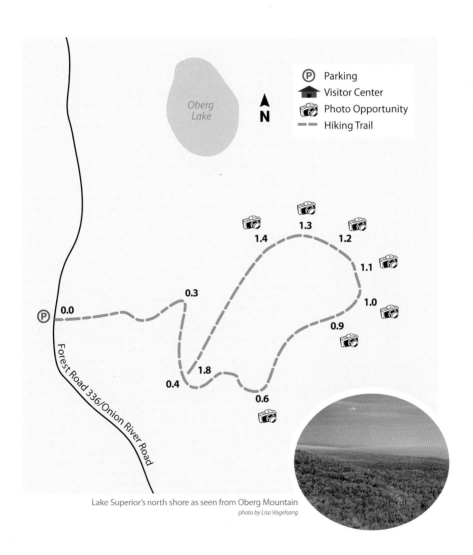

Lake Superior's north shore as seen from Oberg Mountain
photo by Lisa Vogelsang

1.0
INCLINE
PHOTO
In this section you will encounter the area with the steepest incline (18° for 15'). Soon you will come to the third scenic overlook, with a dramatic view of Lake Superior from a flat, lichen-covered rock.

1.1
PHOTO
The fourth rocky overlook features more of Lake Superior, with fabulous views of its shoreline and the Sawtooth Mountains in the distance. Shortly you will descend some rocks, before the trail turns away from the lake.

1.2
PHOTO
The fifth overlook (guardrails) showcases Moose Mountain and delivers the first of three views of Oberg Lake. Each one gets bigger and, we think, better! Keep the camera handy. From here, the trail gradually ascends toward the next overlook.

1.3
BENCH
PHOTO
The sixth overlook features a picturesque vista of Oberg Lake nestled among evergreens. A log bench offers a moment to prolong the tranquility. It's a great photo op, too.

1.4
STEPS
PHOTO
En route to the final overlook, the trail levels out. Cross a few sections of boardwalk and one gentle incline leading up to 9 steps (wood, no handrail). The last overlook is here and it delivers—Oberg Lake, bold and beautiful!

1.8
Farther along on the trail, cross a few more boardwalk sections and eventually end up back at the sign indicating the parking area. This time, turn right and retrace the path to the trailhead. Enjoy the gentle descent back down the trail.

2.3
Trailhead.

View of Oberg Lake from Oberg Mountain   *photo by Lisa Vogelsang*

MODERATE

Poplar River Overlook

Off Highway 61, approximately 90 miles from Duluth •
Superior Hiking Trail section: Lutsen to Caribou Trail

- **A very short trek to see the scenic Poplar River as it plummets over huge boulders through a rocky ravine.**

TRAILHEAD DIRECTIONS:
From Highway 61 at mile marker 90.1 (watch for a sign indicating Lutsen Mountain and Village preceding mile marker 90), turn left on Cook County Road 5 and follow for 2 miles, passing Lutsen Mountain and Village. Here the road surface changes from paved to gravel. Park in the small gravel lot at a sign indicating Superior Hiking Trail Parking Access.

CONTACT:
Superior Hiking Trail: 218-834-2700

TOTAL TRAIL LENGTH, SURFACE, & WIDTH:
0.4 mile; gravel and hard-packed dirt; average 9' wide, then narrows to 2–4' wide. Moderate rock and minimum root.

INCLINES & ALERTS:
No inclines more than 10°, but the trail is not flat. Wet areas are possible. Much of this trail is shared with mountain bikers. Use caution at all turns.

TRAILHEAD FACILITIES & FEES:
None. No fees for trail use.

MILEAGE & DESCRIPTION

0.0 The trailhead begins on a 10-foot-wide gravel path. Shortly you will encounter a trail intersection, turn left and follow a sign toward Mystery Trails; listen for sounds of the river as it rushes downstream.

0.2 In about 300', there will be another trail intersection; veer left to follow the
PHOTO Superior Hiking Trail. Shortly thereafter, cross a bridge (wood, double handrails) over the Poplar River Falls; the river is lined with spruce, cedar, and birch. There are wonderful photo ops up- and downriver. **Note:** This bridge is closed to vehicles. Turn around here and retrace path to trailhead.

0.4 Trailhead.

Says Who?

Got a craving that just won't relent, even though your caloric intake has already been spent? Studies demonstrate that exercise can reduce cravings for high-fat or high-sugar snack foods.

Everyday Health[13]

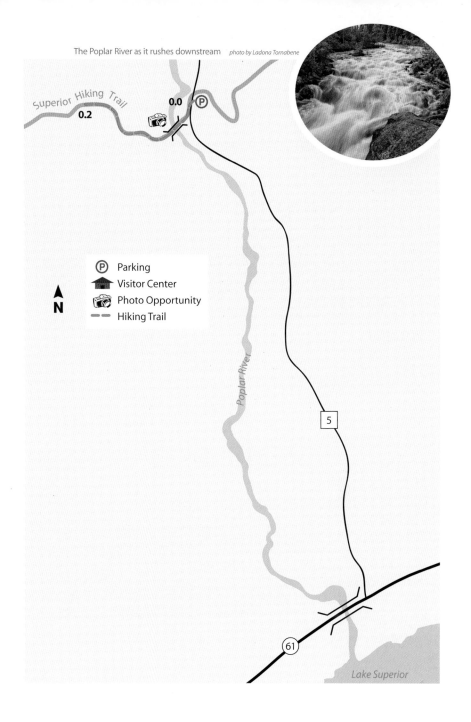

The Poplar River as it rushes downstream   *photo by Ladona Tornabene*

Superior Hiking Trail
0.2
0.0

Ⓟ Parking
🏠 Visitor Center
📷 Photo Opportunity
— — Hiking Trail

N

Poplar River

5

61

Lake Superior

Lower Cascade Falls—Quick Route*

Cascade River State Park • On Highway 61, 100 miles from Duluth •
Gentle Hikes name

- **Take the shortest, easiest walk to a popular, spectacular waterfall—the Lower Cascades!**
- **Here you can photograph the very same image that is featured on many postcards!**

TRAILHEAD DIRECTIONS:
From Highway 61 at mile marker 99.9, pull into the paved parking area opposite Cascade River Wayside.

CONTACT:
Cascade River State Park: 218-387-3053; www.dnr.state.mn.us/state_parks/cascade_river/index.html

TOTAL TRAIL LENGTH, SURFACE, & WIDTH:
0.1 mile; gravel and hard-packed dirt; average 3–4' wide.

INCLINES & ALERTS:
The only incline is 14° for 30' at 80' into the trail. Although there is a guardrail at the overlook, it can easily be navigated by small children; use caution as steep cliffs follow.

TRAILHEAD FACILITIES & FEES:
No facilities available, but there are no fees for trail use from this access point. If you drive into the park, you'll need an annual or a day-use state permit; they are available at the park office. Otherwise, no permit is needed for parking along either side of the highway.

MILEAGE & DESCRIPTION

0.0
INCLINE
BENCH
PHOTO
The trailhead begins at a parking area immediately off Highway 61 (across from Lake Superior) at the Cascade River State Park kiosk (which shows an aerial view of the area). Ascend 11 uneven steps (rock, no handrail, non-continuous). In 80', you'll encounter the area of steepest incline (14° for 30'). After that, you are only 300' away from a most incredible view of the famous Lower Falls of the Cascade River! Bring the camera to this overlook (with guardrails), and pick your best viewing spot. After that, turn around and retrace with your path to the trailhead. If you're curious as to where the rest of the trail leads, see Lower Falls Cascade River Loop pg. 128.

0.1   Trailhead.

 Says Who?

Want to curb your appetite? Get out and take in the sights!

Walking has been shown to reduce appetites in some people.

Everyday Health[13]

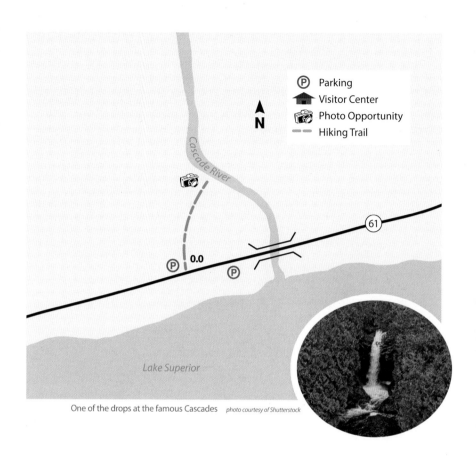

Parking

Visitor Center

Photo Opportunity

Hiking Trail

N

61

Cascade River

0.0

Lake Superior

One of the drops at the famous Cascades   *photo courtesy of Shutterstock*

Lower Falls Cascade River Loop*

Cascade River State Park • On Highway 61, 101 miles from Duluth •
Gentle Hikes name

- **See the cascades—the features that give Cascade River State Park its name.**

- **This trail features some of the most frequently photographed falls and cascades along the North Shore.**

TRAILHEAD DIRECTIONS:

From Highway 61 at mile marker 100.9, turn left into Cascade River State Park. Follow the signs for trail parking; the lot is located about 0.7 mile from the park office, in the campground.

CONTACT:

Cascade River State Park: 218-387-6000 or www.dnr.state.mn.us/state_parks/cascade_river/index.html

TOTAL TRAIL LENGTH, SURFACE, & WIDTH:

0.7 mile; gravel and hard-packed dirt; average 4–5' wide. Minimal rocks and roots.

INCLINES & ALERTS:

No inclines more than 10°. Some areas may be slippery when wet.

TRAILHEAD FACILITIES & FEES:

There is a vault toilet and a picnic table near the parking area. An annual or day-use state park permit is required; they are available at the park office.

MILEAGE & DESCRIPTION

0.0
STEPS

The trailhead begins at the far end of the parking area at a sign indicating "Cascade River Trail" near a blue Hiking Club sign. In this section, ascend and descend 14 steps (wood, handrail) before arriving at a "Y" in the trail; continue straight. Ascend 16 uneven steps (stone, no handrail), then descend 16 steps (wood, handrail).

0.1
STEPS
PHOTO

This brings you to a trail intersection. At this junction, go straight and cross the Cascade River over a bridge (wood, double handrail). Pause while crossing the bridge for beautiful views upriver of the cascades and downriver views of Lake Superior. Immediately to your right after crossing the bridge, descend 12 steps (stone, handrail) for a spectacular overlook; a postcard-quality photo op of the cascades! Back at the end of the bridge, take the trail closest to the river that leads toward Lake Superior. In this section, descend 47 steps (wood, some handrail, non-continuous). This brings you to an overlook (guardrails) and a photo op from a vantage point overlooking the falls.

0.2
STEPS
PHOTO

From there, head down 34 platform-type steps (wood, double handrail, non-continuous) to another postcard-quality photo op—the impressive Lower Cascade Falls! The trails behind you lead to Cascade Lodge and the Highway 61 parking area. Continue straight on the main trail following the river and descend 53 steps (wood, no handrail, non-continuous) to the river.

0.3
STEPS
PHOTO

During the summer, a lovely fern glade grows here. Take some time to explore this area where the river empties into Lake Superior. Then ascend 15 steps (wood, double handrail) toward the highway, turn left and continue across the bridge (pedestrian lane with guardrails) over Cascade River. Photo ops abound here. At the end of the bridge, turn left and ascend 20 uneven steps (stone, no handrail) to the kiosk, where there's a small overlook, then ascend 9 steps (stone, no handrail).

0.4
STEPS
PHOTO

Continue straight on the trail (paths to the right lead to the campground). Farther along, you will descend 10 steps (wood, no handrail) to the bridge (wood, double handrail). At the end of the bridge there is a small spur to the left (very rooted and rocky) but a wonderful view of Cascade River, Highway 61 bridge, and Lake Superior. Ascend 18 steps (wood, no handrail), or at 10 steps, take a spur to the left to a small overlook that lets you bypass the last 8 steps. Back on the trail, ascend 4 steps (wood, no handrail) and continue to another overlook (guardrail) above the river. Ascend an additional 19 steps (stone, no handrail, non-continuous) and yet another overlook (guardrail). Shortly, ascend 3 steps (stone, no handrail), then 23 steps (wood, no handrail). This brings you back to the intersection with the bridge. Turn right and retrace your path to the trailhead.

0.7   Trailhead.

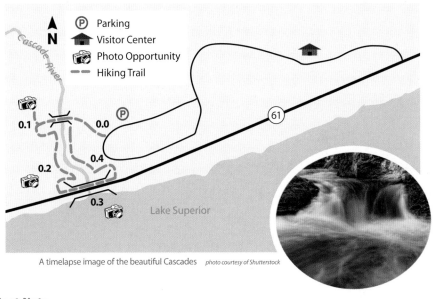

A timelapse image of the beautiful Cascades   *photo courtesy of Shutterstock*

Foot Note:

Can't wait to get here? Have a sneak peek via the Cascade River State Park virtual tour! Visit: www.dnr.state.mn.us/state_parks/virtual_tour/cascade_river/dialup.html

LIGHTER

Lake Loop Trail

Grand Marais, MN • Off Highway 61, 109 miles from Duluth •
Located inside Grand Marais RV Park and Campground

• **Lovely barrier-free wooded path with two lookouts onto Lake Superior.**

TRAILHEAD DIRECTIONS:

From Highway 61 at mile marker 109.1, turn right into Grand Marais RV Park and Campground, and continue 0.3 mile through the campground past picnic area #1 (an open shelter on the left). Look right to locate the last paved road in the campground, then turn right and follow it 0.1 mile to a ballfield. Park in the gravel lot as there are no designated spaces.

CONTACT:

Grand Marais Campground and Marina: 800-998-0959; grandmaraisrecreationarea.com

TOTAL TRAIL LENGTH, SURFACE, & WIDTH:

0.4 mile; hard-packed gravel, average 6' wide.

INCLINES & ALERTS:

No inclines greater than 10°. Trail access necessitates driving through the campground; please use caution.

TRAILHEAD FACILITIES & FEES:

Flush toilets, water, picnic tables (grass surface beneath), and grills are available. No fees for trail use.

MILEAGE & DESCRIPTION

0.0 From the parking area, follow the paved road toward the west, and in a few yards, locate a large metal gate and a nature trail sign. Just beyond is a large grassy/gravel area. Look straight ahead and slightly to the left to locate the official trailhead.

0.1 The trailhead begins at a sign indicating Sweethearts Bluff Nature Area on a 6-foot-wide, hard-packed, barrier-free gravel path. This is a loop, so either path leads back to this point. We ventured right. As you continue through lovely stands of maple and fir, soon you will see a trail to the right, which leads to the much more rugged Sweethearts Bluff trail. Stay on the barrier-free path.

0.2 This section contains two lookout points with benches and great views of
BENCH Lake Superior.
PHOTO

0.4 You have now come full circle. Return to the parking area.

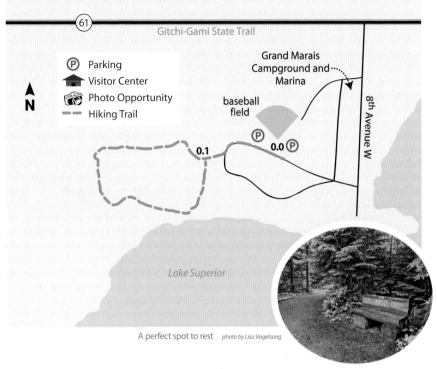

A perfect spot to rest   photo by Lisa Vogelsang

Foot Notes:

The Grand Marais RV Park and Campground hosts 300 campsites, is bordered by a forest and Lake Superior's rocky shores, provides harbor access, and is located a few blocks from downtown, which is walkable via the paved Gitchi-Gami State Trail (www.grandmaraisrecreationarea.com).

The North House Folk School offers sailing aboard its schooner and specializes in teaching traditional northern crafts. Inspired by Scandinavian folkehøjskolers, the school has captured imaginations for years. Plan a visit and experience why . . . For more information: northhouse.org

Beyond Grand Marais
to the Canadian Border

High Falls at Grand Portage   *photo courtesy of Shutterstock*

RUGGED

Kadunce River

On Highway 61, 119 miles from Duluth • Superior Hiking Trail section: Kadunce River to Judge C.R. Magney State Park

- **A scenic hike offering many breathtaking views of the river's gorge.**
- **Follows the Kadunce River in a beautifully wooded setting for first 0.1 mile.**
- **This river is also a designated trout stream.**

TRAILHEAD DIRECTIONS:
Highway 61 at mile marker 118.9, after crossing bridge, turn right into Kadunce River Wayside paved parking lot (highway sign is spelled Kodonce Creek).

CONTACT:
Superior Hiking Trail: 218-834-2700

TOTAL TRAIL LENGTH, SURFACE, & WIDTH:
1.2 miles; gravel and hard-packed dirt; average 3' wide. Moderate root (significant in sections), minimum rock (moderate in sections).

INCLINES & ALERTS:
There is one incline of 16° for 20' at 0.2 mile. Cross Highway 61 to locate the trailhead. There are natural overlooks with erosion beneath, as well as steep cliffs, in various places with no guardrails. The trail entrance can be extremely wet after heavy rain.

TRAILHEAD FACILITIES & FEES:
Picnic table with pavement extending to it. See Kadunce River Wayside (pg. 178). No fees for trail use.

MILEAGE & DESCRIPTION

0.0
PHOTO
From Kadunce River Wayside parking area, cross Highway 61 and proceed toward river along the path that parallels the extended bridge rail. The trailhead officially begins near the river at a Superior Hiking Trail sign noting the Kadunce bridge. This beautifully shaded path meanders along the Kadunce River, and within the first 500', several spur trails beckon a closer walk to the river's edge. Here, miniature waterfall basins serve as home to various species of trout.

0.1
STEPS
PHOTO
As the trail begins to gently climb, notice the moss- and lichen-covered rhyolite cliff walls. Ascend 21 steps (wood, no handrail). Soon, encounter 7 uneven steps (wood, no handrail). Tree roots are present here due to erosion. Shortly, you will find a natural overlook (no guardrail) as the Kadunce rounds a bend. See if you can locate the swirl cave tucked in beneath cedar and spruce.

0.2
INCLINE
PHOTO
At the trail intersection, turn right. (However, if you like adventure, take the spur to the left and have fun carefully exploring this lush forest that takes you to the river's edge. **Alert:** Erosion near cliff edge).

In 100', ascend the area of steepest incline (16° for 20').

Over the next 0.4 mile the trail winds above the river gorge. The trail leads back down to parallel the river for a short time where amazing photo ops await.

0.6
STEPS
PHOTO
As the trail approaches the bridge (steel, double handrail) over Kadunce River, ascend 3 log-like steps (uneven, no handrail). This is near where a SHT journal is housed. You can read sentiments from the trail and/or leave some of your own. SHT publishes selections from these journals in their newsletters. The bridge affords lovely views up- and downriver of gently tumbling cascades or roaring rapids—depending on water levels. Our hike ends on this bridge. Retrace your path to the trailhead.

1.2 Trailhead.

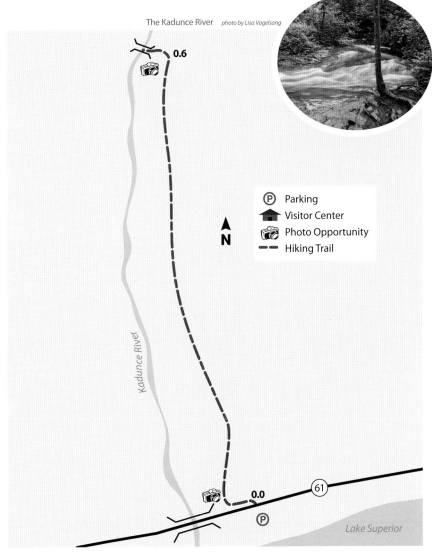

The Kadunce River   *photo by Lisa Vogelsang*

0.6

Parking
Visitor Center
Photo Opportunity
Hiking Trail

N

Kadunce River

61

0.0

Lake Superior

Devil's Kettle

Judge C.R. Magney State Park • On Highway 61, 124 miles from Duluth

- **See the infamous kettle, as 920 gallons of water per second mysteriously "disappear" into a cavernous hole—where it goes, nobody knows . . . until now. Well, maybe. Please see Foot Note. (source: DNR).**

- **A lovely wooded hike along and above the Brule River, with a view of Upper Falls.**

- **This state park is named in honor of Judge C.R. Magney, who was instrumental in the establishment of numerous parks on the North Shore.**

TRAILHEAD DIRECTIONS:
From Highway 61 at mile marker 124, turn left into Judge C.R. Magney State Park. Follow the signs indicating trail parking (0.2 mile from park office). The trailhead is located immediately to the right as you enter the gravel parking area. The trail starts at the sign indicating Devil's Kettle Trail.

CONTACT:
Judge C.R. Magney State Park: 218-387-6300 or www.dnr.state.mn.us/state_parks/judge_cr_magney/index.html

TOTAL TRAIL LENGTH, SURFACE, & WIDTH:
2.8 miles from official trailhead, but 3 miles from the parking area. However, the park lists it as 2 miles. Hard-packed dirt; average 3–4' wide. Minimum roots, moderately rocky sections.

INCLINES & ALERTS:
There are five inclines ranging from 12–16°. The steepest is at mile 2.0 for roughly 20'.

TRAILHEAD FACILITIES & FEES:
Vault toilet, water (seasonal), and picnic tables are available at the trailhead. An annual or day-use state park permit is required; they are available at the park office.

MILEAGE & DESCRIPTION

0.0
PHOTO
From the parking area kiosk, follow the sign indicating Devil's Kettle Trail. It is 0.1 mile to the official trailhead from this sign. Soon you will cross a bridge (wood, double handrail). Follow the path to a monument honoring Judge C.R. Magney (off to the left), the man who played a significant role in establishing several North Shore state parks and waysides. Another bridge (concrete, green handrails) takes you across the Brule River, with marvelous photo ops up- and downstream.

0.1
After crossing this bridge, a vault toilet and a few picnic tables are straight ahead. To the left is the official trailhead and sign indicating Devil's Kettle Trail. Prior to hiking the trail, please use the built-in foot brush to wipe your shoes in order to prevent spreading invasive plants. The path parallels the river for another 0.1 mile, then gradually ascends above it.

0.2 An incline of 12° for approximately 40'. **Alert:** Steep cliff with no guardrail in
INCLINE this section.

0.4 An incline of 14° for approximately 40'.
INCLINE
0.5 Ascend 20 steps (laid-log with dirt, uneven rise, no handrail, non-continuous).
STEPS This area is possibly rutted due to erosion at the top of these steps.

0.6 A bench with a wooded view. Continue straight on the trail.
BENCH
0.7 An incline of 14° for approximately 30'.
INCLINE
0.9 At the intersection, a very short walk to the left leads to two benches with foliage-
BENCH dependent views of the Upper Falls. The trail to the right continues to Devil's Kettle.

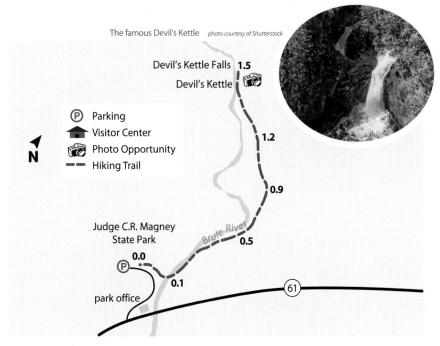

The famous Devil's Kettle *photo courtesy of Shutterstock*

Devil's Kettle Falls **1.5**
Devil's Kettle

- Ⓟ Parking
- 🏠 Visitor Center
- 📷 Photo Opportunity
- ▬ ▬ Hiking Trail

N

1.2

0.9

Judge C.R. Magney
State Park **0.5**

Brule River

0.0
Ⓟ
0.1

park office

61

1.0 Two more benches with views of woods. Look for "Old Man's Beard" lichen in
INCLINE the trees around you. Now the descent via steps (wood, double handrail, non-
BENCH continuous) to Devil's Kettle begins as follows: 65 steps to double benches;
34 steps to another bench; 75 steps to boardwalk that has a decline (which
visually resembles a steep ramp) measuring 14–16° for approximately 20', but
there is a handrail. Another 10 steps lead to a dirt path.

1.2 Soon you will see a set of 21 steps (iron grate, double handrail, non-continuous)
STEPS that leads down to the river's edge where a spectacular view of Upper Falls awaits.
PHOTO **Alert:** Please use caution when exploring this area, as footing consists of rocky,
uneven surfaces. Back on the trail, ascend 3 uneven steps, of which the last step
has a steep rise of 15–17 inches, but the handrail's presence can be of great assistance. However, the rail is only present for the last step.

1.3
STEPS
BENCH
A bench with a partial river view. Soon, ascend 53 laid-log steps (wood/dirt, single rail). At the time of this writing, the handrail was in disrepair and missing for 4 steps.

1.4
BENCH
Another bench with a partial river view. Here the trail has a number of roots.

1.5
INCLINE
PHOTO
An incline of 14° for approximately 60'. **Alert:** This is an area of erosion. Shortly afterward, find a sign indicating "Devil's Kettle Falls." Turn left to the small viewing platform (guardrail). One of the falls drops 50' and is traceable to Lake Superior. The other drops into a mysterious kettle, a phenomenon best seen when water levels are low. At time of this writing, there was a hunch, but no definitive answer, as to where the water exits. Wherever it goes, we think the falls are beautiful anytime they are flowing and worth the trek and the tripod! Our hike ends here. Please turn around and retrace your path to the trailhead.

2.0
INCLINE
The area of the steepest incline. Please see description from mile 1.0 above.

2.8
Trailhead.

 Foot Note:

For the most current info about the mystery of Devil's Kettle, visit www.dnr.state.mn.us/mcvmagazine/issues/2017/mar-apr/devils-kettlemystery.html

Says Who?

Wanna feel "in the pink"? Eat a little pink—fish that is . . .

Lake trout, lake herring, and salmon all have darker (pinkish) colored flesh, which makes them higher in Omega 3 fatty acids. As a result, two servings per week may decrease heart attack/stroke risk, prevent blood clots, and reduce blood pressure.

Minnesota Sea Grant[35]

Seafood Health Facts[36]

It's still not clear where the water in this portion of the falls ends up   *photo courtesy of Shutterstock*

LIGHTER

Brule River Loop*

Judge C.R. Magney State Park • On Highway 61, 124 miles from Duluth •
Gentle Hikes name

- **Impressive views of the Brule River!**
- **This state park is named in honor of Judge C.R. Magney, who was instrumental in the establishment of numerous parks on the North Shore.**
- **During summer, see a wide variety of wildflowers on optional spur trail.**

TRAILHEAD DIRECTIONS:
From Highway 61 at mile marker 124, turn left into Judge C.R. Magney State Park. Follow signs indicating trail parking (0.2 mile from park office). The trailhead is immediately to the right as you enter a gravel parking area. Start at the sign for Devil's Kettle Trail.

CONTACT:
Judge C.R. Magney State Park: 218-387-6300 OR www.dnr.state.mn.us/state_parks/judge_cr_magney/index.html

TOTAL TRAIL LENGTH, SURFACE, & WIDTH:
0.4 mile (*optional spur adds additional 0.4 mile); hard-packed dirt; average 2–3' wide (narrower for optional spur). Minimal rocks and roots.

INCLINES & ALERTS:
No inclines greater than 10°. Optional spur trail may have significant rocks, roots, and vegetation overgrowth.

TRAILHEAD FACILITIES & FEES:
Vault toilet, water (seasonal), and picnic tables are available. An annual or day-use state park permit is required; they are available at the park office.

MILEAGE & DESCRIPTION

0.0
PHOTO
The trailhead begins at a sign indicating Devil's Kettle Trail; soon you will cross a bridge (wood, double handrail). Follow the path to a monument honoring Judge C.R. Magney (off to the left). A bridge (concrete, green handrails) takes you across the Brule River with marvelous photo ops up- and downriver!

0.1
STEPS
PHOTO
After crossing the bridge, veer right and follow the trail along the river to stop and relax. However, in front of you is a wonderful picnic area in a wooded setting. At the "Y" in the trail, veer right and continue past some steps (if you do venture down, there are 17 steps (wood, handrail). You'll get a closer look at the river and maybe even see some waterfowl. There are also beautiful views of the Brule and some small falls. **Alert:** No guardrails; tree roots and erosion.

0.2
STEPS
PHOTO
At the next "Y," veer right (the paths reconnect, but views are better this way) through a fir grove as the trail continues along the river toward Highway 61. There are several paths here that lead to the highway; however, we found that it's best to turn left at the next trail intersection, then take a right. You'll see (and hear) the highway. At the guardrail, take another right, which leads across a bridge (concrete,

double guardrail) running parallel to Highway 61. This is another great place for photo ops of the Brule. Look across the highway for views of Lake Superior and the historic Naniboujou Lodge, open for both lodging and fine dining.

At the end of the bridge, turn right and descend 16 steps (wood, no handrail).

0.3   At the trail intersection, turn right for the optional spur trail* or continue straight and return to the monument via a path through a wooded area along the river. At monument, continue toward the trailhead.

0.4   Trailhead.

*Option: At the trail intersection, the hike may be lengthened by turning right and taking the optional spur trail, which narrows and becomes rocky/rooted as it runs along the Brule River toward Lake Superior. You'll find numerous photo ops along this section.

This is a great trail for viewing a variety of wildflowers (bring the zoom lens). Follow it for 0.2 mile to a place where the trail opens up and the river meets the breakwater. We recommend stopping here because of the excessive overgrowth, very low tree branches, and rooted surfaces beyond this point. Turn around and retrace path back to intersection.

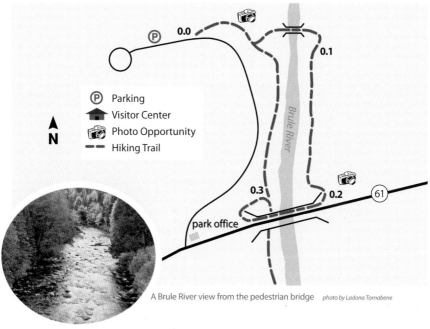

A Brule River view from the pedestrian bridge   *photo by Ladona Tornabene*

Foot Note:

The Naniboujou Lodge is listed in the National Register of Historic Places and is one of the "must-see" locations along the North Shore (218-387-2688 or naniboujou.com).

Webster-Ashburton Trail and Picnic Area*

Grand Portage State Park • On Highway 61, 150 miles from Duluth • *Gentle Hikes* name

---

- **A wonderfully wooded, short trail with picnic sites and views of the Pigeon River.**
- **The border here between the U.S. and Canada was defined by the Webster-Ashburton Treaty of 1842; the marker here commemorates that treaty.**

TRAILHEAD DIRECTIONS:

From Highway 61 at mile marker 150.4, turn left into Grand Portage State Park Welcome Center, which is very close to the Canadian Border. Paved parking is located at the park entrance, with separate lots for cars and RVs/trucks. Designated wheelchair-accessible sites are available.

CONTACT:

218-475-2360 or www.dnr.state.mn.us/state_parks/grand_portage/index.html

TOTAL TRAIL LENGTH, SURFACE, & WIDTH:

0.4 mile; paved; average 8' wide, for first 0.2 mile; after that, grass and hard-packed dirt; average 1–4' wide. Minimal rock and root.

INCLINES & ALERTS:

No inclines greater than 10°. Steep cliffs beyond picnic area (no guardrails).

TRAILHEAD FACILITIES & FEES:

There is no fee to park at Grand Portage Welcome Center (four-hour limit). The Welcome Center hosts interpretative displays that introduce visitors to the culture of the Grand Portage Ojibwe people. It also houses a gift shop and travel information. The flush toilets and water fountains are open 24/7. The grounds have a picnic area, a pavilion, and an observation deck. There are several wheelchair-accessible picnic tables available in the pavilion.

MILEAGE & DESCRIPTION

0.0   The trailhead begins across from the Welcome Center and to the right, in front of the pavilion. This trail is unique in that it also hosts a wonderful picnic site with views of the Pigeon River as it flows through a mixed forest. There are several picnic sites along this trail.

0.2   The pavement ends. Continue on a 2- to 3-feet-wide grass and hard-packed dirt
PHOTO   trail. Shortly you will encounter a bridge (handrails). **Alert:** Steep cliffs with no guardrails on river side. Historical marker just 18' ahead. Take time to read about the interesting treaty that determined the national boundaries of the U.S. and Canada. Retrace path to trailhead.

0.4   Trailhead.

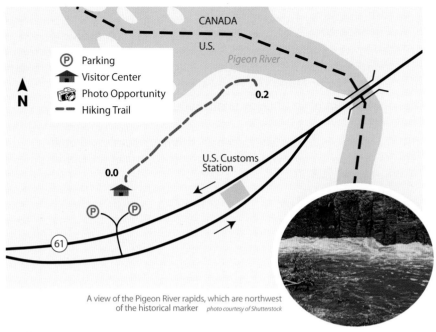

A view of the Pigeon River rapids, which are northwest of the historical marker   *photo courtesy of Shutterstock*

Foot Note:

This is the only state park in Minnesota located on tribally owned land.

Says Who?

Still trying to kick the habit? Move the butt!

Exercise has been shown to reduce cravings for smoking.

Everyday Health[13]

High Falls at Grand Portage

Grand Portage State Park • On Highway 61, 150 miles from Duluth

- **See Minnesota's highest waterfall. Here, an angular, rugged rock face is a majestic stage for the main attraction—3,200 gallons of water per second pouring over the towering 120' High Falls—all from an accessible trail!**

- **View the remains of an 1899 log flume built to prevent timber from "free-falling" over the falls.**

- **Visit the Welcome Center, which houses stunning murals and other artwork, and serves as an introduction to the culture of the Grand Portage Ojibwe people.**

TRAILHEAD DIRECTIONS:
From Highway 61 at mile marker 150.4, turn left into Grand Portage State Park Welcome Center, which is very close to the Canadian Border. Paved parking is located at the park entrance. Designated wheelchair-accessible sites are available.

CONTACT:
218-475-2360 or www.dnr.state.mn.us/state_parks/grand_portage/index.html

TOTAL TRAIL LENGTH, SURFACE, & WIDTH:
1.0 mile; paved; average 8' wide; constructed to meet Universal Design Standards.

INCLINES & ALERTS:
No inclines greater than 10°.

TRAILHEAD FACILITIES & FEES:
There is no fee to park at Grand Portage Welcome Center (four-hour limit). It also houses a gift shop and travel information. The flush toilets and water fountains are open 24/7. The grounds have a picnic area, a pavilion, and an observation deck. There are several wheelchair-accessible picnic tables available in the pavilion.

MILEAGE & DESCRIPTION

0.0
BENCH
PHOTO
There are two options to begin this hike: You can start to the right of the Welcome Center on a paved path marked "Waterfall Trail" or head through the rear doors of the Welcome Center and follow the boardwalk. But before you venture to the Falls, head over to the nearby accessible river overlook deck (wood, guardrails) for lovely views of the Pigeon River and Ontario in the distance.

En route to High Falls, there are a total of nine benches strategically placed approximately every 400' and the pavement extends to each bench. The trail passes through a mixed forest with interpretative signs.

0.2
BENCH
Just past the second bench, you will find an optional spur trail that goes off to the right. If you choose to explore it, descend 20 steps (wood, handrail) to a 1- to 2-foot-wide dirt path (hard-packed, roots). This spur offers views of the rapids. At the end of the spur, ascend 16 steps (wood, handrail) and arrive between the third and fourth benches.

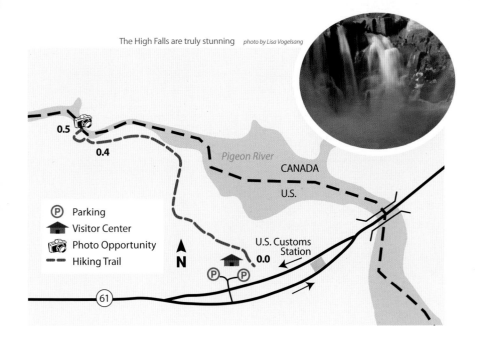

The High Falls are truly stunning   *photo by Lisa Vogelsang*

Map legend:
- (P) Parking
- Visitor Center
- Photo Opportunity
- Hiking Trail

Pigeon River
CANADA
U.S.
U.S. Customs Station
0.0
N
61
0.5
0.4

0.4 There is a vault toilet to the left. Soon boardwalk begins (double handrail), which leads to three options for viewing the falls (two have stairs, one does not).

0.5 Trail intersection.

STEPS
BENCH
PHOTO

Option #1: Veer left and ascend 40 steps (wood, double handrail, non-continuous) that lead to the first viewing platform, equipped with bench and guardrails. This vantage point offers a phenomenal view of the thundering falls. We stood in awe . . . simply put, words cannot do justice.

Notice the trail across the river; look closely to see the remains of an 1899 log flume. To the east, on a clear day, look for Isle Royale and Pigeon Point in the distance.

The other two viewing areas can be accessed from the base of the steps and by staying on the boardwalk.

Option #2: The middle viewing area affords a spectacular falls view and is located on the boardwalk itself (no steps).

Option #3: The upper observation deck can be accessed by ascending 17 steps (wood, double handrail). The falls are mesmerizing and clearly the main event here.

Retrace your path to the trailhead.

1.0 Trailhead.

Foot Note:

Can't wait to get here? Take a sneak peek via a virtual snapshot tour of Grand Portage State Park! Visit: www.dnr.state.mn.us/state_parks/virtual_tour/grand_portage/dialup.html

ALMOST HIKES

An Almost Hike

- is a very short path (read great "leg stretch!"), ranging from 100' to 0.6 mile; Almost Hikes have spectacular scenery, include a location of interest, or are just plain fun.

- may or may not be part of an existing trail, but the route we describe leads to scenic beauty or another attraction.

- may sometimes have an original name, as this concept is unique to our book.

We hope you'll enjoy the following strolls scattered from Duluth to Grand Marais. We provide highlights, total length/surface, safety concerns, amenities, applicable fees, and a brief narrative of what you'll see while there.

Most Almost Hikes are very suitable for families traveling with small children, but please heed any noted safety concerns.

Artists' Point in Grand Marais   *photo by Ladona Tornabene*

Enger Park

Duluth • Off Skyline Parkway

- **One of Minnesota's premier parks, Enger Park features phenomenal panoramic views of Lake Superior, the Aerial Lift Bridge, Duluth Harbor and the iconic Enger Tower, where the 360-degree views magically transform after each flight of stairs!**

- **Picturesque, intimate gardens line the park, including a Japanese Zen Garden and a ringable Peace Bell.**

DIRECTIONS:

From the corner of Superior Street and Lake Avenue, turn northwest (away from the lake) on Lake Avenue, and drive to West 7th Street, where you will turn left. Continue across Mesaba Avenue on West 7th Street, which then merges left onto West Skyline Parkway. After nearly 2 miles, you'll reach a "T" intersection at Twin Ponds. Either way leads to Enger Park; however, the most scenic option is to the left by staying on West Skyline Parkway. At the very next intersection, turn right on Hank Jensen Drive, then very shortly take another right onto Enger Tower Drive. Follow to the paved parking lot (where there is designated wheelchair-accessible parking).

TOTAL TRAIL LENGTH & SURFACE:

0.6 mile (may vary depending upon how much you explore); paved, fine-packed gravel over dirt, crushed stone.

ALERT:

Although overlooks are spacious and taper very gradually, if you explore beyond the bench locations, some areas may be steep. Please use caution. Rock surfaces may be slippery when wet.

AMENITIES & FEES:

Flush toilets as well as water, picnic tables, and grills. No fees for parking or trail use.

NARRATIVE:

This Almost Hike covers three distinct features at Enger Park: the Enger Tower climb and the gazebo picnic area—both with stunning panoramic views—and the Japanese Zen Garden Walk/Peace Bell, all of which are within 0.2 mile of the parking lot.

To climb the tower, head north from the parking lot and take the 8-foot-wide paved path that is farthest to the left, and follow it for 0.2 mile up a gentle grade as it ascends to Enger Tower's base. There, 12 stone steps (no handrail) serve as a prequel to your ascent of 85 additional steps. However, this climb has a unique layout. Each flight of stairs (5 total) consists of 17 steps (concrete, double handrail) and after each flight there are two options: Continue climbing, or stop and circle each floor for a 360-degree view of Duluth. It's magical and fascinating to watch those views transform as you ascend the tower. At the top there are sweeping unobstructed panoramas of Lake Superior, the Aerial Lift Bridge, Duluth Harbor, Superior, Wisconsin, the Enger Golf Course, and the area hillside. Benches are cut into the stone if you need a rest.

To explore the Japanese Zen Garden and ring the Peace Bell, take the same path leading to Enger Tower, but just before the paved path veers left, look straight ahead for the gravel path and follow it toward the garden and bell tower. The gardens are laced with Japanese statuary and artistically designed benches. The bell has a very intriguing history, as it relates to Duluth's sister city in Ohara/Isumi City in Japan and WWII. An informational sign just prior to the garden is definitely worth a read.

To access the gazebo, with covered picnic tables and stellar views similar to those from Enger Tower, take the same path leading to the Tower, but turn right onto the sidewalk in front of the restroom building, and follow it to its east side. Find the accessible crushed stone path, which leads to the Julia Newell Marshall covered gazebo. Here, strategically placed benches offer commanding and awe-inspiring views. If you're visiting in early evening on a summer Wednesday, the Duluth Yacht Club hosts sailboat races. It's a gem to see as they parade under the Aerial Lift Bridge. Pack a dinner picnic and camera because this view is not to be missed any day of the week.

En route to all of the aforementioned Almost Hikes are quaint gardens with intimate paths that beckon you to explore. From the macro flower world to sprawling overlooks, this entire park is one huge photo op!

Foot Note:

The 80-foot-tall Enger Tower is named after native-Norwegian Bert Enger, who donated this land upon which the tower, Enger Park, and golf course now reside. Comprised of indigenous bluestone, the tower was built in 1939 and dedicated by the Crown Prince and Princess of Norway during the same year, then rededicated in 2011 by Norway's King and Queen—all in honor of Mr. Enger. (www.engertowerduluth.com/history.html)

The Zen garden at Enger Park *photo by Ladona Tornabene*

Canal Park Lighthouse Stroll*

Duluth, MN • *Gentle Hikes* name

- **A premier location for boat watching! It just does not get much better than this (see Foot Note for information on schedules).**

- **Peruse Lake Superior's Maritime Visitor Center, which offers free admission to programs/exhibits on maritime history.**

DIRECTIONS:

Take I-35 North to the Lake Avenue South exit, and turn right. Continue straight onto Canal Park Drive. The trailhead begins at the end of Canal Park Drive in front of Lake Superior Maritime Visitor Center. Most parking is fee-based (May 15–October 26) and enforced 24/7. For helpful parking info, visit: canalpark.com/parking-transportation/

TOTAL TRAIL LENGTH & SURFACE:

0.4 mile; paved, with ramp access. Flat with the exception of 15 steps (concrete, double handrail) leading up to the actual lighthouse.

ALERT:

This is a multiuse, non-motorized path. This Almost Hike is on a structure built for navigational purposes, with signage informing visitors to use at their own risk. If it's windy, waves can crest the structure and flood the area.

AMENITIES & FEES:

Flush toilets are available in Lake Superior Maritime Visitor Center. There are no fees for trail use; however, there may be a fee for parking.

NARRATIVE:

The trailhead begins on the paved walkway down the very wide gentle grade near the doorway to Lake Superior Maritime Visitor Center. This center is operated by the U.S. Army Corps of Engineers and houses some fine exhibits and programs. Admission is free. For hours of operation and more, visit lsmma.com/visitors-center/.

There are ample benches in this area for boat watching. Take a stroll out toward the lighthouse via very level concrete. Where you go, photo ops abound.

 Foot Note:

This location is absolutely prime for boat watching!
For schedules visit: duluthshippingnews.com

Leif Erikson Rose Garden
Duluth, MN

- **Here you'll see thousands of roses and the Duluth Peony Garden.**
- **An Italian-style gazebo, an authentic fountain, and a herb garden, all set with a backdrop of Lake Superior and Duluth's most famous landmark—the Aerial Lift Bridge.**

DIRECTIONS:
From I-35 North at Lake Avenue exit, turn left. Turn right at the first traffic light onto Superior Street. At 10th Avenue E, turn right onto London Road (this is where London Road begins and then runs parallel to Superior Street). Drive to the paved parking lot on the right side of street between S 13th Avenue E and S 14th Avenue E.

TOTAL TRAIL LENGTH & SURFACE:
0.2 mile around the perimeter (distance varies depending upon how much you explore); brick cobblestone and concrete. Grassy surfaces offer up-close view of roses.

ALERT:
No pets allowed in Rose Garden. Also, it is illegal to pick the roses. (With more than 70,000 visitors per year, there would be no Rose Garden if everyone picked a rose.) The garden is a tobacco-free area.

AMENITIES & FEES:
Flush toilets and water fountain (all seasonal) are available near parking lot; benches. A grocery store and eateries are nearby. There are no fees for parking or trail use.

NARRATIVE:
The trailhead begins at the parking lot on a path that circles around the Rose Garden. The first half is brick cobblestone yielding to a wide concrete path, including the sidewalk along London Road. To give the olfactory glands a workout, you'll want to venture off the path onto the grass to access the four circles of rose bushes. Strategically placed benches throughout offer ample resting and viewing places.

There are informational markers placed around the rose garden to enhance your visit.

The lovely Italian-style gazebo is often used as a site for wedding pictures, but it makes for great photo ops whatever the occasion. In the center of the largest rose circle stands a fountain with a history. It was built in 1905 and was used for watering horses (and dogs, too—notice the lapping bowl at the base) until the automobile rumbled onto the scene, relegating the fountain to its present ornamental state.

Note: In mid-October, when the roses are put to bed, the remaining blooms are cut and distributed to anyone who is visiting at the time.

Two Rivers, Three Views*

Lester Park • Duluth, MN • *Gentle Hikes* name

- **Incredible vantage points for viewing Lester River and Amity Creek.**

DIRECTIONS:

Follow I-35 North until it ends; at the split, veer left (do not follow North Shore). Cross London Road and begin up 26th Avenue E, turning right onto Superior Street. Continue for 3.5 miles, then turn left onto Lester River Road. A paved parking lot is immediately on the left.

TOTAL TRAIL LENGTH & SURFACE:

0.6 mile; gravel, wood, paved (parts are on sidewalk, the Lakewalk, and a bridge).

ALERT:

The sidewalk to the viewing area runs parallel to Superior Street, and you'll need to cross Superior Street to reach the first viewing area.

AMENITIES & FEES:

Portable toilets (may be seasonal), covered picnic tables, and a playground are available. A major grocery store is nearby. No fees for parking or trail use.

NARRATIVE:

The trailhead begins on a gravel path located at the east end of the parking lot, heading toward Superior Street. The trail travels along the Lester River until ending at the sidewalk. For Lester River view #1, cross Superior Street, and in a few yards, begin looking right for the paved Lakewalk. Turn right and head for the wide wooden bridge

McQuade Small Craft Harbor (Breakwater Loop)   *photo by Lisa Vogelsang*

(double handrails); the views of the river are especially scenic when water flow is high. When conditions are right, waterfalls form. For Lester River view #2, retrace your steps and cross back over Superior Street, then turn left onto the sidewalk and follow it toward another bridge (concrete, double handrails). The first view you'll see is of Lester River, and it is simply fabulous: a quaint stone bridge serves as a backdrop to the terraced rocky river below. This near-perfect tripod-worthy scene draws many photographers, as it is delightful in summer, but fall adds a bit of unforgettable splendor. Viewpoint #3 can be reached from this same sidewalk a few yards farther by continuing straight and looking right for Amity Creek.

McQuade Small Craft Harbor (Breakwater Loop)
On Old Highway 61, 4.5 miles from the highway entrance in Duluth

- **An unobstructed 180-degree view of Lake Superior and its rugged shoreline.**
- **Several fishing piers, a boat launch, and interpretative signage.**
- **A great location for boat watching or a place to stretch your legs or catch some fresh air.**

DIRECTIONS:
From Old Highway 61 (approximately 4.5 miles from the highway entrance in Duluth), turn left onto McQuade Road, and then take the first right into the small gravel parking area, which is located directly across from the wayside. The location is also accessible from MN-61 Expressway (follow signage).

TOTAL TRAIL LENGTH & SURFACE:
0.5 mile paved

ALERT:
The path is paved, wide, and flat, but if you venture off it, loose rock abounds.

AMENITIES & FEES:
Flush toilets and water fountain (seasonal) are available, as is a portable toilet. The site has a boat and kayak launch, a fishing pier, and the ramp and benches are all wheelchair accessible. No fees for parking or trail use.

NARRATIVE:
The trailhead begins from the gravel parking lot on a 6' sidewalk, northeast of the wayside near a brown sign indicating "Pedestrian Access to Breakwater." In 300' a ramp leads to the tunnel that crosses under Highway 61. At the tunnel's end, turn left (the boat launch is to the right). This area is spacious and beautiful with a wide, paved, walkway that leads to spectacular Lake Superior and shoreline views. Several fishing piers and benches dot the landscape. Under the covered shelter there are interpretive signs about area settlers, commercial fishing, tourism, the safe harbor, ships, and fun Lake Superior facts.

Bear Trail

On Old Highway 61, 13 miles from highway entrance in Duluth

- **Come face-to-face with a bear (cutout that is!) on this fun-themed little trail with great photo ops for the young and young at heart.**

DIRECTIONS:

This short little jaunt is on the property of Great! Lakes Candy Kitchen, which is located on Old Highway 61 just past Knife River bridge (on the right side of road). It is 13 miles from the highway entrance in Duluth. A gravel parking area is located in front of the candy shop (no wheelchair or designated RV parking).

TOTAL TRAIL LENGTH & SURFACE:

200 feet; 1–3' wide; dirt and cedar chip.

ALERT:

None.

AMENITIES & FEES:

Great! Lakes Candy Kitchen has a spread of outdoor picnic tables, hammocks, and swing seats.

A vault toilet is located at Knife River Rest Area, 0.5 mile away. To get there, head southwest on Scenic Drive toward Central Avenue, turn right, and follow Central Avenue until reaching the road just prior to MN-61 Expressway. Turn left and follow to the rest area. No fees for parking or trail use.

NARRATIVE:

The trailhead begins at the southwest side of Great! Lakes Candy Kitchen at a sign indicating "Bear Trail" on a 1- to 3-foot-wide dirt/cedar path. Just follow the bear tracks to the fun (with your camera in hand). The myriad props make this a fun adventure for little ones and an adorable family photo op.

 Foot Note:

Great! Lakes Candy Kitchen is comprised of third-generation candymakers who honor 100 years of family tradition by making candy the old-fashioned way—hand-stirred and cooked in copper kettles. www.greatlakescandy.com

 Says Who?

The dark side of chocolate isn't all that dark . . .

Eating dark chocolate can help prevent heart disease, some cancers, Alzheimer's, and stroke while slowing aging, improving immune function, and reducing high blood pressure. Keep the portion to about an ounce, though, since it is high in fat and calories.

Journal of Advanced Drug Delivery[33]

Agate Bay Breakwater
Off Highway 61, 26 miles from Duluth

- **One of the few places on the shore where you can get a nearly 360° sweep of Lake Superior.**
- **Terrific views of the ore docks and the city of Two Harbors. Look closely to spot the *Edna G*, a retired tug.**
- **A magnificent view of the old Two Harbors Lighthouse nestled among a forest of birch and spruce.**

DIRECTIONS:
From Highway 61 at mile marker 26 (**Note:** you will not find the actual mile marker— use your odometer reading from marker 25), turn right onto Waterfront Drive (at the corner of Dairy Queen and Black Woods Grill and Bar) and follow for 0.5 mile to South Avenue. Turn left and follow for 0.3 mile to 3rd Street; turn right and follow for 0.2 mile to the paved parking area (there are ample spaces for RVs).

TOTAL TRAIL LENGTH & SURFACE:
0.6 mile; paved, with access ramp.

ALERT:
No railing on one side of the breakwater walkway.

AMENITIES & FEES:
A vault toilet, picnic tables, a boat launch, a small gift shop in the lighthouse. No fees for parking or trail use.

NARRATIVE:
The trailhead begins at the far end of the parking area facing the lake. Descend 10 steps (concrete, double handrail) or take the alternative paved ramp toward the foghorn/light. A cable railing has been placed on one side of the 8-foot-wide concrete walkway. Follow the breakwater path 0.3 mile to the end. After enjoying the above highlights, turn around and retrace the walkway to the trailhead. This area also features a wayside (pg. 168).

 Foot Note:

Two Harbors' breakwater was constructed between 1947 and 1951 by the U.S. Army Corps of Engineers.

Split Rock River Beach

On Highway 61, 43 miles from Duluth

- **Access the beautiful Split Rock River pebble beach on Lake Superior via a tunnel under Highway 61.**

- **A popular canoe/kayak entry with gorgeous views of Lake Superior shoreline.**

- **The area has Gitchi-Gami State Trail access and is a popular fishing spot.**

DIRECTIONS:

From Highway 61 at mile marker 43.3, turn left into paved parking area.

TOTAL TRAIL LENGTH & SURFACE:

0.3 mile (depending on how much you explore); asphalt, concrete, hard-packed dirt, rock steps, grass, and pebble beach.

ALERT:

At time of writing, the last of the 16 steps from the bridge area down to the beach was broken. However, there are two grass paths that split off from steps 12 and 13 (left or right) that lead safely to the beach. When emerging from the Highway 61 underpass, use caution and look both ways, since you are crossing the non-motorized, multiuse Gitchi-Gami State Trail.

Bayside Park and Silver Bay Marina   *photo by Ladona Tornabene*

AMENITIES & FEES:

No amenities. No fees for parking or trail use.

NARRATIVE:

The trailhead begins at the southwest end of parking area near a kiosk and Inukshuk sculpture. Take time to read the informational display about Larry Moon, who spearheaded the initiative to have the North Shore Scenic Drive awarded a Scenic Byway status, as well as about the logging operation that occupied this area in the 1800s, trout fishing, and other trail information. Head north down the path, which gradually declines, and follow the trail as it veers right toward the tunnel under Highway 61. When exiting the tunnel, you must cross the multiuse Gitchi-Gami State Trail. Please use caution, as cyclists may be descending a downhill area and pass by very quickly. Descend the stone steps until you come to one of the grassy paths to the left or right. To avoid the last broken step, take one of those grassy paths to the pebble beach area. Photo ops abound here! We also recommend meandering up and down the Gitchi-Gami State Trail for additional photos and great views of Lake Superior.

 Says Who?

Need an energy boost? Take a hike.

Walking has been shown to increase energy levels for several hours afterwards.

Harvard Medical School Report[3]

Bayside Park

Silver Bay, MN • On Highway 61, 52 miles from Duluth

- **A short trek to this scenic overlook delivers great views of Lake Superior, Pellet Island, the marina, and the hills of Silver Bay.**

DIRECTIONS:

From Highway 61 at mile marker 52.4 (watch for a sign indicating Marina/Park at the preceding marker), turn right onto Bayside Park Road to enter the park. Take the next right, and drive beyond the boat launch to the upper paved parking lot, with ample pull-throughs for trailers and RVs.

TOTAL TRAIL LENGTH & SURFACE:

Approximately 350'; gravel and hard-packed dirt.

ALERT:

Two inclines of 12° each, for 15' and 20'.

AMENITIES & FEES:

A portable toilet (seasonal) is available near picnic area. No fees for parking or trail use.

NARRATIVE:

The trailhead begins in the upper parking area at a sign indicating the overlook. A large platform (guardrails) at the trail's end makes for a nice viewing area for the above highlights. We think it's worth the trek up!

Father Baraga's Cross
Cross River • On Highway 61, 79 miles from Duluth

- **A lovely memorial to one of the early Christian missionaries along the North Shore.**
- **A beautiful photo op of the stunning granite cross, with Lake Superior as a backdrop.**
- **Dynamic views of Lake Superior and the Cross River rushing into it.**

DIRECTIONS:
From Highway 61 at mile marker 79.3, turn right onto Father Baraga Road and follow for 0.2 mile to a paved parking area. **Note:** This is a residential area, so please drive cautiously. Parking is limited.

TOTAL TRAIL LENGTH & SURFACE:
Approximately 200'; hard-packed dirt.

ALERT:
Steep cliffs with no guardrail.

AMENITIES & FEES:
A portable toilet (seasonal) at nearby wayside and two picnic tables (with a gorgeous lakeside view), a grill, a BBQ pit, and a boat launch are available. No fees for parking or trail use.

NARRATIVE:
The trailhead begins at the west side of the parking area near a sign indicating Father Baraga's Cross. A very short walk reveals a lovely memorial to Father Baraga, missionary to the Native Americans of Madeline Island. The year was 1846, when a raging storm on Lake Superior almost took Father Baraga's life while he was returning from Madeline Island in a small boat. This granite cross today serves as a reminder of the original cross that a grateful Father Baraga placed here after his safe journey across Lake Superior.

Temperance River Bridge View
Temperance River State Park • On Highway 61, 80 miles from Duluth

- **Experience dramatic views of the lower Temperance River rushing through narrow canyon walls, with Lake Superior as a backdrop!**
- **Opposite the lake, an expansive view of the Temperance River is impressive as it curves around a birch-lined bend.**

DIRECTIONS:
From Highway 61 at mile marker 80.2, pull into the paved parking areas on either side of the highway and on either side of Temperance River. There is a special pullout for RVs and campers on the left side prior to the river.

TOTAL TRAIL LENGTH & SURFACE:
100–200' (depending on location of parked vehicle); hard-packed dirt, gravel.

ALERT:
Use caution when crossing Highway 61, and keep children in hand.

AMENITIES & FEES:
Vault toilets are available in the campground on the lake side of highway. No fees for parking or trail use.

NARRATIVE:
The trailhead begins at the pedestrian walkways located on either side of the highway bridge. A very short paved walk delivers a great view and instant photo ops of highlights on this river!

We encourage you to further explore this area via several short hikes and a picnic site that can be accessed from these parking areas (see pp. 114-118, 187).

Tofte Park
On Highway 61, 82 miles from Duluth

- **Gorgeous, continuous views of Lake Superior and her rugged shoreline.**
- **See Tofte Park's restored charming cobblestone bridges from 1924.**
- **A unique bronze sculpture of a trout in pursuit of herring.**

DIRECTIONS:
From Highway 61 at mile marker 81.9, look for a sign indicating Sugar Beach Lakeside Cabins. Immediately veer right onto Tofte Park Road and follow for 0.2 mile. It's easy to miss the entry to the park, so look for fire marker #7270, and immediately turn right onto a paved, narrow driveway that leads into a paved parking area with no designated parking places for cars/RVs.

TOTAL TRAIL LENGTH & SURFACE:
0.4 mile; paved.

ALERT:
No trash cans; please pack out refuse. If travelling by bicycle, please dismount and walk. No motorized vehicles. No inclines more than 10°, but the trail is not completely flat.

AMENITIES & FEES:
A wheelchair-accessible vault toilet is available; however, a 5-inch-high lip topped by a 3-inch-wide door threshold may pose an entry challenge. There's also a boat launch, picnic tables (grass underneath), and grills. No fees for parking or trail use.

NARRATIVE:
The trailhead starts on the northeast side at a 5-foot-wide paved path near white fences. Much is packed into this little trail, starting with uninterrupted views of Lake Superior and her beautiful rugged shoreline. There's also a covered picnic shelter and mammoth-size grill (there are no trash cans anywhere in the park), a unique bronze

sculpture of a trout pursuing herring, and an interpretative sign where you can read about lake herring and trout (the North Shore's two most important commercial fish) and how they nearly became extinct. You'll also find a set of quaint, picturesque cobblestone bridges and a former cobblestone well, which was constructed in 1924 and subsequently restored. Last but not least, you'll find signage about the interesting history of Tofte Park. The trail officially ends under the "Tofte Park" arch just prior to Bluefin Bay Resort.

Foot Note:

Minor Power is Major! Tofte Park was donated by Elizabeth Tofte, a minor at the time, whose father had to sign as her agent.

Says Who?

Gone Fishing or Fish Going?

Overfishing and global warming have caused a decline in Lake Superior herring, which also puts lake trout and whitefish at risk because they feed on the herring. Fortunately, conservation efforts have been successful in increasing fish populations.

Minnesota Public Radio News [34]

Tofte Park   *photo by Lisa Vogelsang*

Best-Kept Secret of Grand Marais*

Grand Marais, MN • Off Highway 61, 109 miles from Duluth • *Gentle Hikes* name

- **This spot showcases the jagged ridges of the Sawtooth Mountain Range, thought to be worn remains of ancient volcanoes, which is beautifully silhouetted against Lake Superior.**
- **Vibrant orange lichen nearly covers the rocks.**
- **Commanding views of Grand Marais Lighthouse, the harbor, Artists' Point (The Point), and Lake Superior.**

DIRECTIONS:
From Highway 61 at mile marker 109.1, turn right into Grand Marais Recreation Area, and drive 0.3 mile to picnic area #1 (an open shelter on the left). Park in the gravel lot near the boat launch.

TOTAL TRAIL LENGTH & SURFACE:
Length depends on how much you explore. Gravel and some flat, level sections of rock.

ALERT:
Some rock surfaces in this area are uneven.

AMENITIES & FEES:
A portable toilet (seasonal) is available, and there is also a picnic area (Grand Marais Recreation Area pg. 188) and a boat launch. No fees for parking or trail use.

NARRATIVE:
The trailhead begins at the stairs (two sets of 6 wood steps, 3.5' wide, double handrails) situated between two municipal buildings. These buildings are located off the gravel parking area, close to Lake Superior. There is one bench at the bottom of the steps. As you ascend, another bench is located at the top of the stairs and affords endless viewing pleasure. To the right are the jagged ridges of the Sawtooth Mountains. Lake Superior lies directly in front of you, and Grand Marais Lighthouse, the harbor and Artists' Point are to the left. The rock in this area has some large, very flat sections that can be immediately accessed from the bench. Spend a little time exploring up here.

 Foot Note:

In 2015, *Budget Travel* named Grand Marais "America's Coolest Little Town," and in 2017, *USA Today* readers voted it "Best Midwestern Small Town." And we don't want that to be kept secret!

Reference: *StarTribune*. Retrieved July 17, 2017, from www.startribune.com/grand-marais-wins-best-midwestern-small-town-award/420790383/

Harbor Park/Bear Tree Park

Gitchi Gami State Trail section: Grand Marais • Off Highway 61, approximately 109 miles from Duluth

- **Two parks and one amazing walk with uninterrupted, fabulous views of Grand Marais Harbor.**
- **One nonstop photo op with ample benches for sailboat watching—look for the iconic schooner *Hjørdis* (see below).**
- **Access to a cobblestone beach, where rock-skipping is a popular pastime.**

DIRECTIONS:

Highway 61 leads through downtown Grand Marais less than 1 mile after passing mile marker 109. This Almost Hike begins at the corner of Wisconsin Street and 1st Avenue West near Harbor Park, directly across from the Blue Water Cafe on the walkway parallel to Wisconsin Street. **Note:** 1st Avenue West and Harbor Park are unmarked.

PARKING INFORMATION:

There is ample street parking throughout downtown Grand Marais, but please be respectful of businesses. There is sufficient RV parking and car parking in Boulder Park (see pg. 176).

TOTAL TRAIL LENGTH & SURFACE:

0.5 mile; paved. Optional hard-packed dirt paths with light layer of small pebbles in Harbor Park; small cobblestones in beach area.

ALERT:

Multiuse Path is part of the Gitchi-Gami State Trail.

AMENITIES & FEES:

Benches and a boat launch are available, with portable restrooms at nearby Boulder Park (see pg. 176). No fees for parking or trail use.

NARRATIVE:

The entirety of this Almost Hike is on a barrier-free path that showcases superb harbor views with strategically placed benches; however, there is ample opportunity to explore the unpaved routes of lovely Harbor Park, which lead to the pebbled-laced beach. Continuing on the paved path, the Bear Tree statue marks Bear Tree Park. A few yards farther, pause for an interesting read about the harbor's history or learn more about geology in Minnesota. The path is now transformed by picturesque lampposts and quaint rope-draped railings that guard the rocky shoreline. Benches invite otter watching and, if fortunate, a sighting of the iconic area schooner, *Hjørdis*. The hike officially ends where the roped-draped railing ceases. However, if you want to continue on this path, fine eateries soon await on both sides of the street, as does the North House Folk School, which takes visitors aboard the *Hjørdis*. Also, some amazing eateries and shopping await near the trailhead as well. Honestly, the entire town of Grand Marais is chock full of these and more! It is one of our favorite getaways.

Artists' Point (a.k.a. "The Point")

Grand Marais, MN • Off Highway 61, 109 miles from Duluth

- **A slice of heaven on Earth, where woods and lake meet, and verdant flora yields to rugged rock jetties, which burst with spectacular orange lichen!**
- **This place is popular with tourists, but it also attracts a plethora of artists.**

DIRECTIONS:

From Highway 61 at mile marker 109.8, turn right onto Broadway Avenue and follow 0.3 mile to a public water access. There is a paved parking lot with wheelchair-accessible spots and RV spaces.

TOTAL TRAIL LENGTH & SURFACE:

0.4 mile (depending on how explored); rock, root, hard-packed dirt, and grass.

ALERT:

The gravel driveway en route to Artists' Point is shared with vehicles. The natural rock may be challenging to negotiate in places.

AMENITIES & FEES:

Portable toilets (seasonal), several picnic tables (one with extension), benches, and boat launch are available. No fees for parking or trail use.

NARRATIVE:

The trailhead is located at the rear left of the parking area behind the Coast Guard station on a gravel road. (**Alert:** This portion of the road is shared with vehicles.) Soon you'll see the photo-rich kiosks that display information about The Point and its natural history. A bit farther up the path toward the lake, ascend 3 steps (stone, no handrail), then immediately turn left onto the concrete seawall. This leads to some uneven rocks and eventually to a solid rock surface that is predominantly flat and boasts some incredible Lake Superior views! This area's 0.4 mile of trails are not definitively marked, but they are suitable for exploration. However, you'll need to carefully navigate this natural habitat, as its paths are rocky and rooted and skirt unguarded edges. While the terrain is relatively flat, there are a few small inclines/declines that you can avoid, depending on how the area is traveled. In summary, you don't need to travel far to realize that this highly scenic peninsula juxtaposes a deep-woods feel with the sublime spaciousness of the vast lake. One also does not have to venture very far to realize that this is not just a trail to explore, but a place to experience.

Foot Note:

This location is still referred to by the locals (and even listed on some maps) as Artists' Point. Historically, it was called "The Point." Regardless of the name, the photo-rich kiosk near the trailhead provides an interesting history of this point of land.

WAYSIDES AND SCENIC LOCALES

We have included some of the most scenic waysides and locales that the North Shore has to offer, and while we are quick to encourage physical activity in the outdoors, we also acknowledge the benefits of simply being in nature and enjoying the view. Therefore, we have included some sites that can be enjoyed from the car, including scenic drives.

We also tell you which sites are paved as well as which have designated wheelchair accessible and RV parking, plus highlights, amenities, and a brief narrative of what to expect while there.

Keep in mind that many waysides are closed during snow season, and some only operate seasonally (roughly from mid-May to mid-October).

And don't forget to bring the camera!

Grand Marais Harbor as seen from Boulder Park   *photo by Ladona Tornabene*

Duluth Skyline Parkway
Duluth

This scenic byway meanders nearly 20 miles along a ridgeline and showcases the city from end to end. Incredibly picturesque panoramas of the Duluth Harbor, Lake Superior, and St. Louis River Bay are accompanied by numerous pullouts perfect for photo ops. Our Enger Tower Almost Hike (pg. 148) can be reached from this parkway as well. From playgrounds to city parks, and golfing to watching hawks, Skyline Parkway takes you there. For a complete listing of scenic highlights, visit www.duluthmn.gov/parks/parks-listing/skyline-parkway

North Shore Scenic Drive (Highway 61)
Originates in Duluth and continues 150 miles to the Canadian Border

This drive has been likened to California's Pacific Coast Highway and with good reason. Although on a smaller scale than the Pacific Coast Highway, it too boasts rugged cliffs towering over a vast body of water, evergreens that dot the landscape, water cascading over vertical drops, and highways threaded through cut rock. Best of all, both share the prestigious status as All-American Roads, which is the top designation in the National Scenic Byway System. Few roads are awarded such status because to obtain that, . . . "a road must possess multiple intrinsic qualities that are nationally significant and contain one-of-a-kind features that do not exist elsewhere. The road or highway must also be considered a destination unto itself."[ii] Indeed, the North Shore Scenic Drive is a destination unto itself, yet it is also the gateway to many other adventures, including our trailheads. While by no means comprehensive, below is a list of activities to help you maximize your northern getaway!

To best showcase the region, we refer to the 19-mile stretch of North Shore Scenic Drive from Duluth to Two Harbors as "Old Highway 61" and the stretch from Two Harbors to the Canadian border as "Highway 61" or, when activities span "Old Highway 61" and "Highway 61," we state "All."

EXPLORE
All: Numerous waysides/pulloffs (several with picnic tables—and many with breathtaking Lake Superior views).

HIKE
All: Most of our trailheads and scenic locales can be reached from this road.

BICYCLE
Old Highway 61: Its shoulder is a designated bike path, and views of Lake Superior are stupendous!

Highway 61: The spectacular Gitchi-Gami State Trail parallels Highway 61 and passes through several state parks. It too offers up some incredible Lake Superior and wooded views. When completed, this multiuse, non-motorized paved path will span 89 miles between Two Harbors and Grand Marais. Visit www.ggta.org to see which sections are complete.

RUN

Old Highway 61: Each June, more than 12,000 runners and thousands of volunteers/spectators line the road for Grandma's Marathon and the Garry Bjorklund Half-Marathon. This "Superior" race along the Great Lake's shore culminates in Canal Park (grandmasmarathon.com).

Highway 61: Some of our trails are conducive to runners seeking a bit of off-road adventure, whereas the highly scenic sections of the Gitchi-Gami State Trail that we feature may be more appealing to those seeking a paved, even surface underfoot.

FISH

Old Highway 61: French and Knife Rivers are designated trout streams. Please visit MN Fishing Regulations (www.dnr.state.mn.us) before casting your line.

EAT

All: Many good eats throughout. Grab a taste of them at www.northshorevisitor.com/dining/

CREATE

All: Art can be good for the heart, be it art you make or art you take home with you. For current art events and longstanding venues, visit www.northshorevisitor.com/attractions/the-arts/

SHOP

All: Quaint gift and specialty shops offer items unique to this geographical region.

STAY

All: Be it a campground, cabin, cottage, hotel, resort, or inn, let the reservations begin—because you'll most likely need them! (www.northshorevisitor.com/lodging/)

A view from Old Highway 61   *photo by Ladona Tornabene*

[ii]Retrieved September 1, 2017 from www.fhwa.dot.gov/pressroom/fhwa0227.cfm

Buchanan Historical Marker

On Old Highway 61, 11 miles from highway entrance in Duluth

- **This old wayside was built to commemorate the town of Buchanan, named for the fifteenth President, James Buchanan.**
- **Buchanan was the seat of the land office for the northeastern district of Minnesota.**
- **There is a beautiful vista of Lake Superior here.**

DIRECTIONS:
On Old Highway 61, opposite fire marker #5875. Parking is available at the pulloff.

PARKING INFORMATION:
Paved.

AMENITIES:
None.

NARRATIVE:
Descend 12 steps (stone, no handrail), or take the wheelchair-accessible hard-packed gravel ramp to the viewing area of this quaint wayside and a historical marker. A few feet beyond that is Lake Superior's glorious shore.

Lake Superior Agate Bay Public Water Access

Off Highway 61, 26 miles from Duluth

- **Various picnic tables offer delightful views of Lake Superior and Agate Bay, with the active ore docks in close proximity; the boats that pick up ore here are the size of three football fields!**
- **Here you'll see a striking view of the original Two Harbors Lighthouse, which began operation in 1892 and continues today, making it the oldest operating lighthouse in Minnesota. It is also a bed-and-breakfast.**
- **See the fishing boat *Crusader II* that was built in 1939 and christened by Norway's Crown Prince Olav.**

DIRECTIONS:
From Highway 61 at mile marker 26 (**Note:** you will not find an actual mile marker—use your odometer reading from marker 25), turn right onto Waterfront Drive (at the corner of Dairy Queen and Black Woods Grill and Bar and follow for 0.5 mile to South Avenue. Turn left and follow for 0.3 mile to 3rd Street; turn right and follow for 0.2 mile to the parking area.

PARKING INFORMATION:
Paved; ample RV parking.

AMENITIES:

Vault toilets, picnic tables, boat launch, and a small gift shop in lighthouse are on-site.

NARRATIVE:

Photo ops abound from the parking area! There are stunning views of the Lighthouse, which is especially photo-worthy during the "golden light" just prior to sunset, and then there are the ore docks, which are visited by massive ships. Add to these the sweeping vistas of Agate Bay and Lake Superior, which make this locale a wonderful stop for a leg stretch, a final destination, or entry point to Agate Bay Trail (Lighthouse Loop) hike and Agate Bay Breakwater Almost Hike (pg. 54, pg. 155).

Foot Note:

Tours of the lighthouse are available (888-832-5606 or visit them online at lighthousebb.org/).

Flood Bay Wayside

On Highway 61, 27 miles from Duluth

- **A hotspot for agate hounds, with direct access to a pebble beach.**
- **Learn more about agates and their formation via the educational plaque.**
- **Incredible views of Lake Superior—and especially striking if waves are crashing.**

DIRECTIONS:

From Highway 61 at mile marker 27.5 (watch for a sign preceding the marker), turn right into the Flood Bay Wayside parking area.

PARKING INFORMATION:

Paved; designated wheelchair-accessible and RV pull-through parking. Day-use area only.

AMENITIES:

There is a wheelchair-accessible vault toilet located down a paved path northeast of the parking area.

NARRATIVE:

Every storm washes stones up on the beach, making this an agate adventure zone. There are four entry points via sets of 6 to 8 stone steps (uneven and no handrails) that lead to Lake Superior's pebble beach just around the bay from Superior Shores Resort. Also, this is one of the best waysides for viewing wave action.

Says Who?

Want to improve your relationship with each other? Hike together!

Walking together improves relationships because of the time spent talking without distractions.

Journal of Positive Psychology[28]

Split Rock Scenic Overlook*

On Highway 61, 45 miles from Duluth •*Gentle Hikes* name

- **A grand view of Split Rock Lighthouse—right from your car!**
- **A marker here provides information about the geology of the Split Rock and Beaver Bay area.**

DIRECTIONS:
From Highway 61 at mile marker 45.2 (watch for a sign indicating the wayside preceding the marker), turn right into the pullout.

PARKING INFORMATION:
Paved; highway pullout.

AMENITIES:
None.

NARRATIVE:
Excellent and popular photo op. On a clear day, this is a lovely area from which to view the lighthouse.

 Foot Note:

The paved Gitchi-Gami State Trail runs through the wooded area of this wayside and we have highlighted a phenomenal section of it (see Split Rock: Birch to Beacon Trail, pg. 82). When complete, this multiuse trail will stretch from Two Harbors to Grand Marais. For updates and status, visit www.ggta.org.

Black Beach Park

Off Highway 61, approximately 55 miles from Duluth

- **One location, two super-scenic destinations: Agate Beach and Black Beach, both of which have Lake Superior as their prodigious and dazzling backdrop!**
- **A short 0.1-mile walk to Black Beach from the last parking area.**

DIRECTIONS:
Form Highway 61 at mile marker 54.7, turn right onto Mensing Drive and follow signs to Black Beach. It is about a mile drive to Black Beach proper, but it's worth a stop into the first parking area because the overlook of the unmarked Agate Beach is stunningly beautiful.

PARKING INFORMATION:
There are three parking areas. The first gravel lot is on the left and marked by a sign indicating "Black Beach" and "Beach Parking." The second lot is gravel and also on the left and states "Beach Parking Handicap Only"; therefore, if you want to visit this strikingly beautiful unmarked Agate Beach, please park in the first lot and walk on the dirt

road for less than 0.1 mile to this area. The third gravel lot is a bit farther down the road on the left and does not seem suitable for RVs, due to a tighter turning radius.

AMENITIES:
Vault toilets are at parking lots 1 and 3, and there are picnic tables at all locations.

NARRATIVE:
The first gravel parking lot has a terrific overlook of the unmarked Agate Beach and Lake Superior. It features a large grassy area, a beautiful granite memorial bench, and several picnic tables, but no beach access that is at all gentle. There are much safer ways to arrive at Agate Beach. If your vehicle has a permit to use wheelchair-accessible parking, then park in the second gravel lot, which reads, "Beach Parking Handicap Only." While it may be challenging to roll a wheelchair along the pebble beach, the views from the small parking area are magnificent. If you do not have a handicap permit, then please park in the first lot and walk less than 0.1 mile on the dirt road to the second parking lot. Farther down the unpaved road, the last gravel parking lot has a 0.1-mile path that leads directly to Black Beach. To find it, follow the 10-foot hard-packed gravel trail at the southwest end of the parking lot down a 12° decline for approximately 50' to reach the beach. The views of the beach, Lake Superior, and the small, unmarked Turtle Island are superb.

Foot Note:

Why is this beach "black"? In 1956, the now defunct Reserve Mining Company began depositing up to 67,000 tons of taconite tailings (fine-rock byproduct of iron ore extraction) per day into Lake Superior*. While this practice ceased in 1980, the remaining tailings have mixed with sand to give Black Beach its namesake hue as a Silver Bay Gem. However, releasing tailings into the lake was not without controversy. For details about this landmark case, visit: www.mnopedia.org/event/united-states-america-v-reserve-mining-company

*Source of info: www.seagrant.umn.edu/newsletter/2005/06/readers_want_to_know.html

Black Beach, which gets its color from the taconite tailings that were once dumped into the lake   *photo by Ladona Tornabene*

Palisade Head Overlook

On Highway 61, 57 miles from Duluth

- **A glorious view of Shovel Point to the left and the Sawtooth Range to the right. On a clear day, look for the Apostle Islands in the distance.**
- **Flows of igneous rhyolite overlaying softer basalt, with both combining to form Palisade Head and Shovel Point.**
- **Before driving up, stop at the initial pullout and read the marker about how the North Shore formed.**

DIRECTIONS:

From Highway 61 at mile marker 57, turn right and travel 0.4 mile to the top on a curvy, paved road through a splendid mixed forest. **Alert:** There are sharp curves; no trailers or RVs are allowed. The two-way road is very narrow and steep in places.

PARKING INFORMATION:

Paved.

AMENITIES:

None.

NARRATIVE:

Not only are the views striking from the top, but the short drive as you wind your way up the narrow road through a splendid mixed forest is spectacular in and of itself. It all makes it seem like you're entering another world just yards off the highway. Palisade Head is a favorite of area rock climbers.

ALERT:

When at the top, use extreme caution when walking over to view Palisade Head. There is no trail, and its rock surfaces require careful negotiation. The cliff is very steep and there are no guardrails, only a brick barrier.

Says Who?

Do you have high blood pressure?

Physical activity, such as walking, can reduce and prevent high blood pressure.

BC Medical Journal[2]

Taconite Harbor Public Water Access and Safe Harbor

On Highway 61, 77 miles from Duluth

- **See a 6,100-pound taconite rock and other massive artifacts.**
- **View Bear and Gull Islands, which gave nearby Two Island River its name.**[iii]
- **Look for ships through the Hi-Spy viewing machines (binocular viewfinders).**

DIRECTIONS:
From Highway 61 at mile marker 76.9 (watch for a sign preceding the marker), turn right onto paved road and travel 0.4 mile to the gravel parking area on the right.

PARKING INFORMATION:
There are two lots. We recommend using the huge gravel lot. One paved spot is designated for wheelchair-accessible parking. Boat-launch parking is on the opposite side down the decline, and is paved.

AMENITIES:
There's a picnic table on the grass and a bench (paved underneath) with a view of Gull and Bear Islands. There are seasonal portable toilets near the boat launch.

NARRATIVE:
Here you'll find massive palpable artifacts of the area's history, including a 6,100-pound taconite rock, an enormous anchor, and a colossal tire from a mining truck, all of which make for intriguing selfies or fun family photos! Interpretative signs about a steam-powered tugboat, log rafting on Lake Superior, and Sugarloaf Cove and Taconite Harbor make this an interesting and informative stop.

Cross River Wayside

On Highway 61, 79 miles from Duluth

- **Dramatic cascades of the Cross River can be seen from the highway, but we highly recommend a stop and a camera!**
- **Overlooks on both sides of the bridge are visible from a pedestrian walkway.**
- **A memorial to Father Frederic Baraga, a missionary to the early residents along the North Shore, is found here.**

DIRECTIONS:
From Highway 61 at mile marker 78.9, pull into the parking area on the left side of the highway prior to the bridge.

[iii]Upham, W. (1920). *Minnesota Geographic Names: Their Origin and Historic Significance, Volume 17*, Minnesota Historical Society, St Paul

PARKING INFORMATION:
Paved.

AMENITIES:
Vault toilets and polished granite benches are on-site.

NARRATIVE:
We highly recommend parking in one of the designated waterfall-viewing areas, as there is no stopping allowed on the highway.

The cascades are very visible from the 6- to 8-foot-wide concrete sidewalk on the bridge (wheelchair accessible). **Alert:** Use caution if crossing Highway 61, and keep children in hand.

In addition to the stunning cascades, an overlook (guardrail) is located on the lake side of the highway, providing a view of the Cross River's lower gorge. A trek down 37 steps (wood, handrail, non-continuous) offers a closer look.

Cascade River Wayside
On Highway 61, 100 miles from Duluth

- **A gorgeous view of Lake Superior!**
- **A short trek down a few steps showcases the Cascade River as it flows into Lake Superior.**

DIRECTIONS:
From Highway 61 at mile marker 99.9, veer right into the pullout.

PARKING INFORMATION:
Paved; highway pull-through.

AMENITIES:
None.

NARRATIVE:
This site is often crowded and with good reason. The breathtaking lake views, combined with the proximity to Cascade River State Park and the Lower Cascade Falls Quick Route (pg. 126), make it an ideal stopping place.

To get a view of the Cascade as it flows under the bridge into Lake Superior, descend the 24 steps (stone and wood, some handrail, non-continuous) located at the northeast side of the parking area.

Says Who?

Joint pain keeping you off the trail?

Jarring forces on knees and other joints can be reduced by using hiking poles, especially when walking downhill.

Journal of Physical Therapy Science[40]

Good Harbor Bay Scenic Locale

On Highway 61, 104 miles from Duluth

- **See and read about what happened when lava flows explosively encountered standing water.**

- **A beautiful view of Good Harbor Bay and the rugged shoreline of Lake Superior.**

DIRECTIONS:
From Highway 61 at mile marker 104.1 (watch for the historical marker sign preceding mile marker), veer right into the pullout.

PARKING INFORMATION:
Paved; highway pull-through.

AMENITIES:
None.

NARRATIVE:
A must-see for rockhounds and fans of geology! Wheelchair accessible informational plaques reveal the geology of the region and area history.

Cutface Creek Rest Area

On Highway 61, 104 miles from Duluth

- **Sit among old growth pine and stately birch.**

- **Manicured lawns sport very nice picnic tables overlooking the lake; paved walkways lead to strategically placed benches for Superior views!**

- **There is walking access to the water's edge.**

DIRECTIONS:
From Highway 61 at mile marker 104.5, turn right into the Cutface Creek rest area.

PARKING INFORMATION:
Paved; designated wheelchair-accessible and RV parking.

AMENITIES:
Vault toilets, picnic tables (paved path extends to one table), and benches are all on-site.

NARRATIVE:
We think this wayside has something for nearly everyone. It brings you to the water's edge via a paved path leading to 11 wide steps (rock, no handrail), then onto a pebble beach. Strategically placed benches afford viewing pleasure from any angle. To date, we say it's one of the best-groomed waysides on the shore.

Pincushion Mountain Overlook

Off Highway 61, approximately 109 miles from Duluth

- **The only designated drive-to overlook that features an aerial view of Grand Marais Harbor, the Lighthouse, and Artists' Point, with nearly panoramic views of Lake Superior.**

DIRECTIONS:

From Highway 61 at mile marker 109.2 in Grand Marais, turn left at 5th Avenue W (County Road 15) and follow for 0.7 mile to a stop sign at the junction with County Road 12 (Gunflint Trail). Turn left again and follow for 1.5 miles to County Road 53 (Pincushion Drive). Turn right and follow for 0.1 mile to the overlook.

PARKING INFORMATION:

Paved; no designated spaces. The parking area is loop-shaped, which may accommodate an RV pull-through.

AMENITIES:

Vault toilet.

NARRATIVE:

The delightful views expressed in the highlights are framed by evergreens. An informational board provided is wheelchair accessible.

Boulder Park (a.k.a. Grand Marais Public Water Access)

Off Highway 61, approximately 109 miles from Duluth

- **A drive-to view of Grand Marais Harbor, Artists' Point (or "The Point"), Lighthouse, Eagle Mountain, Pincushion Mountain, and the Sawtooth Mountain Range.**
- **Picnic tables with great lake and harbor views.**
- **The former site of a pulpwood rafting operation.**

DIRECTIONS:

From Highway 61 at mile marker 109.8, turn right onto Broadway Avenue, and follow 0.3 mile to the public water access.

PARKING INFORMATION:

Paved; designated wheelchair-accessible and RV parking.

AMENITIES:

Portable toilets (seasonal), several picnic tables (one with extension), benches, and a boat launch are on-site.

NARRATIVE:

This popular area is conveniently located in the heart of Grand Marais, with several restaurants and specialty shops nearby. This is also the parking area for the Artists' Point Almost Hike. The scenery is rich—right from the car! There are views of Pincushion Mountain to the north, Eagle Mountain to the west, and the Sawtooth Mountain Range located 30 miles to the southwest. Enjoy!

Foot Note:

There's much to see and do in Grand Marais. Visit: www.exploreminnesota.com/where-to-go/cities-towns/2904/grand-marais-area-tourism-association

The shoreline from Cutface Creek Wayside   *photo by Ladona Tornabene*

Kadunce River Wayside

On Highway 61, 119 miles from Duluth

- **The town of Colvill was named in honor of Colonel William Colvill, Commander of 1st Minnesota Volunteer Infantry Regiment, which was present at many major battles during the Civil War.**
- **This is a great place for a sunrise or sunset picnic.**
- **Listen for the comforting sounds of waves on the pebble beach.**

DIRECTIONS:
From Highway 61 at mile marker 118.9, after crossing the bridge, turn right into Kadunce River Wayside paved parking lot (highway sign is spelled Kodonce).

PARKING INFORMATION:
Paved; designated wheelchair-accessible and motorcycle parking.

AMENITIES:
A picnic table with pavement extending to it.

NARRATIVE:
A small, lovely wayside showcasing Lake Superior with access to the water's edge via a pebble beach. Kadunce River empties into the lake here.

Old Dog Trail*

Off Highway 61, 128 miles from Duluth • *Gentle Hikes* name

- **This is part of the historic John Beargrease sled-dog route. When roadways were impassable due to snow, mail and supplies were shipped to this location, then packed on a dog sled for delivery.**
- **A great view of Superior's rugged shoreline.**

DIRECTIONS:
From Highway 61 at mile marker 128.4 (as you enter Hovland), turn right onto Chicago Bay Street, and follow for 0.1 mile to the old pier and a boat launch.

PARKING INFORMATION:
The site is paved but not well maintained, and there's minimal parking—but it's heavy on historical significance and views!

AMENITIES:
Boat launch.

NARRATIVE:
This Hovland Dock brings you within feet of the waters of Superior; however, do not drive on the pier, due to instability issues. Old Dog Trail, which ran along the North Shore for 130 miles, was used for mail delivery between Grand Marais and Fort William, Canada. This is the original mail drop location. A full restoration of this dock is planned.

Susie Islands Overlook

On Highway 61, 147 miles from Duluth

- **A sweeping panorama of the Susie Islands, and if it's crystal clear, look for Isle Royale and Rock of Ages Lighthouse!**
- **The viewing platform overlooks beautiful Wauswaugoning Bay.**

DIRECTIONS:
From Highway 61 at mile marker 147.5 (watch for a sign indicating Scenic Overlook at the preceding marker), turn right into the parking area. The actual wayside is partially hidden from the highway.

PARKING INFORMATION:
Paved; designated wheelchair-accessible and RV parking.

AMENITIES:
The site has an informational kiosk, vault toilets, benches, and small wooden tables with seating for picnicking. The tables have an overhang to accommodate a wheelchair. There is also a viewing platform.

NARRATIVE:
A nice "away from the highway" parking area offering some lovely scenery on a clear day. Views abound from the car, but it's a great stretch break! About 1 mile farther up Highway 61, there is another highway pull-through with similar views, but no facilities.

Says Who?

Have trouble drinking enough? (Water, that is!)

Studies show that some people have an easier time drinking sports drinks than water during physical activity, not only because they taste good, but because they can help reduce fatigue on long treks.

Journal of the International Society of Sports Nutrition[41]

PICNIC AREAS

Whether you want to grill or pack a lunch, we have selected some of the most scenic picnic areas along Lake Superior and the North Shore. From woods to rivers and plenty of views of the Big Lake, you'll find it listed here.

To arouse your appetite for nature and other nearby points of interests, we had a little fun with format as described below:

Appetizer: Typically, we list what is en route to the picnic area (what precedes it—as an appetizer precedes a meal), whether it's an Almost Hike, trail, or wayside.

Main Course: Here's where we describe what the actual picnic area is like.

Dessert: Usually we list what is nearby the picnic area—whether an Almost Hike, a trail to explore, or just somewhere to enjoy nature. It's what we recommend as a great finish to a good meal, and in most cases, actually burns calories instead!

In addition to this fun format, we include amenities that are located at the picnic sites, applicable fees, parking surface, and designated wheelchair accessible spaces. We also note sites that have pavement extending to tables and/or table extensions.

Please note: There are no drive-up tables; you'll need to park and carry your gear unless otherwise noted.

The Breakwall at Bayside Park   *photo by Ladona Tornabene*

Kitchi Gammi Park (Brighton Beach)
Duluth, MN

- **Appetizer: En route to this picnic area, stop for a family photo op. There is a gazebo just prior to the entrance of Brighton Beach that affords glorious views of Lake Superior and is a great resting place for the travel-weary.**

- **Main Course: This scenic 0.8-mile stretch of road hugs Lake Superior and offers numerous places to picnic by the gorgeous lake and among wooded sites. There is also a playground and a fire shelter. It's a true luxury—right here in Duluth.**

- **Dessert: Explore the shore! This area is prime.**

DIRECTIONS:

From I-35 North, continue until it ends. Follow the sign for North Shore, veering right onto London Road. Follow London Road, which then becomes Congdon Boulevard. At mile marker 5.1, veer right onto the paved road for the Brighton Beach entrance.

PARKING INFORMATION:

Gravel and paved areas available. Some tables can be driven to; all others are park and carry. Tables are movable.

AMENITIES & FEES:

The site has portable toilets (seasonal), playground, a fire shelter, an open-sided shelter, grills, and BBQ pits. No fees for parking or picnic area use.

Sunrise over Lake Superior at the gazebo near Kitchi Gammi Park picnic areas   *photo by Ladona Tornabene*

Gooseberry Falls Picnic Areas

Gooseberry Falls State Park • On Highway 61, 39 miles from Duluth

- **Appetizer: Take the 5-minute stroll on a paved path to see spectacular Gooseberry Falls (pg. 64), the most visited area on the North Shore!**

- **Main Course: There are several options here. The historic Lakeview Shelter (fully enclosed) is equipped with fireplace, lots of windows, and is reservable. A variety of tables surround it, some in wooded areas, others with commanding lake views. A short spur north of the parking lot leads to more tables near Gooseberry River. The last option (Picnic Flow) is best reached from the next parking lot just 0.1 mile south of this one. The paved Gitchi-Gami State Trail splits the area, with tables on either side. However, remarkable views of Lake Superior are straight ahead, just over a gentle unpaved grade. On a sunny day, the vast rocky open area bursts with vivid orange lichen juxtaposed against the vibrant blue lake, combining to provide picnicking like no other place on the shore. If very windy, waves crashing on the shore may rival those seen on the West Coast.**

- **Dessert: Nibble on the history at Plaza Overlook Loop (pg. 66).**

DIRECTIONS:

From Highway 61 at mile marker 38.9, turn right into Gooseberry Falls State Park, and follow the signs to the picnic area that is located approximately 1 mile from the visitor center.

PARKING INFORMATION:

The small paved parking is located in front of the Lakeview Picnic Shelter; larger paved parking is less than 0.1 mile farther at the picnic area.

AMENITIES & FEES:

Flush toilets and water (both seasonal) are available at Lakeview Shelter, as is a vault toilet, BBQ pits, and grills. An annual or day-use state park permit is required; they are available at the visitor center. There are fees to rent the Lakeview Shelter. Contact park office: 218-595-7100.

 Foot Note:

Lakeview Shelter was constructed in 1934 by the Civilian Conservation Corps (CCC) and is part of 624 acres at the park listed on the Historic Registry.

Trail Center/Lakeview Picnic Area

Split Rock Lighthouse State Park • On Highway 61, 46 miles from Duluth

- **Appetizer: Take a spur off the Little Two Harbors trail located directly outside the shelter for unsurpassed, iconic views of Split Rock Lighthouse. This short trek is over uneven rock, but the views are sweet!**

- **Main Course: Near a birch forest, there are two shelters that offer a unique dining experience. A wood-burning stove, beautifully finished picnic tables, and reading materials about the North Shore, as well as photos of Split Rock Lighthouse State Park, are all located in the fully enclosed side of the shelter. The partially enclosed side of the shelter provides enough tables and two grills to accommodate even the biggest of families.**

- **Dessert: Take the Little Two Harbors & Pebble Beach Trail (pg. 80) to scope out your next picnic spot.**

DIRECTIONS:
From Highway 61 at mile marker 45.9, turn right into Split Rock Lighthouse State Park. Follow past the park office, turning right onto the first street you encounter. Follow it for 0.4 mile, and turn left at the sign indicating Trail Center and picnic area.

PARKING INFORMATION:
Paved; designated wheelchair-accessible and RV parking.

AMENITIES & FEES:
Flush toilets and water fountain are open year-round. Both shelters are wheelchair accessible. An annual or day-use state park permit is required; they are available at the park office. For shelter reservations, call the park office: 218-595-ROCK (7625).

Bayside Park Picnic Area

Silver Bay Marina & Park • On Highway 61, 52 miles from Duluth

- **Appetizer: Take the paved walk out toward the flag circle. If fog is lingering on the lake, you may experience an especially striking view of Pellet Island. The harbor views make for interesting photo ops.**

- **Main Course: Picnic areas are generously scattered around the park, offering a variety of Lake Superior and wooded views. A boat launch is available too.**

- **Dessert: Take the Bayside Park Almost Hike (pg. 157) up to a scenic overlook with first-rate views of the safe harbor and lake.**

DIRECTIONS:
From Highway 61 at mile marker 52.4 (watch for a sign indicating Marina/Park preceding the marker), turn right onto Bayside Park Road to enter the park.

PARKING INFORMATION:

Parking (paved and gravel) is plentiful and scattered throughout the marina; however, no trailers are allowed in picnic areas. A generous paved lot for RVs and trailers is available by taking the first left upon entering the park.

There is designated parking for wheelchair accessibility. Picnic tables (with extensions) are available at open-sided shelters and throughout the area.

AMENITIES & FEES:

Vault toilets, BBQ pits, grills, and a playground are on-site, as is Silver Bay Safe Harbor and boat launch. No fees for parking or picnic area use.

Tettegouche General Picnic Areas*

Tettegouche State Park • On Highway 61, 58 miles from Duluth •
Gentle Hikes name

- **Appetizer: Hike the gorgeous Shovel Point Trail (pg. 94).**
- **Main Course: Plenty of table options, from covered open-sided shelters to lake views.**
- **Dessert: Take the 0.4-mile Baptism River Loop trail (pg. 98) nearby.**

DIRECTIONS:

From Highway 61 at mile marker 58.6, turn right into Tettegouche State Park.

Picnic areas are accessible from the parking lot. A covered shelter is near the parking area, and several tables are scattered in the back of the visitor center.

PARKING INFORMATION:

Paved; there is designated wheelchair-accessible parking and a separate lot for RVs.

AMENITIES & FEES:

Herein is a spectacular visitor center that houses a gift shop, an interpretive center, as well as a snack counter serving coffee/light refreshments. There is 24/7 access to flush toilets, water, and vending machines. An amphitheater is also on-site, as is a massive indoor fireplace, and an enormous outdoor stone fireplace, which is available for public use with purchase of wood.

There is no fee to park at Tettegouche Visitor Center (four-hour limit). However, if vehicles are driven to or parked at other areas within the park, a day-use or annual permit is required; these are available at the park office.

High Falls Picnic Area

Tettegouche State Park • On Highway 61, 58 miles from Duluth

- **Appetizer: A trek to High Falls at Tettegouche (pg. 100).**

- **Main Course: Sip the sweetness of silence in a beautiful wooded environment preserved with attention to privacy.**

- **Dessert: Savor more of this park and peruse the interpretative display at the visitor center, then stroll through the Triple Overlook Loop (pg. 90)**

DIRECTIONS:

From Highway 61 at mile marker 58.6, turn right into Tettegouche State Park, and immediately take another right passing the visitor center. Soon you will drive over a bridge. Continue on this curvy road for 1.5 miles. **Note:** At an intersection at approximately 1.2 miles, do not turn right into camping area; instead, follow signs to the Trail Center, where a paved parking lot is located. Locate sign indicating picnic area.

PARKING INFORMATION:

Paved/gravel lot.

AMENITIES & FEES:

The site has a vault toilet, a picnic area, and BBQ pits. An annual or day-use state park permit is required; they are available at the park office.

 Says Who?

Hiking + soda pop = discomfort!

Soft drinks are not recommended as a fluid replacement because of their concentrated sugars, carbonation, and/or caffeine contents. Carbonation takes up space in the stomach that could be used by additional fluids. And caffeine causes you to lose more fluid than contained in the drink itself.

Nutrition: Concepts and Controversies (Fourteenth Edition), [42]

Benson Lake Picnic Area

George H. Crosby Manitou State Park • Off Highway 61, approximately 59 miles from Duluth

- **Appetizer: Relax on the strategically placed bench that affords a full view of Benson Lake. Watch for otters and loons.**
- **Main Course: This beautiful gem of a lake has shaded and sunny lakeside picnic sites.**
- **Dessert: Hike the Benson Lake Trail (pg. 104).**

DIRECTIONS:

From Highway 61 at mile marker 59.3, turn left onto Highway 1 and follow for 6.2 miles (you will travel through Finland). Turn right onto County Road 7, and follow for 7.6 miles. Turn right onto Benson Lake Road (also fire marker #7616) into George H. Crosby Manitou State Park, and follow it for 0.5 mile to a gravel parking lot on the left.

PARKING INFORMATION:

The picnic area is 0.1 mile from the gravel parking lot (follow a sign for Benson Lake Trail); however, there is a spot where you can park temporarily to unload picnic supplies.

AMENITIES & FEES:

The site has a vault toilet, BBQ pit, and water is available seasonally at the park entrance. An annual or day-use state park permit is required. A pay box is available at the park entrance.

 Foot Note:

This is the most remote of all North Shore state parks and is managed by Tettegouche State Park. And did you know that "the name Tettegouche comes from a French-Canadian phrase meaning 'meeting place?'" Retrieved from: www.duluthnewstribune.com/content/long-awaited-tettegouche-state-park-visitor-center-opens

Temperance River Picnic Area

Temperance River State Park • On Highway 61, 80 miles from Duluth

- **Appetizer: We recommend the extraordinary Temperance River Gorge Trail (pg. 116) nearby, which features seven dramatic overlooks!**
- **Main Course: A fabulous vista of Lake Superior and its pebble beach.**
- **Dessert: Check out the Temperance River Lower Loop (pg. 114).**

DIRECTIONS:

From Highway 61 at mile marker 80.2 (the turnoff is easy to miss; watch for fire marker #7680), turn right at picnic area sign prior to Temperance River, and follow for 0.1 mile to the picnic area.

PARKING INFORMATION:
One spot is paved, the remainder are gravel. In some places, parking can be very close to tables.

AMENITIES & FEES:
The site has vault toilets, water (seasonal), and a barbeque pit. An annual or day-use state park permit is required to enter park or picnic area; they are available at the park office.

Cascade River State Park Picnic Area
Cascade River State Park • On Highway 61, 100 miles from Duluth

- **Appetizer: If you like waterfalls, take the Lower Cascade Falls Quick Route (pg. 126).**
- **Main Course: Picnic in a secluded wooded environment with stunning views of Lake Superior.**
- **Dessert: Take the Lower Falls Cascade River Loop (pg. 128) for postcard-worthy river views.**

DIRECTIONS:
From Highway 61 at mile marker 100.3, veer right into Cascade River State Park Picnic Area (a long pull-through section of road). Although there is no parking lot per se, parking is permitted in this area. **Note:** The Gitchi-Gami State Trail is slated to travel along this parking area, which will change the way this picnic area is accessed in the future.

PARKING INFORMATION:
Paved/gravel pull-through alongside a section of road. Nearest tables are located approximately 200' from parking area; others are farther.

AMENITIES & FEES:
Vault toilet, grills, barbeque pits are on-site. An annual or day-use state park permit is required to enter park or picnic area; they are available at the park office.

Grand Marais Recreation Area
Grand Marais, MN • On Highway 61, 109 miles from Duluth

- **Appetizer: Enjoy uninterrupted panoramas along the paved Harbor Park/ Bear Tree Park Almost Hike (pg. 162)**
- **Main Course: Indulge in views of Grand Marais Harbor, Artists' Point, and the Lighthouse from a covered open-sided shelter.**
- **Dessert: Discover the Best-Kept Secret of Grand Marais. Hint: It's an Almost Hike (pg. 161).**

DIRECTIONS:
From Highway 61 at mile marker 109.1, turn right into Grand Marais Recreation Area, and follow for 0.3 mile to Picnic Area 1 (an open-sided shelter on the left).

PARKING INFORMATION:

The gravel parking area is less than 10' from the paved shelter. **Note:** There is no ramp access from gravel lot to shelter 1, but tables are movable.

AMENITIES & FEES:

The site has a portable toilet (seasonal), a grill, and one table with extensions at both ends. No fees for parking or picnic area use.

Grand Portage National Monument Picnic Area

Grand Portage, MN • Off Highway 61, approximately 144 miles from Duluth

- **Appetizer: Excellent opportunity to visit the Grand Portage National Monument.**
- **Main Course: Picnic by Lake Superior, nestled beneath the hills of Grand Portage and majestic white spruce.**
- **Dessert: Take a stroll on the spur trails that lead to the lake, the monument, and through a refreshing stand of pine.**

DIRECTIONS:

From Highway 61 at mile marker 144, turn right on Cook County 17. At the stop sign, turn left. Follow past the Grand Portage National Monument Heritage Center and parking lot, and continue to a small gravel parking area on the right just beyond Cook County 73.

PARKING INFORMATION:

The gravel parking area has no designated spaces. You can also park at the Heritage Center or the National Monument, both of which have paved parking plus designated wheelchair-accessible spaces. There is a paved wheelchair-accessible trail from the Heritage Center to the National Monument.

AMENITIES & FEES:

Flush toilets (seasonal at Monument, open 8 a.m.–5 p.m.) are available at the Heritage Center and the National Monument. Restrooms are wheelchair accessible. Parking at the picnic area, the Heritage Center, and the National Monument is free; however, fees are charged for entrance to the Monument.

 Foot Note:

Experience Grand Portage National Monument, where history of worldwide importance was made by the North West Company and the Ojibwe people. Plan your visit today: www.nps.gov/grpo

Hiking for Health

INCREDIBLE STUFF EVEN WE COULDN'T MAKE UP!

Imagine being able to take a pill that could:

- stimulate weight loss
- reduce risk of heart disease, cancer, and stroke
- decrease development of or drop high blood pressure
- improve cholesterol levels
- cut risk for type 2 diabetes
- lessen risk of Alzheimer's and other forms of dementia
- facilitate better sleep
- help you manage stress better
- improve cognitive functioning
- manage lower back and knee pain
- function better with arthritis
- reduce the risk and symptoms of depression
- lessen risk of osteoporosis
- lower risk of falls and injury
- sustain the ability to live independently
- improve the quality of your life!

No such pill exists; however, all of the above benefits and more can be derived from doing one thing. That one "thing"? Physical activity.[1,2,3] If the benefits of physical activity could be packaged in pill form, it could easily become a trillion-dollar seller!

But currently our nation as a whole is not capitalizing on these benefits; approximately a quarter of a million deaths occur annually in the United States because of sedentary living.[4] Other major causes of death include heart disease, cancer, and stroke.

HEART DISEASE

The bad news: Cardiovascular disease is the No. 1 killer of men and women currently and has been for decades. Surprisingly, more women died yearly from cardiovascular disease than men, until recently.[5] Even though there is increased awareness for heart disease, most don't realize that heart disease kills more women than all other cancers combined.[5] The same is true for men, and cardiovascular disease causes 800,000 deaths annually, or nearly 1 in 3 deaths.[5] Someone in the United States has a heart attack every 40 seconds.[5] Inactivity is a major risk factor for heart disease.[5]

The good news: Regular moderate-intensity physical activity (such as brisk walking) offers considerable protection against heart disease.[6,7] Even walking for 10 minutes at a time, or less than the recommended 150 min/week, is associated with decreased disease risk.[7,8]

CANCER

The bad news: Men have a 1 in 2 chance and women have a 1 in 3 chance of obtaining some form of cancer in their lifetimes.[9] While breast cancer in women and prostate cancer in men claim the highest occurrence rates, lung cancer claims almost twice as many lives of women as does breast cancer and more than three times as many men as prostate cancer.[9] Smoking can be credited for more than 80 percent of lung cancer deaths and nearly 50 percent of 12 other types of cancer.[10] More than 90 percent of colorectal cancer cases occur after age 50.[11] Inactivity is a major risk factor for cancer as well.[12]

The good news: Quitting smoking pays enormous health benefits. Kick butt with physical activity, as it helps to ease cravings, withdrawal symptoms, appetite, stress, and weight gain.[13] A recent study has shown an 18 percent reduction of risk for breast cancer with as little as 1.25 to 2.5 hours per week of brisk walking.[14] Risk of lung and colon cancer as well as 12 other cancers can also be reduced through exercise.[12]

STROKE

The bad news: Men have a 1 in 6 chance and women have a 1 in 5 chance of stroke in their lifetimes.[15] While approximately 795,000 people will have a stroke yearly in the USA, only about 130,000 will die from that stroke.[16] Someone in the United States has a stroke every 40 seconds.[16]

The good news: Adults who are moderately to highly active (including moderate intensity exercise, such as walking) have a 20–27 percent (respectively) risk reduction for a stroke.[16]

Let's use our FEET to DE-FEAT these many disease risks due to inactivity!

A view from Gooseberry Falls State Park   *photo by Lisa Vogelsang*

HOW MUCH DO THE FEET HAVE TO MOVE?

The Centers for Disease Control and the American College of Sports Medicine recommend 150 minutes per week of moderate-intensity exercise or 75 minutes of vigorous-intensity exercise per week, or a combination of both.[8,17] This works out to be 30 minutes of moderate-intensity activities 5 days per week or 15 minutes of vigorous-intensity activities 5 days per week. Examples of moderate-intensity activities include a 30-minute brisk walk for 2 miles, wheeling in a wheelchair for 30 minutes, or bicycling 5 miles in 30 minutes. Examples of more-vigorous activity include a 15-minute run for 1.5 miles, shoveling heavy snow for 15 minutes, or cycling for 4 miles in 15 minutes.[18,19] Certain trails in this book can accommodate all of the above activities, depending on the season. For weight management or improved cardiovascular benefits, 150–250 minutes of moderate-to-vigorous-intensity activity per week is recommended, whereas more than 250 minutes will produce more clinically significant results while maintaining healthy caloric intake requirements.[20] **Note:** If you are new to a moderate or vigorous physical activity program (less than 150 minutes per week) and are over age 35, have high blood pressure, high cholesterol, prediabetes, type 1/type 2 diabetes, or are overweight, it is recommended that you first consult your doctor to ensure that you are in good health before engaging in vigorous exercise.[8]

HOW FAST DO THE FEET HAVE TO MOVE?

Hiking can be done at light-, moderate-, or vigorous-intensity levels depending on the speed at which you walk and diversity of terrain. If you hike at a light intensity, do so for longer than 30 minutes; 60 minutes if possible. Trails with a Lighter Side of Gentle rating are relatively flat, providing an excellent location for light-intensity hiking. For vigorous intensity, seek out our more-rugged-rated trails, with steps and inclines, or jog along the easier-rated trails.

WHAT IF THE FEET CAN'T MOVE MUCH?

If you are unable to engage in 30 minutes of continuous activity, start slowly, increasing no more than 10 percent of total minutes or mileage per week. If you are inactive, even increments of 10 minutes to achieve 150 minutes per week can improve heart health.[8] Our Almost Hikes (pg. 146) range from 80' to 0.6 mile, making them ideal for smaller increments of physical activity. **Note:** If you have chronic health problems, such as heart disease, obesity, diabetes, or are at high risk for these problems, you are advised to consult your physician prior to beginning a new program of physical activity.[8]

Health Is More Than Just the Physical . . .

PHYSICAL ACTIVITY IS GOOD FOR MENTAL HEALTH

Depression can have devastating effects on people's lives, relationships, employment, or academics.[21] It is also the leading cause of disability worldwide and is associated with increased death and disease.[22] Many studies have been done on the relationship between exercise and decreased depression, and results have shown that a significant reduction in depression can be brought about through exercise, regardless if the activity was a single bout or done on a regular basis.[23] Exercise has been shown to be effective for preventing both depression and anxiety, as well as the relapse of depression.[23] The benefits of exercise are consistent across age and gender.[23] So, whether it's one hike or adherence to a regular exercise program, physical activity can reduce depression.

Other mental and emotional benefits of physical activity include reducing stress, anxiety, and feelings of loneliness, while promoting overall psychological well-being.[2,23]

Cognitive functioning, such as memory and thinking ability, has also been shown to improve in older men and women who engage in regular physical activity, like walking.[2]

FOR BETTER HEALTH ON THE INSIDE—GET OUTSIDE!

Hiking outdoors produces many benefits for mental health that go beyond the effects of the exercise itself. Simply being in the outdoors adds a sense of calm and peace.[24] In fact, the first few minutes of exercising in nature causes an increase of self-esteem and a reduction of negative mood, like tension, anger, or depression.[24] Additionally, there is less perception of effort in outdoor environments, compared to indoor, and people tend to move farther and faster with less effort outside.[24] Several studies demonstrated that exercise outdoors improved measures of mental well-being, both after one session and across time.[25] People are also more likely to repeat exercise in green environments, and exercise adherence is improved.[25] Actually, just looking at the color "green" has been shown to have a calming effect and contributes to the positive effects of "green exercise."[26] As a matter of fact, physical activity in natural environments might produce greater mental health benefits than exercising in human-built environments.[27]

SOCIAL BENEFITS OF WALKING/HIKING

Outdoor pursuits can effect changes in interpersonal relationships. In one study, walking in nature was found to produce more positive feelings, more connectedness to others, nature, and life as a whole, as well as a more general prosocial orientation than walking in human built environments.[28] A major report from the UK suggested that walking in green spaces, such as state or city parks, trails, and community gardens, had a number of social benefits, such as social interaction, social inclusion, interracial interaction, social support, and social cohesion.[29] They found that hiking can lead to more interaction among many different types of people from all walks of life. Since many of the state park trail locations in this book are major tourist destinations, there can be opportunities to interact with people from all over the world!

Hiking may be more of a social activity than walking. Most people take along another person or more when venturing out for a hike, for safety as well as other reasons. Additionally, people often want to share the special beauty, sights, and sounds of the outdoors with someone. There are no TVs blaring, no phones ringing (leave the cell phone off!), and no chores calling while outside. New terrain to explore and discuss gives additional advantage to hiking. Couples and friends can improve their relationships by talking while walking.

So, grab a friend and/or loved one to share a trail with you. But please remember that others on the trail may be seeking solitude or a spiritual experience. Therefore, remember to keep conversation volume down, as voices travel a long way in the woods, especially near water.

SPIRITUAL BENEFITS OF WALKING/HIKING

There is no question that being out in nature can awaken a deep part of us like nothing else can. For many people, walking in the woods or other natural settings can help them to realize or even access feelings of spirituality in ways not possible through other methods. It seems that natural environments serve as a type of connection to spiritual experience.[30] "The elevating feelings of awe and inspiration, connection to a greater whole, and spiritual exaltation . . . have been linked with nature as well." [30] Even imagined experiences of nature can create the same types of feelings of connectedness, awe, and a sense of being in the presence of something greater than oneself.[30] Such imagined experiences of nature are often used in guided imagery or guided meditation experiences for stress reduction and health promotion. Appreciating the world's natural beauty has been a part of most spiritual traditions from the very beginning of time. Since time is at such a premium in most people's lives, it has been suggested to use exercise time (walking, running, hiking, etc.) to commune with God or to pray.[31]

UNTIL OUR PATHS MEET AGAIN . . .

It is the authors' hope that all of this information will encourage you to get out and explore the trails in this guide. But don't wait until you are near the North Shore area to hike. Explore local trails and neighborhood parks. Start or join a walking/hiking club in your own community. Treat yourself to a mental workout by reading some of our recommendations in Recommended Reading and Resources, pg. 206.

Remember: The steps you take toward a healthy lifestyle today will eventually create a path to that same destination. Wishing you a lifetime of healthy trails—however you travel them.

Note: The information presented herein is in no way intended to substitute for medical advice. It is best to seek medical advice from a reputable medical professional. For your maximum well-being, we strongly recommend getting your doctor's approval before beginning any physical activity program.

For Travelers with Specific Needs

FOR OUR READERS WITH PHYSICAL CHALLENGES

This chapter augments some of the information included throughout this book that may be helpful to our readers with physical challenges. For a full description of each trail, almost hike, and scenic locale (including waysides or picnic areas), please see their respective sections.

CANDID MESSAGE

Deeply moved by one person's tenacity of spirit, we wanted to share his story. His name is Paul Hlina. In 1995, he was the first documented through-hiker of the Superior Hiking Trail (SHT). We found this to be an impressive accomplishment in and of itself, but there's more. Paul hiked the entire 200 miles of this trail (the length of SHT at that time) on crutches, due to his partially paralyzed lower extremities.[iiii]

[iiii]Slade, A. (Ed.), *Guide to the Superior Hiking Trail* (Two Harbors, MN: Ridgeline Press, 2007).

Deeply moved by Paul's achievement and that of another man who took his wife in a wheelchair on a trail that contained more than 300 steps, and inclines at a 20° grade—we had to pause and reflect on what we say regarding accessibility.

OUR APPROACH TO ACCESSIBILITY

While we do report trails that meet Universal Design Standards for accessibility, we also provide significant details in 0.1-mile increments as applicable so our readers can decide if a trail is within their ability level. This "know before you go" approach empowers readers with the following information:

- total round-trip trail length
- trail surface (e.g. paved, dirt, hard-packed gravel, rock/root rating)
- location and total number of steps, presence of handrails
- location of bridge crossings
- bench placements
- safety concerns
- total number and location of inclines that exceed 10° (18 percent grade)

Additionally, we note the steepest and longest incline, typically when those exceed 30'. We used a clinometer to measure their running slope (not cross-slope), and we report in degrees rather than percent grade (please see pg. 211 for conversion chart).

FINDING FLAT AMIDST RUGGED TERRAIN

In a geographical region known for its rugged cliffs and terrain, we have aspired to showcase its gentlest side. However, even though a trail may not have inclines that exceed 10°, it could (and often does) have inclines of lesser degrees. Many of our paved trails have inclines of lesser degrees (see Authors' Corner (pg. 10), but their surfaces are wheelchair friendly. Also see Authors' Corner (pg. 10) to view the flattest trails and Almost Hikes that we could find. We also recommend reading all subsequent descriptions for paved and flat trails throughout this book.

TRAILS THAT MEET UNIVERSAL DESIGN STANDARDS

The following trails meet Universal Design Standards: Gooseberry Falls (pg. 64), the Plaza Overlook Loop (pg. 66) at Gooseberry Falls State Park, Triple Overlook Loop (pg. 90) at Tettegouche State Park, Lake Loop Trail (pg. 130), and the High Falls at Grand Portage State Park (pg. 144).

Additionally, the following trail sections meet Universal Design Standards: The first 0.2 mile of Caribou Falls (pg. 108) and the first 230' of Temperance River Gorge Trail, which is paved to the bench at the Hidden Falls viewing platform (pg. 116).

BEST WHEELCHAIR-FRIENDLY SECTIONS OF THE SUPERIOR HIKING TRAIL

In addition to the Caribou Falls section mentioned above, the Superior Hiking Trail shares passage with the following paved sections of Duluth Lakewalk: Canal Wall to Bayfront Festival Park (pg. 28) and Canal Wall to Fitger's (pg. 32).

TRAILHEAD RESTROOMS AND ACCESSIBILITY

The "Trailhead Restroom Accessibility" chart below contains features such as type of toilet (flush, vault, portable) and surface to restrooms as applicable for our trails and Almost Hikes. All restrooms are wheelchair accessible unless otherwise noted. However, a wheelchair accessible restroom at a trailhead does not mean that the trail is wheelchair accessible, which is why we recommend consulting the detailed descriptions throughout this book to determine if such is within your ability level. Most flush toilets are housed in venues that are not open 24/7. Yet if available 24/7, we state that in the chart under restroom type. Some portable and flush toilets are only available seasonally.

Note: This chart is organized geographically, from south (in or near Duluth) to the Canadian border.

Trail/Almost Hike	Type	Surface to Restroom
Enger Park (pg. 148)	Flush	Paved
Bayfront Festival Park (pg. 26)	Flush	Paved
Shared Trailhead **Lakewalk: Canal Wall to Bayfront Festival Park** (pg. 28) **Lakewalk: Canal Wall to Fitger's** (pg. 32) **Canal Park Lighthouse Stroll** (pg. 150)	Flush	Paved
Shared Trailhead **Lakewalk: Rose Garden to Fitger's** (pg. 36) **Lakewalk East: Rose Garden to Water Street** (pg. 38) **Leif Erikson Rose Garden** (pg. 151)	Flush (seasonal)	Paved
Shared Trailhead **Lakewalk East Extension: London Road to Water Street** (pg. 40) **Lakewalk East Extension: S 26th Ave E to N 40th Ave E (i.e., Duluth East High School)** (pg. 42)	Portable (not wheelchair accessible)	Paved/grass
Bagley Nature Area (pg. 44)	Portable	Dirt/gravel (slight paved decline prior to entry)
Shared Trailhead **Rock Knob** (pg. 48) **Hartley Pond & Tischer Creek Loop** (pg. 50)	Flush	Paved, but not a smooth surface
Shared Trailhead **Lester Park Trail** (pg. 52) **Two Rivers, Three Views** (pg. 152)	Portable	Paved
McQuade Small Craft Harbor (Breakwater Loop) (pg. 153)	Flush	Paved
Shared Trailhead **Agate Bay Trail: Lighthouse Loop to Paul Van Hoven Park** (pg. 54) **Agate Bay Breakwater** (pg. 155)	Vault	Paved
Bear Trail (pg. 154)	Nearby (see Bear Trail description, pg. 154)	Paved

Trail/Almost Hike	Type	Surface to Restroom
Shared Trailhead **Gooseberry Falls** *(pg. 64)* **Plaza Overlook Loop** *(pg. 66)* **River View Trail** *(pg. 68)* **Gitchi Gummi** *(pg. 70)* **Gooseberry River Loop** *(pg. 74)*	Flush (24/7); Designated assisted restroom, 8 a.m. to midnight	Paved
Iona's Beach *(pg. 78)*	Portable (located near boat launch)	Paved
Little Two Harbors Trail & **Pebble Beach** *(pg. 80)*	Vault	Dirt/gravel
Shared Trailhead **Split Rock: Birch to Beacon** *(pg. 82)* **Split Rock: Tour de Park** *(pg. 86)* **Little Two Harbors Trail** *(pg. 84)*	Flush	Paved
Shared Trailhead **Triple Overlook Loop** *(pg. 90)* **Shovel Point Trail** *(pg. 94)* **Baptism River Loop** *(pg. 98)*	Flush (24/7)	Paved
High Falls at Tettegouche *(pg. 100)*	Vault	Dirt/gravel
Bayside Park *(pg. 157)*	Vault Portable	Paved/grass
Benson Lake Trail *(pg. 104)*	Vault	Gravel
Caribou Falls *(pg. 108)*	Vault	Paved
Sugarloaf Cove Trail *(pg. 110)*	Flush (seasonal) Portable (seasonal), not wheelchair accessible	Dirt/gravel
Father Baraga's Cross *(pg. 158)*	Vault at nearby Cross River Wayside *(pg. 173)*	Paved
Temperance River Gorge View **(paved route)** *(pg. 118)*	Vault	Dirt/gravel
Tofte Park *(pg. 159)*	Vault	Paved
Lower Falls Cascade River Loop *(pg. 128)*	Vault	Dirt/gravel
Shared Trailhead **Best-Kept Secret of Grand Marais** *(pg. 161)* **Lake Loop Trail** *(pg. 130)*	Flush (seasonal) in campground	Paved, but parking lot is gravel
Artists' Point (a.k.a. "The Point") *(pg. 163)*	Portable	Gravel
Shared Trailhead **Devil's Kettle** *(pg. 136)* **Brule River Loop** *(pg. 140)*	Vault	Dirt
Shared Trailhead **Webster–Ashburton Trail and** **Picnic Area** *(pg. 142)* **High Falls at Grand Portage** *(pg. 144)*	Flush (24/7)	Paved

All locations listed in this chart provide designated wheelchair-accessible parking with the exception of Bear Trail.

WAYSIDES, SCENIC LOCALES, AND PICNIC AREAS ACCESSIBILITY FEATURES

The chart below contains features such as type of toilet (flush, vault, portable), surface to restrooms, and picnic table information as applicable for our scenic locales, waysides, and picnic areas. Most flush toilets are housed in venues that are not open 24/7. If available 24/7, we state that in the chart under restroom type. Some portable and flush toilets are only available seasonally.

Note: This chart is organized geographically, from south (in or near Duluth) to the Canadian border.

Scenic Locale, Wayside, Picnic Areas	Restroom Type	♿	Surface to Restroom
Kitchi Gammi Park (Brighton Beach) *(pg. 182)*	Portable	✔	Grass/dirt
Lake Superior Agate Bay Public Water Access *(pg. 168)*	Vault at boat launch	✔	Paved
Flood Bay Wayside *(pg. 169)*	Vault	✔	Paved
Gooseberry Falls Picnic Areas *(pg. 183)*	Flush (seasonal) Vault	✔	Uneven cobblestone/grass
Trail Center/Lakeview Picnic Area *(pg. 184)*	Flush	✔	Paved
Bayside Park Picnic Area *(pg. 184)*	Vault Portable	✔	Paved/grass
Black Beach Park *(pg. 170)*	Vault	✔	Gravel
Tettegouche General Picnic Areas *(pg. 185)*	Flush (24/7)	✔	Paved
High Falls Picnic Area *(pg. 186)*	Vault	✔	Dirt/gravel
Benson Lake Picnic Area *(pg. 187)*	Vault	✔	Dirt
Taconite Harbor Public Water Access and Safe Harbor *(pg. 173)*	Portable nearby at boat launch (seasonal)	✔	Paved
Cross River Wayside *(pg. 173)*	Vault	✔	Paved
Temperance River Picnic Area *(pg. 187)*	Vault	✔	Dirt
Cascade River State Park Picnic Area *(pg. 188)*	Vault	✔	Dirt/gravel
Cutface Creek Rest Area *(pg. 175)*	Vault	✔	Paved
Grand Marais Recreation Area *(pg. 188)*	Portable (not wheelchair accessible)		Loose gravel
Pincushion Mountain Overlook *(pg. 176)*	Vault	✔	Paved
Boulder Park (Grand Marais Public Water Access) *(pg. 176)*	Portable (not wheelchair accessible)		Dirt/gravel
Susie Islands Overlook *(pg. 179)*	Vault	✔	Yes

Seeking more inclusive outdoor adventure? Visit: www.wildernessinquiry.org and dnr.state.mn.us/accessible_outdoors/index.htm

Surface to Tables	Surface Under Tables	Table Extension/ Universal Design	Wheelchair-Accessible Designated Parking
Grass/dirt, hard-packed gravel	Grass/dirt, paved		
Paved	Paved	Yes	Yes
n/a	n/a	n/a	Yes
Grass	Paved/grass	Yes	Yes
Paved, crushed limestone, grass	Paved, crushed limestone, grass	Yes	Yes
Paved, gravel	Paved, gravel	Yes	Yes
Grass/gravel	Grass/gravel	Yes	Yes
Paved	Paved	Yes	Yes
Grass/dirt	Grass/dirt		Yes
Grass	Grass		
Grass	Grass		Yes
n/a	n/a	n/a	Yes
Grass, dirt, gravel	Grass, dirt, gravel		Yes
Dirt	Dirt		
Paved/grass	Paved	Yes	Yes
Loose gravel	Paved	Yes	
n/a	n/a	n/a	
Grass/gravel	Grass/gravel	Yes	Yes
Yes	Yes	Yes	Yes

For Our Readers Traveling in RVs

Welcome to Minnesota's North Shore and Highway 61, the "All-American Road"! The North Shore Scenic Drive originates in Duluth and continues 150 miles to the Canadian Border. We recommend allowing plenty of time as this road is not only highly scenic and beautiful, but is also a two-lane highway (occasional passing lanes) with frequent curves and deer crossings. But the main reason we advocate for allowing plenty of time is because there is an abundance of fabulous things to experience in this amazing region (please see the North Shore Scenic Drive (pg. 166) and About the Trails and Those Who Host Them (pg. 208).

The chart below features parking information for selected trails, Almost Hikes, and scenic locales and picnic areas and waysides. If a trail/scenic locale is not listed, it either

Scenic Locale or Trailhead	Parking Information
Bayfront Festival Park (pg. 26)	Designated parking at the DECC (Duluth Entertainment and Convention Center), which is nearby. No reservations accepted and availability is on a first-come, first-served basis. decc.org/parking-directions/parking/
Lakewalk Sections **Canal Wall to Bayfront Festival Park** (pg. 28) **Canal Wall to Fitger's** (pg. 32) **Canal Park Lighthouse Stroll** (pg. 150)	Designated parking at the DECC, which is across the slip bridge from Canal Park (see above information).
Lakewalk Sections **Rose Garden to Fitger's** (pg. 36) **Rose Garden to Water Street** (pg. 38) **Leif Erikson Rose Garden** (pg. 151)	Potential parallel street parking along either side of London Road near Rose Garden. Also, limited parallel parking in paved lot next to Rose Garden.
Lakewalk Sections **London Road to Water Street** (pg. 40) **S 26th Ave E to N 40th Ave E (i.e., Duluth East High School)** (pg. 42)	Potential parking in gravel lot at trailhead. **Alert:** Potholes and uneven surfaces abound.
Bagley Nature Area (pg. 44)	Potential parking along St. Marie Street on UMD's campus; however, when classes are in session, virtually impossible to find.
Kitchi Gammi Park (Brighton Beach) (pg. 182)	On/off street parallel parking depending on how cars are situated. Area can get very crowded. Paved and gravel surfaces.
North Shore Scenic Drive (Highway 61) (pg. 166)	Many pull-through areas along Old Highway 61 and waysides along Highway 61.
McQuade Small Craft Harbor (Breakwater Loop) (pg. 153)	Paved parking lot with many pull-through spaces, since it is a boat launch.
Buchanan Historical Marker (pg. 168)	Parallel parking on Old Highway 61 shoulder.

has no designated RV parking, or we speculate that parking an RV may be challenging. However, if in doubt about any RV parking, please call ahead to the number listed on our trails or contact the DNR. As an added bonus, we list contact information for campgrounds that are near our trails/scenic locales and also accommodate RVs. We recommend checking their website or calling ahead, as sites vary in length accommodation and range from full to no hookups.

Note: This chart is organized geographically, from south (in or near Duluth) to the Canadian border.

 Foot Note:

For additional information on camping in the North Shore region (including Gunflint Trail), please visit www.northshorevisitor.com/lodging/campgrounds/

Fee for Parking	Nearby Campgrounds That Accommodate RVs
Yes	
Yes	Lakehead Boat Basin on Park Point www.lakeheadboatbasin.com/rv.html 218-722-1757 Full hookups available **Note:** This location is only 3 blocks from Canal Park, where the hikes listed to the left start
	Penmarallter Campground (closer to Two Harbors) www.penmaralltercampsite.com 218-834-4603 Full hookups available.

Scenic Locale or Trailhead	Parking Information
Agate Bay Trail: Burlington Bay to First Street (pg. 58)	Open gravel lot.
Agate Bay Trail: Lighthouse Loop to Paul Van Hoven Park (pg. 54) **Agate Bay Breakwater** (pg. 155) **Lake Superior Agate Bay Public Water Access** (pg. 168)	Paved parking lot with many pull-through spaces since it shares a boat launch.
Silver Creek Cliff Trail (pg. 62)	Paved pull-through lot with a few parallel parking places.
Flood Bay Wayside (pg. 169)	Paved parking with many pull-through spaces that are shared with cars.
Gooseberry Falls (pg. 64) **Plaza Overlook Loop** (pg. 66) **River View Trail** (pg. 68) **Gitchi Gummi** (pg. 70) **Gooseberry River Loop** (pg. 74)	Designated paved RV parking lot near visitor center.
Gooseberry Falls Picnic Areas (pg. 183)	Potential parallel parking in paved lot depending on how cars are situated.
Iona's Beach (pg. 78)	Paved parking lot with many pull-through spaces since it shares a boat launch.
Split Rock Scenic Overlook (pg. 170)	Highway pull-through.
Split Rock Lighthouse State Park: **Split Rock: Birch to Beacon** (pg. 82) **Split Rock: Tour de Park** (pg. 86) **Little Two Harbors Trail & Pebble Beach** (pg. 80) **Little Two Harbors Trail** (pg. 84) **Trail Center/Lakeview Picnic Area** (pg. 184)	Paved parking lot with many pull-through spaces that are shared with cars.
Northshore Scenic Overlook and Trails (pg. 88)	A lower lot provides RV parking.
Bayside Park (pg. 157)	Paved parking lot with many pull-through spaces since it shares a boat launch.
Tettegouche State Park **Triple Overlook Loop** (pg. 90) **Shovel Point Trail** (pg. 94) **Baptism River Loop** (pg. 98) **Tettegouche General Picnic Areas** (pg. 185)	Designated paved RV parking lot to left of visitor center.
High Falls at Tettegouche (pg. 100) **High Falls Picnic Area** (pg. 186)	Depending on how cars are situated, there may be parking in paved/gravel, but when crowded, turning radius might be challenging.

Fee for Parking	Nearby Campgrounds That Accommodate RVs
	Burlington Bay Campground www.twoharborsmn.gov/city_departments/burlington_bay_campground/index.php 218-834-2021 Full hookups available.
	See Burlington Bay Campground
Limit to two hours	Gooseberry Falls State Park Campground www.dnr.state.mn.us/state_parks/gooseberry_falls Requires reservations. No hookups.
Yes	
Limit to four hours.	Tettegouche State Park Campground www.dnr.state.mn.us/state_parks/tettegouche Requires reservations Electric hookups only.
Yes	See above

Scenic Locale or Trailhead	Parking Information
Caribou Falls *(pg. 108)*	Parallel paved parking for one to two RVs
Taconite Harbor Public Water Access and Safe Harbor *(pg. 173)*	Very large open gravel lot with no designated parking places for cars/RVs. Nearby boat launch with paved pull-through spaces.
Cross River Wayside *(pg. 173)*	Several paved highway pull-throughs with potential parallel parking depending on how cars are situated.
Temperance River Lower Loop *(pg. 114)* **Temperance River Gorge Trail** *(pg. 116)*	Potential parallel parking beside Highway 61 on left side just prior to crossing bridge. Paved.
Tofte Park *(pg. 159)*	Modest paved lot, which houses a small boat launch. No designated parking places for cars/RVs.
Cascade River State Park Picnic Area *(pg. 188)*	Gravel parallel parking alongside road. No designated parking places for cars/RVs.
Cascade River Wayside *(pg. 174)*	Highway pull-through that is typically crowded.
Good Harbor Bay Scenic Locale *(pg. 175)*	Highway pull-through.
Cutface Creek Rest Area *(pg. 175)*	A couple parallel parking places.
Grand Marais Recreation Area *(pg. 188)* **Best-Kept Secret of Grand Marais** *(pg. 161)*	Open gravel lot. No designated parking places for cars/RVs.
Lake Loop Trail *(pg. 130)*	Parking is located in Grand Marais Campground near ballfield in gravel area.
Harbor Park/Bear Tree Park *(pg. 162)* **Artists' Point (or "The Point")** *(pg. 163)* **Boulder Park (a.k.a. Grand Marais Public Water Access)** *(pg. 176)*	Paved parking lot with many pull-through spaces since it shares a boat launch.
Pincushion Mountain Overlook *(pg. 176)*	Paved lot with potential parallel parking depending on how cars are situated.
Judge C.R. Magney State Park **Devil's Kettle** *(pg. 136)* **Brule River Loop** *(pg. 140)*	Gravel lot with signage inviting RV parallel parking when area is not used by cars.
Grand Portage State Park **Webster-Ashburton Trail and Picnic Area** *(pg. 142)* **High Falls at Grand Portage** *(pg. 144)*	Designated paved RV parking lot.
Susie Islands Overlook *(pg. 179)*	A couple parallel parking places in this highway pull through.

Lamb's Resort Campground
lambsresort.com
218-663-7292
Full hookups available

Temperance River Campground
www.dnr.state.mn.us/state_parks/temperance_river
Electric hookups only.

Yes   Cascade River State Park campground
www.dnr.state.mn.us/state_parks/cascade_river
Electric hookups only.

See above.

Grand Marais Campground and Marina
800-998-0959
www.grandmaraisrecreationarea.com
Full hookups available

See Grand Marais Campground and Marina above

See Grand Marais Campground and Marina above

See Grand Marais Campground and Marina above

Yes

Limit
to four
hours.

Grand Portage Marina & RV Park
www.grandportage.com/index.php/staying/the-rv-park
218-475-2476.
Full hookups available

Recommended Reading and Resources

The following are recommended resources for your health and enjoyment.

HIKING

Slade, A. *Hiking the North Shore: 50 Fabulous Day Hikes in Minnesota's Spectacular Lake Superior Region, 2nd Ed.* Duluth, MN: There & Back Guides, 2017.

Superior Hiking Trail Association. *Guide to the Superior Hiking Trail, 8th Ed.* Two Harbors, MN: Superior Hiking Trail Association, 2017.

Tornabene, L., Morgan, M. and Vogelsang, L. *Gentle Hikes: Northern Wisconsin's Most Scenic Lake Superior Hikes Under 3 Miles.* Cambridge, MN: Adventure Publications, 2004

Wallinga, E. and Wallinga, G. *Waterfalls of Minnesota's North Shore: A Guide for Sightseers, Hikers & Romantics, 2nd Ed.* North Shore Press, 2015.

STATE PARKS

Keigan, M. *Minnesota State Parks: A Camper's Guide.* Bloomington, IN: Authorhouse, 2011.

HISTORY

Anderson, C. and Fischer, A. *North Shore: A Natural History of Minnesota's Superior Coast.* Minneapolis, MN: University of Minnesota Press, 2015.

Aubut, S.T. and Norton, M.C. *Images of America: Duluth, Minnesota.* Chicago: Arcadia Publishing, 2001.

Beattie Bogue, M. *Around the Shores of Lake Superior: A Guide to Historic Sites, 2nd Ed.* Madison, WI: University of Wisconsin Press, 2007.

Morse-Kahn, D. *Lake Superior's Historic North Shore: A Guided Tour.* St. Paul, MN: Minnesota Historical Society Press, 2008.

Young, F. A. *Duluth's Ship Canal and Aerial Bridge: How They Came to Be.* Duluth, MN: Stewart-Taylor Company, 1977.

BIKING

Rails-to-Trails Conservancy. *Rail-Trails Minnesota: The Definitive Guide to The State's Best Multiuse Trails.* Birmingham, AL: Wilderness Press, 2016.

CROSS-COUNTRY SKIING

Slade, A. *Skiing the North Shore: A Guide to Cross Country Trails in Minnesota's Spectacular Lake Superior Region.* Duluth, MN: There and Back Books, 2007.

FIELD GUIDES

McCarthy, A. *Critters of Minnesota Pocket Guide.* Cambridge, MN: Adventure Publications, 2000.

Tekiela, S. *Birds of Minnesota Field Guide.* Cambridge, MN: Adventure Publications, 1998.

Tekiela, S. *Birds of Prey of Minnesota Field Guide.* Cambridge, MN: Adventure Publications, 2002.

Tekiela, S. *Birds of Wisconsin Field Guide.* Cambridge, MN: Adventure Publications, 1999.

Tekiela, S. *Trees of Minnesota Field Guide.* Cambridge, MN: Adventure Publications, 2001.

Tekiela, S. *Trees of Wisconsin Field Guide.* Cambridge, MN: Adventure Publications, 2002.

Tekiela, S. *Wildflowers of Minnesota Field Guide.* Cambridge, MN: Adventure Publications, 1999.

Tekiela, S. *Wildflowers of Wisconsin Field Guide.* Cambridge, MN: Adventure Publications, 2000.

DULUTH & NORTH SHORE

Blacklock, C. *Minnesota's North Shore*. Moose Lake, MN: Blacklock Nature Photography, 2007.

Mayo, K. and Mayo, W. *61 Gems on Highway 61: A Guide to Minnesota's North Shore—From Well-Known Attractions to Best-Kept Secrets*. Cambridge, MN: Adventure Publications, 2009.

Zager, Anita. *Duluth: Gem of the Freshwater Sea*. Cambridge, MN: Adventure Publications, 2004.

MINNESOTA

Perich, S. *Backroads of Minnesota: Your Guide to Scenic Getaways & Adventures*. McGregor, MN: Voyageur Press, 2011.

Weinberger, M. *Minnesota Off the Beaten Path®: A Guide To Unique Places*. Guilford, CT: Globe Pequot Press, 1992.

CIRCLE TOUR

Berg, R. and Lemay, K. *Lake Superior: The Ultimate Guide to the Region, 2nd Ed*. Duluth, MN: Lake Superior Port Cities, 2010.

Morgan, M., Tornabene, L., and Vogelsang, L. *Gentle Hikes of Upper Michigan: Upper Michigan's Most Scenic Lake Superior Hikes Under 3 Miles*. Cambridge, MN: Adventure Publications, 2006.

STRETCHING

Anderson, B. and Anderson, J. *Stretching: Pocket Book Edition*. Bolinas, CA: Shelter Publications, 2015.

About the Trails and Those Who Host Them

Maximize your Duluth and North Shore experience! The following resources not only introduce many of the cities/organizations that house our trails, but they can also be used to empower your best sojourn. Be it your first or fiftieth visit, we hope that this information inspires you to explore a new hobby, activity, city or state park, gift shop, place to eat/stay, and of course, adventure onto a new trail.

DULUTH CHAMBER OF COMMERCE

225 W. Superior St., Suite 110
Duluth, MN 55802
800-438-5884
www.visitduluth.com

DULUTH'S LAKEWALK

Duluth Parks and Recreation
City Hall, Ground Floor
411 West First Street
Duluth, MN 55802
218-730-4303 (for winter conditions)
www.duluthmn.gov/parks/parks-listing/lakewalk/

TWO HARBORS AREA CHAMBER OF COMMERCE

1330 MN-61
Two Harbors, MN 55616
218-834-2600
www.twoharborschamber.com

SILVER BAY CITY HALL

7 Davis Drive
Silver Bay, MN, 55614
218-226-4408
www.silverbay.com/

COOK COUNTY

218-387-2524
www.visitcookcounty.com

BAGLEY NATURE AREA

153 Sports and Health Center
1216 Ordean Court
Duluth, MN 55812
218-726-7128
http://d.umn.edu/recreational-sports-outdoor-program/facilities/bagley-nature-center

Camping and gear rental: d.umn.edu/recreational-sports-outdoor-program/programs/rental-center/bagley-nature-area-campground

UNIVERSITY OF MINNESOTA DULUTH RECREATIONAL SPORTS OUTDOOR PROGRAM
218-726-7128
d.umn.edu/recreational-sports-outdoor-program/

HARTLEY PARK & NATURE CENTER
3001 Woodland Ave
Duluth, MN 55803
218-724-6735
hartleynature.org

SUGARLOAF COVE NATURE
218-663-7679
sugarloafnorthshore.org

SUPERIOR HIKING TRAIL ASSOCIATION
731 Seventh Ave, Suite 2
Two Harbors, MN 55616
218-834-2700
shta.org

GITCHI-GAMI TRAIL ASSOCIATION
1130 11th Street
Two Harbors, MN 55616
www.ggta.org

WILDERNESS INQUIRY (INCLUSIVE OUTDOOR ADVENTURE TRAVEL)
808 14th Avenue SE
Minneapolis, MN 55414
612-676-9400
www.wildernessinquiry.org

MINNESOTA STATE PARKS ON THE NORTH SHORE
Minnesota Department of Natural Resources
500 Lafayette Rd.
St. Paul, MN 55155
888-646-6367
http://dnr.state.mn.us/accessible_outdoors/index.html (for accessibility details)

GOOSEBERRY FALLS STATE PARK
3206 Highway 61 East
Two Harbors, MN 55616
218-595-7100
www.dnr.state.mn.us/state_parks/gooseberry_falls/index.html

SPLIT ROCK LIGHTHOUSE STATE PARK
3755 Split Rock Lighthouse Road
Two Harbors, MN 55616
218-595-ROCK (7625)
www.dnr.state.mn.us/state_parks/split_rock_lighthouse/index.html

TETTEGOUCHE STATE PARK
5702 Highway 61
Silver Bay, MN 55614
218-353-8800
www.dnr.state.mn.us/state_parks/tettegouche/index.html

GEORGE H. CROSBY MANITOU STATE PARK
7616 Lake County Road 7
Finland, MN 55603
218-353-8800
www.dnr.state.mn.us/state_parks/george_crosby_manitou/index.html

TEMPERANCE RIVER STATE PARK
7620 West Hwy 61, Schroeder, MN 55613
218-663-3100
www.dnr.state.mn.us/state_parks/temperance_river/index.html

CASCADE RIVER STATE PARK
3481 West Highway 61
Lutsen, MN 55612
218-387-6000
www.dnr.state.mn.us/state_parks/cascade_river/index.html

JUDGE C.R. MAGNEY STATE PARK
4051 East Highway 61
Grand Marais, MN 55604
218-387-6300
www.dnr.state.mn.us/state_parks/judge_cr_magney/index.html

GRAND PORTAGE STATE PARK
9393 East Highway 61
Grand Portage, MN 55605
218-475-2360
www.dnr.state.mn.us/state_parks/grand_portage/index.html

Technical Details

Forgive us, but remember that two of us are professors and the other—
a bookkeeper!

MEASURING DISTANCES

All trails were initially rolled with a Rolotape (400 series—professional). Distances were recorded in feet, then rounded to the nearest tenth of a mile. Subsequent measurements were taken via a Garmin Forerunner 235.

MEASURING INCLINES

Inclines were measured with a clinometer (Suunto MC-2G Global Navigator).

Inclines were reported on an average of various places on the slope.

All were reported in this book in degrees. The following is a conversion chart for those desiring the same information reported in percent grade.

CONVERSION OF DEGREES TO PERCENT GRADE

10 degrees is 18 percent grade
12 degrees is 21 percent grade
14 degrees is 25 percent grade
16 degrees is 29 percent grade
18 degrees is 32 percent grade
20 degrees is 36 percent grade
22 degrees is 40 percent grade

Formula: To convert degrees to percent grade, use a calculator with a tangent function. Enter the number of degrees, then press the "tan" button. For an approximation, double the degrees and the answer will be close to the percent grade.

Bibliography

1. Reiner M., Niermann C., Jekauc D., Woll A. Long-term health benefits of physical activity—a systematic review of longitudinal studies. Biomed Cent Public Heal. 2013;13:813-822. doi:10.1186/1471-2458-13-813.

2. Mckinney J., Lithwick D.J., Morrison B.N., et al. The health benefits of physical activity and cardiorespiratory fitness. bc Med J. 2016;58(3):131-137. www.bcmj.org/sites/default/files/BCMJ_Vol58_No_3_cardiorespiratory_fitness.pdf. Accessed August 23, 2017.

3. Minter-Jordan M., Davis I., Arany Z. Healthy Mind, Healthy Body: Benefits of Exercise. Boston; 2014. https://hms.harvard.edu/sites/default/files/assets/Sites/Longwood_Seminars/Exercise3.14.pdf. Accessed August 23, 2017.

4. Knight J.A. Physical Inactivity: Associated Diseases and Disorders. Ann Clin Lab Sci. 2012;42(3):320-337. www.ncbi.nlm.nih.gov/pubmed/22964623. Accessed August 30, 2017.

5. Benjamin E.J., Blaha M.J., Chiuve S.E., et al. Heart Disease and Stroke Statistics—2017 Update: A Report From the American Heart Association. Circulation. 2017;135(10). http://circ.ahajournals.org/content/135/10/e146. Accessed August 31, 2017.

6. Murtagh E.M., Murphy M.H., Boone-Heinonen J. Walking: the first steps in cardiovascular disease prevention. Curr Opin Cardiol. 2010;25(5):490-496. doi:10.1097/HCO.0b013e32833ce972.

7. Warburton D.E., Bredin S.S. Health benefits of physical activity. Curr Opin Cardiol. 2017;32(5):541-556. doi:10.1097/HCO.0000000000000437.

8. Garber C.E., Blissmer B., Deschenes M.R., et al. Quantity and quality of exercise for developing and maintaining cardiorespiratory, musculoskeletal, and neuromotor fitness in apparently healthy adults: Guidance for prescribing exercise. Med Sci Sports Exerc. 2011;43(7):1334-1359. doi:10.1249/MSS.0b013e318213fefb.

9. Siegel R.L., Miller K.D., Jemal A. Cancer statistics, 2017. CA Cancer J Clin. 2017;67(1):7-30. doi:10.3322/caac.21387.

10. Simon S. and the ACS medical and editorial content team. Study: Smoking Causes Almost Half of Deaths from 12 Cancer Types. www.cancer.org/latest-news/study-smoking-causes-almost-half-of-deaths-from-12-cancer-types.html. Published 2015. Accessed September 1, 2017.

11. Cancer.net Editorial Board. Colorectal Cancer: Risk Factors and Prevention | Cancer.Net. www.cancer.net/cancer-types/colorectal-cancer/risk-factors-and-prevention. Published 2017. Accessed September 1, 2017.

12. Cancer.net Editorial Board. Physical Activity and Cancer Risk | Cancer.Net. www.cancer.net/navigating-cancer-care/prevention-and-healthy-living/physical-activity-and-cancer-risk. Published 2016. Accessed September 1, 2017.

13. Robb B., Editor: Carson-DeWitt R. Exercise Away the Urge to Smoke | Everyday Health. www.everyday-health.com/smoking-cessation/living/exercise-can-help-you-quit-smoking.aspx. Published 2017. Accessed September 1, 2017.

14. Simon S. Five Ways to Reduce Your Breast Cancer Risk. www.cancer.org/latest-news/five-ways-to-reduce-your-breast-cancer-risk.html. Published 2016. Accessed September 1, 2017.

15. Kelly-Hayes M. Influence of age and health behaviors on stroke risk: Lessons from longitudinal studies. J Am Geriatr Soc. 2010;58(SUPPL. 2):S325-8. doi:10.1111/j.1532-5415.2010.02915.x.

16. CDC. Stroke Fact Sheet | Data & amp; Statistics | DHDSP | CDC. www.cdc.gov/dhdsp/data_statistics/fact_sheets/fs_stroke.htm. Published 2017. Accessed September 1, 2017.

17. CDC. How much physical activity do adults need? | Physical Activity | CDC. www.cdc.gov/physicalactivity/basics/adults/index.htm. Published 2015. Accessed September 2, 2017.

18. Harvard School of Public Health. Examples of Moderate and Vigorous Physical Activity | Obesity Prevention Source | Harvard T.H. Chan School of Public Health. www.hsph.harvard.edu/obesity-prevention-source/moderate-and-vigorous-physical-activity/. Published 2017. Accessed September 2, 2017.

19. AHA. Moderate to Vigorous—What is your level of intensity? www.heart.org/HEARTORG/HealthyLiving/PhysicalActivity/FitnessBasics/Moderate-to-Vigorous—What-is-your-level-of-intensity_UCM_463775_Article.jsp#.WapAXsh942w. Published 2017. Accessed September 2, 2017.

20. Donnelly J.E., Blair S.N., Jakicic J.M., Manore M.M., Rankin J.W., Smith B.K. Appropriate physical activity intervention strategies for weight loss and prevention of weight regain for adults. Med Sci Sports Exerc. 2009;41(2):459-471. doi:10.1249/MSS.0b013e3181949333.

21. Mayo Clinic Staff. Depression (major depressive disorder)—Symptoms and causes—Mayo Clinic. www.mayoclinic.org/diseases-conditions/depression/symptoms-causes/dxc-20321472. Published 2017. Accessed September 2, 2017.

22. United Nations News Service. UN News—UN health agency reports depression now "leading cause of disability worldwide." 2017. www.un.org/apps/news/story.asp?NewsID=56230#.WasqC8h942x. Accessed September 2, 2017.

23. Weir K. The exercise effect. Am Psychol Assoc Monit. 2011;42(11):48. www.apa.org/monitor/2011/12/exercise.aspx. Accessed September 2, 2017.

24. Gladwell V.F., Brown D.K., Wood C., Sandercock G.R., Barton J.L. The great outdoors: how a green exercise environment can benefit all. Extrem Physiol Med. 2013;2(1):3. doi:10.1186/2046-7648-2-3.

25. Thompson Coon J., Boddy K., Stein K., Whear R., Barton J., Depledge M.H. Does Participating in Physical Activity in Outdoor Natural Environments Have a Greater Effect on Physical and Mental Wellbeing than Physical Activity Indoors? A Systematic Review. Environ Sci Technol. 2011;45(5):1761-1772. doi:10.1021/es102947t.

26. Akers A., Barton J., Cossey R., Gainsford P., Griffin M., Micklewright D. Visual color perception in green exercise: Positive effects on mood and perceived exertion. Environ Sci Technol. 2012;46(16):8661-8666. doi:10.1021/es301685g.

27. Mitchell R. Is physical activity in natural environments better for mental health than physical activity in other environments? Soc Sci Med. 2013;91:130-134. doi:10.1016/j.socscimed.2012.04.012.

28. Passmore H-A., Holder M.D. Noticing nature: Individual and social benefits of a two-week intervention. J Posit Psychol. 2017;12(6):537-546. doi:10.1080/17439760.2016.1221126.

29. Ten Brink P., Mutafoglu K., Schweitzer J-P., et al. The Health and Social Benefits of Nature and Biodiversity Protection; 2016. doi:10.13140/RG.2.1.4312.2807.

30. Capaldi C., Passmore H-A., Nisbet E., Zelenski J., Dopko R. Flourishing in nature: A review of the benefits of connecting with nature and its application as a wellbeing intervention. Int J Wellbeing. 2015;5(4):1-16. doi:10.5502/ijw.v5i4.449.

31. Hostetler B. 6 ways to pray while you exercise | Guideposts. Guideposts: Exercise. www.guideposts.org/better-living/health-and-wellness/exercise/6-ways-to-pray-while-you-exercise. Published 2016. Accessed September 4, 2017.

32. de Gaetano G., Costanzo S., Di Castelnuovo A., et al. Effects of moderate beer consumption on health and disease: A consensus document. Nutr Metab Cardiovasc Dis. 2016;26(6):443-467. doi:10.1016/j.numecd.2016.03.007.

33. Haritha K., Kalyani L., Rao A.L. Health Benefits of Dark Chocolate. J Adv Drug Deliv. 2014;1(4):184-194. http://jadd.in/aug/5.pdf. Accessed September 4, 2017.

34. Kraker D. Concerns linger over Lake Superior's historic herring fishery | Minnesota Public Radio News. MPR News. www.mprnews.org/story/2016/12/27/concerns-linger-over-lake-superior-historic-herring-fishery. Published 2016. Accessed September 5, 2017.

35. Moen S. Eat More and Better Fish | Minnesota Sea Grant. Minnesota Sea Grant. www.seagrant.umn.edu/fisheries/eat_fish. Published 2008. Accessed September 5, 2017.

36. www.seafoodhealthfacts.org. Seafood Health Facts: Making Smart Choices Balancing the Benefits and Risks of Seafood Consumption Seafood & Nutrition; 2017. www.seafoodhealthfacts.org/printpdf/seafood-nutrition/healthcare-professionals/omega-3-content-frequently-consumed-seafood-products. Accessed September 5, 2017.

37. Stuckey H.L., Nobel J. The connection between art, healing, and public health: a review of current literature. Am J Public Health. 2010;100(2):254-263. doi:10.2105/AJPH.2008.156497.

38. Sifferlin A. Exercise As Effective As Drugs For Treating Heart Disease, Diabetes | TIME.com. Time. http://healthland.time.com/2013/10/01/exercise-as-effective-as-drugs-for-treating-heart-disease-diabetes/. Published 2013. Accessed September 5, 2017.

39. National Health Service: NHS Choices. Osteoporosis—Prevention—NHS Choices. NHS Choices. 2016. www.nhs.uk/Conditions/Osteoporosis/Pages/Prevention.aspx. Accessed September 5, 2017.

40. Cho S.Y., Roh H.T. Trekking poles reduce downhill walking-induced muscle and cartilage damage in obese women. J Phys Ther Sci. 2016;28(5):1574-1576. doi:10.1589/jpts.28.1574.

41. Snell P., Ward R., Kandaswami C., Stohs S. Comparative effects of selected non-caffeinated rehydration sports drinks on short-term performance following moderate dehydration. J Int Soc Sport Nutr 2. 210AD;7(28):1-8. doi:10.1016/j.scispo.2004.05.003.

42. Webb F.S., Whitney E.N. Nutrition: Concepts and Controversies 14th Ed. (Cole B, ed.). Pacific Grove, CA: Brooks Cole; 2016.

SUPERIOR CALLS

Come home to my shores, where your soul longs to be
Bring your worries and cares, spend time with me

Rest from life in the shade of my birch
Daydream like a child as peace you search

Hear the laughter in my soul as waves crash my shore
Embrace the calm in your heart as you open the door

Feel contentment as my crystal waters refresh your soul
Hold tight to the passion that deep within you rolls

Walk my gentle trails and soon you'll begin to smile
Come to Superior and rest for awhile

peeje

(this poem was written as a tribute to this book)
copyright 2001

TRIBUTE TO SPLIT ROCK LIGHTHOUSE

Split Rock Lighthouse perched high
keeping watch, standing solid
guarding the shore

Your light will shine forever
commemorating the memory
you have engraved on so many souls.

written 8-14-01 by Ladona Tornabene

Glossary

AMENITIES: Availability of restrooms, water fountains, visitor centers, picnic tables, play-grounds, grills, shelters, boat launches, etc. **Note:** For clarity, we indicate restrooms by toilet type: flush (modern), vault (pit), portable (port-a-potties, portalets).

BOARDWALK: Long boards laid side by side or end to end, to assist walking over a particular section. These may be slippery if wet/frosted, loose in areas, challenging to navigate when narrow or to use with hiking poles. Always use caution when crossing them.

GGST: Abbreviation for the Gitchi-Gami State Trail, a multiuse, non-motorized paved path that when finalized will span 89 miles between Two Harbors and Grand Marais.

LAID-LOG PATHS: Sometimes referred to as cut-log paths, these are normally laid side by side across the trail to facilitate crossing a muddy section, and are often unsecured or loose. These may be challenging to navigate regardless of conditions. Always use caution when crossing them.

SEASONAL: Typically defined as mid-May to mid-October, but can vary due to ground freezing/thawing. Many waysides are closed during snow season, as they are not plowed.

SHT: Abbreviation for the Superior Hiking Trail, a 326-mile path beginning in Duluth and continuing to the Canadian Border.

SPUR TRAIL: A trail that connects to the main trail, typically leading to a point of interest or scenic overlook.

UNIVERSAL DESIGN STANDARDS: Meets accessibility standards for persons of all abilities.

WHEELCHAIR ACCESSIBLE: A location that can be accessed by someone in a wheelchair.

CHECKLIST *(use the boxes to check the trails you've hiked!)*

TRAILS

Duluth to Two Harbors

- Bayfront Festival Park
- Lakewalk: Canal Wall to Bayfront Festival Park
- Lakewalk: Canal Wall to Fitger's
- Lakewalk: Rose Garden to Fitger's
- Lakewalk East: Rose Garden to Water Street
- Lakewalk East Extension: London Road to Water Street
- Lakewalk East Extension: S 26th Ave E to N 40th Ave E (i.e., Duluth East High School)
- Bagley Nature Area
- Rock Knob
- Hartley Pond & Tischer Creek Loop
- Lester Park Trail
- Agate Bay Trail: Lighthouse Loop to Paul Van Hoven Park
- Agate Bay Trail: Burlington Bay to First Street

Beyond Two Harbors to Little Marais

- Silver Creek Cliff Trail
- Gooseberry Falls (Gooseberry Falls State Park)
- Plaza Overlook Loop (Gooseberry Falls State Park)
- River View Trail (Gooseberry Falls State Park)
- Gitchi Gummi (Gooseberry Falls State Park)
- Gooseberry River Loop (Gooseberry Falls State Park)
- Iona's Beach
- Little Two Harbors Trail & Pebble Beach (Split Rock Lighthouse State Park)
- Split Rock: Birch to Beacon (Split Rock Lighthouse State Park)
- Little Two Harbors Trail (Split Rock Lighthouse State Park)
- Split Rock: Tour de Park (Split Rock Lighthouse State Park)
- North Shore Scenic Overlooks and Trails
- Triple Overlook Loop (Tettegouche State Park)
- Shovel Point Trail (Tettegouche State Park)
- Baptism River Loop (Tettegouche State Park)

High Falls at Tettegouche (Tettegouche State Park)

Benson Lake Trail (George H. Crosby Manitou State Park)

Beyond Little Marais to Grand Marais

Caribou Falls

Sugarloaf Cove Trail

Dyers Creek

Temperance River Lower Loop (Temperance River State Park)

Temperance River Gorge Trail (Temperance River State Park)

Temperance River Gorge View (Temperance River State Park)

Oberg Mountain

Poplar River Overlook

Lower Cascade Falls–Quick Route (Cascade River State Park)

Lower Falls Cascade River Loop (Cascade River State Park)

Lake Loop Trail

Beyond Grand Marais to the Canadian Border

Kadunce River

Devil's Kettle (Judge C.R. Magney State Park)

Brule River Loop (Judge C.R. Magney State Park)

Webster-Ashburton Trail and Picnic Area (Grand Portage State Park)

High Falls at Grand Portage (Grand Portage State Park)

ALMOST HIKES

Duluth to Two Harbors

Enger Park

Canal Park Lighthouse Stroll

Leif Erikson Rose Garden

Two Rivers, Three Views

McQuade Small Craft Harbor (Breakwater Loop)

Bear Trail

Agate Bay Breakwater

Beyond Two Harbors to Little Marais

Split Rock River Beach

Bayside Park

Beyond Little Marais to Grand Marais

- Father Baraga's Cross
- Temperance River Bridge View (Temperance River State Park)
- Tofte Park
- Best-Kept Secret of Grand Marais
- Harbor Park/Bear Tree Park
- Artists' Point (a.k.a. "The Point")

WAYSIDES AND SCENIC LOCALES

Duluth to Two Harbors

- Duluth Skyline Parkway
- North Shore Scenic Drive (Highway 61)
- Buchanan Historical Marker
- Lake Superior Agate Bay Public Water Access

Beyond Two Harbors to Little Marais

- Flood Bay Wayside
- Split Rock Scenic Overlook
- Black Beach Park
- Palisade Head Overlook

Beyond Little Marais to Grand Marais

- Taconite Harbor Public Water Access and Safe Harbor
- Cross River Wayside
- Cascade River Wayside
- Good Harbor Bay Scenic Locale
- Cutface Creek Rest Area
- Pincushion Mountain Overlook
- Boulder Park (a.k.a Grand Marais Public Water Access)

Beyond Grand Marais to the Canadian Border

- Kadunce River Wayside
- Old Dog Trail
- Susie Islands Overlook

PICNIC AREAS

Duluth to Two Harbors

▨ Kitchi Gammi Park (Brighton Beach)

Beyond Two Harbors to Little Marais

▨ Gooseberry Falls Picnic Areas (Gooseberry Falls State Park)

▨ Trail Center/Lakeview Picnic Area (Split Rock Lighthouse State Park)

▨ Bayside Park Picnic Area

▨ Tettegouche General Picnic Areas (Tettegouche State Park)

▨ High Falls Picnic Area (Tettegouche State Park)

Beyond Little Marais to Grand Marais

▨ Benson Lake Picnic Area (George H. Crosby Manitou State Park)

▨ Temperance River Picnic Area (Temperance River State Park)

▨ Cascade River State Park Picnic Area (Cascade River State Park)

▨ Grand Marais Recreation Area

Beyond Grand Marais to the Canadian Border

▨ Grand Portage National Monument Picnic Area

About the Authors

Ladona Tornabene, Ph.D., MCHES, is an Associate Professor of Public Health Education and Promotion at the University of Minnesota Duluth (UMD). Avid in promoting health via the outdoors, she believes that better health on the inside is supported through access to the outside. This belief has shaped her academic curiosity, leading to numerous conference presentations and to the innovative *Gentle Hikes* series (MN, WI, MI). Such books aim to empower people of all physical ability levels to access the outdoors by creating a know-before-you-go approach via significant trail detail (e.g. width/surface, number of steps, rock/root ratings, inclines). The books also incorporate research-based info on the health benefits of hiking and of simply being in nature. Another academic curiosity of Ladona's is the visual arts' role in promoting health, which led to the development of a photo-based data collection method, and numerous publications/presentations. As a fine-art nature photographer, she shares best spots along the trails for happy-snapping! Furthermore, she uses her photography for philanthropic purposes with her "Picture Your Passion" UMD scholarship fund (www.d.umn.edu/~ltornabe/photography/) and through the Foundation for Photo/Art in Hospitals (healingphotoart.org). Her work is represented by Master Framing Gallery in Duluth, MN, and is displayed internationally through the Foundation.

Lisa Vogelsang, Ph.D., has taught at the University of Minnesota Duluth, primarily in Public Health Education and Promotion. She has presented internationally on the importance of green space to health and informs others that the benefits of being in nature extend beyond the hiking. As an avid photographer, her academic interests encompass the health impact of viewing photos of nature, particularly in Hospital/healthcare settings. Her photos are displayed locally and internationally through the Foundation for Photo Art in Hospitals, as well as marketed regionally.

A former two-time Olympian in two different sports, Lisa sustained a devastating ankle injury while training. Seven surgeries over 34 years could not remedy the progressive bone spurs and arthritis. To continue hiking, she needed more details about trails before venturing out, which fueled a desire to "make the outdoors accessible to everyone," and the *Gentle Hikes* concept was born. While the books can be used by anyone seeking short yet scenic hikes within the Lake Superior region, the amount of detail included may be especially helpful to parents with strollers/young children and people with physical challenges. Since the book's publication, her ankle replacement has afforded her many miles of hiking!

Melanie Morgan is a Minnesota native who grew up exploring the woods near her family cabin as a child. There she developed a love of the natural world, learning the names of many wildflowers, trees, and animals. Many happy family vacations were spent camping along the North Shore and up the Gunflint Trail, always exploring the great outdoors. Being involved in the hiking and writing of *Gentle Hikes* seemed like an extension of those good feelings and brought a sense of nostalgia and fond memories. From those early beginnings, Melanie still enjoys a sense of adventure and the love of exploration. She and her husband encourage a love of nature in their children and now their grandchildren. And they continue to hike and explore whenever and wherever they happen to be. Melanie enjoys sewing and quilting, spending time with family and friends, snowshoeing in the quiet winter wonderland, and working with her husband on home projects.

For more *Gentle Hikes* pictures and information, visit the authors on the web at www.d.umn.edu/~ltornabe/gh

TRAILS OF A "CHAMP"-ION

To support public health education and promotion majors in pursuing their passion, Ladona Tornabene has established the Trails of a "Champ"-ion Scholarship Fund through the University of Minnesota Duluth. A portion of the proceeds from the sale of this book go to that scholarship fund.

THE BEST OF THE NORTH SHORE

There's a reason why people flock to Minnesota's North Shore from across the state and throughout the Midwest. It's one of the most amazing regions around. Add these popular books to your collection, and keep the North Shore's majesty at your fingertips.

GUIDEBOOKS
61 Gems on Highway 61

Explore Duluth Outdoors

North Shore Adventures

NATURE GUIDES
Invaders of the Great Lakes

Things That Bite: Great Lake States

CHILDREN'S BOOKS
Emma's First Agate

Great Lakes Activity Book

SPECIAL INTEREST
Duluth: Gem of the Freshwater Sea

The Mysterious North Shore

Sea Stories

Tall Ships

Lake Superior is literally the North Shore's biggest draw. Not only is it breathtakingly beautiful, it also provides excellent opportunities for hobbyists of all ages. Give rock hounding and ship watching a try on your next visit. These titles will get you started.

ROCK HOUNDING

Agate Hunting Made Easy

Agates of Lake Superior

Agates of Lake Superior Playing Cards

Gemstone Tumbling, Cutting, Drilling & Cabochon Making

Lake Superior Agates Field Guide

Lake Superior Agates Quick Guide

Lake Superior Rocks & Minerals

The Storied Agate

SHIP WATCHING

A Beginner's Guide to Ship Watching on the Great Lakes

Ships of the Great Lakes Playing Cards

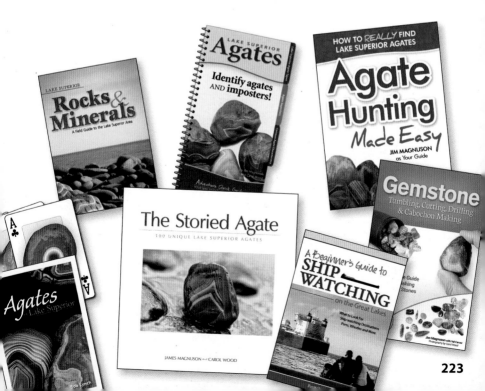

Notes